The Influence of National Culture on Customers' Cross-Buying Intentions in Asian Banking Services

The traditional walls between banking, insurance and securities markets are breaking down as a result of deregulation and liberalization of financial services. The cross-buying of financial services has become a global trend as a part of the convergence of financial services. This trend has recently commenced in East Asian countries, such as Taiwan and Korea, where the tremendous growth of these activities has been noticed. The book explores what the determinants of this growth in East Asia, particularly in Korea and Taiwan, are, and how these determinants have different influences on the customers of these two countries when compared with the studies conducted on other countries (e.g. Europe and North America).

The book opens the view on the subject of customers' behavioural intentions of cross-buying banking services in East Asian countries, especially from a cross-cultural perspective. Empirically tested findings will help marketing personnel in financial institutions, marketing practitioners in banks and researchers of financial services and marketing in their understanding of East Asia, particularly Taiwan and Korea, where the tremendous growth of these activities has been noticed in recent years.

Jung Kee Hong is an active contributor and researcher in the field of international business with a focal interest of cross-cultural management, global consumer dynamics, marketing innovation and strategies, and entrepreneurship in different cultures. As a practitioner, he has produced various reports on customer behaviours and strategic positioning for multinational financial service companies, based on his 15 years' experience of working in the international financial services arena in New York, Seoul, Hong Kong, Taipei and Singapore.

You-il Lee is Associate Professor in International Business and Deputy Director of the Australian Centre for Asian Business leading the research on Globalization and Asian Capitalism in the International Graduate School of Business at the University of South Australia. Professor Lee is a political economist, working on socio-economic and political changes and dynamics of globalization/regional integration in Northeast Asia. He has published widely in leading journals in the areas of Asian Studies, Asian business management and Asian political economy. Professor Lee is currently completing a research book, *The Impact of Foreign Multinational Corporations in South Korea: Evolution, Dynamics and Contradictions* (Cheltenham: Edward Elgar).

The Influence of National Culture on Customers' Cross-Buying Intentions in Asian Banking Services

Evidence from Korea and Taiwan

Jung Kee Hong and You-il Lee

Routledge
Taylor & Francis Group

LONDON AND NEW YORK

First published 2014
by Routledge
2 Park Square, Milton Park, Abingdon, Oxon OX14 4RN

and by Routledge
711 Third Avenue, New York, NY 10017

Routledge is an imprint of the Taylor & Francis Group, an informa business

British Library Cataloguing in Publication Data
A catalogue record for this book is available from the British Library

Library of Congress Cataloging in Publication Data
Lee, You-Il.
Customers' cross buying behaviours in Asian banking services : cases of
South Korea and Taiwan / You-il Lee.
  pages cm
  Includes bibliographical references and index.
  1. Cross-selling financial services–East Asia–Cross-cultural studies.
  2. Banks and banking–Customer services–East Asia–Cross-cultural
  studies. 3. Consumer behavior–East Asia–Cross-cultural studies.
  I. Title.
  HG1616.M3L44 2014
  332.1'7095–dc23   2013043660

ISBN: 978-0-415-82864-2 (hbk)
ISBN: 978-1-315-77658-3 (ebk)

Typeset in Times New Roman
by Wearset Ltd, Boldon, Tyne and Wear

Printed and bound in the United States of America by Publishers Graphics,
LLC on sustainably sourced paper.

Contents

Figures

Tables

Acknowledgements

It is not possible in words to express the extent of our gratitude to various organizations and individuals who provided us with invaluable advice, comments and unremitting encouragement in the course of writing this book.

Jung Kee Hong would like to thank his family, loving wife (Seung Hee Sarah SEO) and kids (Jin Ho and Jin Young Victoria), for their sacrifices of their weekends due to his late studies. The completion of the book would not have been possible without their unremitting supply of joy, love and prayer.

You-il Lee is grateful to the research and financial support for this work provided by the Australian Centre for Asian Business and the International Graduate School of Business at the University of South Australia Business School.

The authors benefited immensely from discussions and conversations with a good group of people who were kind enough to share their knowledge and experience in Korea and Taiwan while being interviewed in those countries.

Last but not least, the authors would like to thank Yongling Lam, Commissioning Editor at Routledge, her colleagues and the Routledge editorial team for their promptness and kind assistance.

Jung Kee Hong and You-il Lee
October 2013

Abbreviations

ADB	Asian Development Bank
AVE	Average variance extracted
BI	Behavioural intention
CAGR	Compound annual growth rate
CB	Cross-buying
CEA	Central Europe Association
CFA	Confirmatory factor analysis
CL	Collectivism
CRM	Customer relationship management
DC	Data classification
EFA	Exploratory factor analysis
GDP	Gross Domestic Product
GLOBE	Global Leadership and Organizational Behaviour Effectiveness
IM	Image
IT	Information technology
KMO	Kaiser-Meyer-Olkin measurement
M2	Money supply (money and close substitute of money)
SERVPERF	Service performance (measurement scale of service performance)
SERVQUAL	Service quality (measurement scale of quality in the service sectors)
ST	Satisfaction
TR	Trust
UK	United Kingdom
US	United States of America
WTO	World Trade Organization

1 Introduction

1.1 Background

Over the years, financial markets have undergone dynamic changes due to the consolidation of the industry, globalization of the market and convergence of the financial services (Chen *et al.* 2009; Claessens 2009; Moshirian 2008). Specifically, the convergence of financial services has caused the traditional walls between banking, insurance and securities markets to break down, as a result of deregulation and the liberalization of financial services (Claessens 2009; Singhal and Vij 2006; Yeager *et al.* 2007). However, this change – the convergence of financial services – occurred comparatively late in East Asian countries, such as Korea, Taiwan and China, compared to European countries.[1] This was mainly because the regulatory frameworks of financial services in these East Asian countries were mostly based on the model of the United States (US) (Calomiris 1998; Hellmann *et al.* 2000; Rajan and Zingales 2003), which prohibits the convergence of financial services through a regulatory separation of banking, insurance and securities services (Francis *et al.* 2010; Kroszner and Rajan 1994).[2] However, since the early 2000s, these regulatory constraints in East Asian countries have been gradually demolished. Following the Asian financial crisis in 1997, the local regulators of these countries – except in Mongolia – have been allowing the cross-buying of financial products in the banking industry (Claessens *et al.* 2010; Corbett 2007; Ghosh 2006).

Despite the late changes in these regulations, the emergence of this sector, including the cross-buying of financial products in the banking industry, has shown remarkable growth compared to countries in Europe (ADB 2009; Prasad 2009). For example, the cross-buying of insurance products from the bank, popularly known as 'bancassurance' (Fields *et al.* 2007), in Korea and Taiwan was lagging behind European countries due to the late establishment of the regulatory frameworks and guidelines in the Asian financial services industry. Most countries in Europe began bancassurance in the early 1970s and 1980s, whereas Taiwan began bancassurance in 1998, and Korea in 2002 (Artikis *et al.* 2008; Chen *et al.* 2009). However, despite this late start, the Swiss Re (2007) reported bancassurance activity in the East Asian region has shown significant growth in the past decade, mainly led by Korea, and is coupled with a high sales performance in Taiwan. In Korea, despite the financial crisis in 2008, the bancassurance market had a Compound Annual Growth Rate (CAGR) of 16 per cent from the fiscal year 2005 to the fiscal year 2009 (Korea Life Insurance Association 2010). In Taiwan, the bancassurance market currently represents 69 per cent of all new insurance policies issued, which means that out of any ten new insurance premiums collected, almost seven are generated by customers' cross-buying activities at bank branches (Taiwan Life Insurance Association 2010). The growth of these two countries in the bancassurance sector should be observed with great interest, as the growth of European countries in the same sector during the same period had less than 2 per cent CAGR, and the average market share of bancassurance was less than 12 per cent (CEA European Insurance and Reinsurance Federation 2010).[3]

Therefore, it is imperative to consider what drives this growth in Korea and Taiwan. What values do the customers in these countries commonly appreciate that have accelerated this phenomenon? What are the differences in how these values influence the customers of Korea and Taiwan compared to customers in other countries?

Taiwan and Korea have close resemblance in a number of aspects. In terms of the industrialization process over the last four decades, both economies were strictly governed and led by their governments, who strongly supported the local industry players in return for political support (Jacobs 2007; Lim 2009). Both countries are recognized as being highly democratic due to the presence of multi-party governments and social evolutions in democratization since 1987 (Chia *et al.* 2007; Peng *et al.* 2010). In some studies, such as those of Abe *et al.* (1999) and Hsieh (2011), it has been suggested that Korea and Taiwan have taken different paths of development – Korea undertook 'path-breaking' to restructure the local financial market, while Taiwan undertook 'path-reforming' in their financial sectors. Regardless of the political paths they pursued, it is clear that Korea and Taiwan have records of strong economic growth and success in the financial market. This places these countries in important positions, not only in the East Asian market, but also in the world's economies. The report from the Asian Development Bank (2009) indicated that Korea and Taiwan represent 49 per cent of the money supply in the East Asian market.[4] As of 2010, Korea and Taiwan were respectively the thirteenth and nineteenth largest Gross Domestic Product (GDP) countries at purchasing power parity.[5]

This suggests that Korea and Taiwan's strong economic growth and rapid financial reformation were the one of reasons for their success in the cross-buying of financial products in the banking industry. However, considering that their industrialization and democratization occurred during the 1980s and 1990s, whereas the cross-buying of financial products emerged in the late 1990s and early 2000s, there must have been a different moderating factor that influenced these two countries. Furthermore, if industrialization and democratization were the factors that influenced the growth of customers' cross-buying activities, then some European countries should have shown a superior outcome to Korea and Taiwan.

Korea and Taiwan share similar cultural values, including collectivism. Both countries have been recognized by cross-cultural studies as countries with highly collectivistic cultures (Abe *et al.* 1999; Brewer and Chen 2007; Bruton and Lau 2008; Hofstede *et al.* 2010; House *et al.* 2004; Kongsompong *et al.* 2009; Zhang *et al.* 2008). For example, Hofstede has undertaken numerous studies (Hofstede 1984a, 2004, 2007; Hofstede and Hofstede 1991; Hofstede *et al.* 2010) examining countries' individualism-collectivism scores. These studies indicated that Korea and Taiwan have individualism scores of 18 and 17, respectively, in Hofstede's individualism-collectivism cross-cultural dimensions, whereas most European countries scored an average higher than 55. Korea and Taiwan also scored relatively lower than their peer Asian countries. For example, Hong Kong scored 25 and Japan scored 46. House *et al.* (2004) confirmed that Korea and Taiwan rank among the lowest countries with societal collectivism. In a review of 20 years of cross-cultural studies by Zhang *et al.* (2008), Korea and Taiwan were frequently selected as countries representative of high collectivism.

Customers or personnel in high collectivistic cultures express different buying behaviour and buying intentions to their counterparts in high individualistic cultures (Cunningham *et al.* 2005; Furrer *et al.* 2000; Kacen and Lee 2002; Lee and Kacen 2008; Liu *et al.* 2001; Moon *et al.* 2008; Ozdemir and Hewett 2010; Sternquist *et al.* 2004; Ueltschy *et al.* 2009). For example, Furrer *et al.* (2000) and Liu *et al.* (2001), based on a survey of personnel from 16 different countries, found that customers from a collectivistic culture tend to have a higher intention to praise the service provider when they experience positive service quality than customers from an individualistic culture. At the same time, collectivistic customers are less likely to change to another service provider or to voice a negative opinion of their service provider, even after experiencing poor service quality. From samples from New Zealand, Moon and Chadee (2008) found that collectivistic customers, such as those from Asia, concentrate less on price sensitivities than individualistic customers – particularly in relation to their purchasing intentions. Ozdemir and Hewett (2010) confirmed that collectivism generally increases the importance of a relationship quality, rather than the service quality for behavioural intentions.

Therefore, it could be assumed that the high level of collectivism in Korea and Taiwan could explain the rapid growth of customers' cross-buying of financial products. While Korea and Taiwan have other similar cultural values – such as power distance, uncertainty avoidance, masculinity-femininity and long-term orientation – collectivism is the most homogenous value between Korea and Taiwan. In addition, in terms of the overall comparison of cultural values between European countries and Korea and Taiwan, collectivism is the cultural value that expresses the most divergence from other cultural values (Hofstede 1984a, 2004, 2007; Hofstede and Hofstede 1991; Hofstede *et al.* 2010). Moreover, collectivism has been considered the most important dimension of cultural differences in social behaviour (Triandis 2006; Triandis and Gelfand 1998), and one of the most active constructs in studies of psychology (Schimmack *et al.* 2005; Vandello and Cohen 1999).

1.2 Critical issues of studies on cross-buying in East Asia

Despite the importance of collectivism in the buying behaviour and buying intentions of customers, only a handful of studies have been conducted on the influence of collectivism on Korean and Taiwanese customers, particularly in the financial service sectors. Equally and importantly, there seems to be little work on cultural values, such as collectivism among the literature of cross-buying activity. In fact, the recent studies found that cross-buying activity is recognized as the most significant trend in banking services, not only in Korea and Taiwan, but also in other Asian countries (Claessens *et al.* 2010; Corbett 2007; Ghosh 2006).

The importance of cross-selling and cross-buying has been a point of interest in several studies in European countries. In the Netherlands, Verhoef (2001), Verhoef *et al.* (2002) and Verhoef and Donkers (2005) repeatedly confirmed that cross-selling increases customer retention and the value of each customer in the context of the financial services industry. Ngobo (2004) and Soureli *et al.* (2008), based on studies in France and Greece, respectively, addressed the fact that, if financial institutions can create more opportunities for customers to cross-buy financial products, this will eventually increase the retention of customer relationships, which will enhance the profit of financial institutions. Harrison *et al.* (2007) and Ormeci and Aksin (2009) substantiated these findings in studies of international insurance companies based in the United Kingdom (UK). They confirmed that customers' cross-buying of financial products generates additional income for financial institutions. These studies and other related studies have demonstrated the various factors that influence cross-selling or stimulate customers in their cross-buying of financial products (Güneş *et al.* 2010; Kamakura *et al.* 2003; Knott *et al.* 2002; Kumar *et al.* 2008; Lymberopoulos *et al.* 2004; Ngobo 2004; Reinartz *et al.* 2008; Salazar *et al.* 2007; Soureli *et al.* 2008; Verhoef and Donkers 2005; Verhoef *et al.* 2001; Vyas and Math 2006). However, none of these studies have addressed the notion that collectivism or other cultural factors may also be moderators.

The situation in the Asian context is even more pressing. There have been only a limited number of studies conducted on the topic of the cross-buying of financial products in Asian countries, and most of these studies were based in Taiwan. Liu and Wu (2007, 2009) investigated the determinants of customers' cross-buying in the banking industry and the correlation they have to customer retention. Fan *et al.* (2011) identified eight factors that affect cross-buying intentions in the Taiwanese bancassurance market. Among these few studies conducted in Asia, as with those conducted in European countries, none considered cultural values as a key factor. In fact, the determinants and factors mentioned in these studies of Taiwanese cross-buying activities were similar to those suggested in the studies from European countries. However, some of the outcomes of these influential factors on Taiwanese customers' cross-buying activities were different to those found in the studies of European customers.

Considering that Taiwan has different cultural values to European countries – such as collectivism – it is reasonable to assume that there may be academic merit in investigating the effect of collectivism on the relationships between these factors and customers' cross-buying intentions. Furthermore, there is also a clear lack of studies conducted in the context of the Korean market. There is only one study by Kim and Kim (2010), which aimed to identify the cross-buying intentions of bank customers based on five factors adopted from various studies in Europe. However, Kim and Kim (2010) did not consider collectivism or other cultural values as moderators in the conceptual model, even though the study included 'emotional bonding' as one of the key variables, which is a core value initiated by high collectivism (Hofstede 1984b, 2007; Hofstede *et al.* 2010). Therefore, empirically testing cross-buying factors in Korea and Taiwan, with consideration of their similar cultural value (collectivism), and offering a particular perspective (culture), will contribute to research in the area of customers' cross-buying intentions in financial products. This attempt places a significant importance on the fact that this activity of cross-buying of financial products is not only a growing trend in these two countries, but also a frequent subject of studies undertaken in European countries.

Prior to beginning this study on cross-buying activities in Korea and Taiwan, there are a number of critical issues that must be fundamentally noted, reviewed and offered keen consideration. First, most of these studies on financial services – both in general and including those studies in Korea and Taiwan – viewed cross-buying from the financial service providers' perspectives, not from the customers' perspectives. This is the reason that the majority of these studies focus on the cross-selling efforts of the financial service providers (Ansell *et al.* 2007; Kamakura *et al.* 2003; Knott *et al.* 2002; Li *et al.* 2005; Ormeci and Aksin 2009; Salazar *et al.* 2007; Vyas and Math 2006). Only a few focus on cross-buying or the intention of customers' to cross-buy in financial services (Liu and Wu 2009; Ngobo 2004; Reinartz *et al.* 2008; Shih-Ping 2008; Soureli *et al.* 2008; Verhoef *et al.* 2001). The reason for the absence of this topic is that these studies are inclined to focus on the financial service providers' strategies, rather than the customers' responses to these strategies (Kamakura *et al.* 2003; Reinartz *et al.* 2005, 2008). Kamakura *et al.* (2003) explained that this is because, in the past, there was a lack of customer information to identify customers' responses to these strategies. Reinartz *et al.* (2008) stated that firms and service providers often undertake simple correlation analyses of cross-selling and customers' reactive behaviour, without identifying the actual causes of this behaviour.

Nevertheless, cross-buying – which is defined as purchasing different types of products from the same provider (Reinartz *et al.* 2008; Verhoef *et al.* 2001) – should have been given greater consideration than cross-selling. This is because cross-selling is unlikely to occur if customers are unwilling to buy different products from the same service provider (Day 2000; Ngobo 2004). Kamakura *et al.* (2003) found that, without identifying customers' intentions to cross-buy, efforts to cross-sell can potentially weaken the relationship between the customers and the company. Gunes *et al.* (2010) further strengthened this view by noting that attempting to cross-sell without understanding the intentions of the customers' to cross-buy may actually motivate customers to switch to other companies. Therefore, there is a need to study the factors that influence customers' cross-buying intentions, rather than focusing on studying the strategic tools that financial service providers are deploying in the market.

Second, in addition to this critical view on the lack of studies on cross-buying activities from the customers' perspectives, there is concern that there is a literature gap and contradicting opinions on the factors that influence customers' cross-buying activities. There have been a few studies that have explored the factors that influence customers' cross-buying behaviour and intentions, most of which were based on European customers. Verhoef and Franses (2001) expressed 'payment equity' and 'satisfaction' as the factors that affect the cross-buying of financial products. Ngobo (2004) indicated that 'perceived value', 'trust', 'image' and 'satisfaction' were the key variables to the conceptual model for cross-buying. Soureli (2008) synthesized these factors and defined the interrelationship between them with the cross-buying intentions of banking customers. These factors were similarly implemented in the conceptual models of studies by Liu and Wu (2009, 2007), Fan *et al.* (2011) and Kim and Kim (2010), which have been the only studies in Taiwan and Korea that investigated customers' cross-buying intentions in the banking industry. However, although the factors and conceptual models in the studies from Korea, Taiwan and European countries were theoretically identical, the outcomes of the empirical test results were surprisingly different.

Few examples can be found comparing existing studies. In the Netherlands, customers' trust towards banks and financial service providers was recognized as the factor that had the smallest effect on customers' cross-buying intentions (Verhoef and Donkers 2005; Verhoef *et al.* 2002). However, in the studies from Korea and Taiwan, customers' trust played a significant role in their cross-buying intentions (Fan *et al.* 2011; Kim and Kim 2010; Liu and Wu 2007, 2009). As for customers' perceived value of banks and financial service providers, Ngobo's (2004) study, based in France, found this to be the most influential factor. Verhoef (2002) also confirmed that customers' perceived value of the bank, such as price equity, strongly affects their decision to cross-buy financial products from the same service provider. Interestingly, in Korea and Taiwan, some of the measurements of perceived value were not considered as important as they were in the studies from European countries (Fan *et al.* 2011; Kim and Kim 2010; Liu and Wu 2007, 2009). There were also relative differences noted between the European studies and the Korean and Taiwanese studies regarding customers' image of financial service providers and customers' satisfaction with financial service providers.

This leads to the final issue – that there could be another moderating factor influencing the relationship between the factors of perceived value, trust, image and satisfaction, and customers' cross-buying intentions. However, there seems to be a lack of studies conducted to provide answers to this question. Other studies have shown that the cultural value of a nation influences how customers think and behave (Craig and Douglas 2006; De Mooij and Hofstede 2002;

Laroche *et al.* 2004; Ozdemir and Hewett 2010; Zhang *et al.* 2008; Zourrig *et al.* 2009). Customers in East Asian countries – specifically Korea and Taiwan – who are commonly referred to as customers with a collectivistic culture (Brewer and Chen 2007; Bruton and Lau 2008; Hofstede 2010; House *et al.* 2004; Kongsompong *et al.* 2009; Zhang *et al.* 2008) express themselves differently in terms of buying behaviour and buying intentions than their counterparts in European countries, who are commonly referred to as high individualistic customers (De Mooij and Hofstede 2002; Hofstede *et al.* 2010; Liu *et al.* 2001; Oyserman and Lee 2008; Schwartz and Bardi 2001; Triandis 2006). However, this theoretical premise has not been applied to studies of customers' cross-buying intentions of financial products in the banking services of Korea and Taiwan. For example, the studies of Verhoef *et al.* (2002) and Verhoef and Donkers (2005) were undertaken in the Netherlands, where the score of individualism-collectivism was 80, based on Hofstede's (2010) cultural dimension. Ngobo (2004) conducted a study on the drivers of cross-buying financial services in France, where the score of individualism-collectivism was 71, based on the same dimension scale. Both studies showed different outcomes from similar studies in Korea and Taiwan, where individualism-collectivism was 18 and 17, respectively. It is not difficult to discern that collectivism has played a moderate role in the outcomes of the studies on cross-buying activities in Korea and Taiwan. Simultaneously, it is recognized that collectivism is the cultural value that shows the most divergence between the Netherlands and France, and Korea and Taiwan. Compared to the other cultural values mentioned in the study of Hofstede (2010), collectivism seems most likely to be the main moderator of the outcomes.

It is understandable that this lack of studies in Korea and Taiwan is because the cross-buying of financial services in these countries started relatively later than in European countries. However, Korea and Taiwan now have more than 10 years of history of deregulation in cross-buying financial products in the banking industry (Artikis *et al.* 2008; Chen *et al.* 2009), as well as a rapid growth in cross-buying activities (Swiss Re 2007; Teunissen 2008). This means that there is now a legitimate need to scrutinize the factors driving customers to cross-buy financial products in the banking services of Korea and Taiwan.

This book was undertaken in response to this clear demand to identify the drivers of the cross-buying intentions of Korean and Taiwanese customers in the banking services, and to investigate the influence of collectivism on these factors. This book also explores whether collectivism has different moderating effect in Korea and Taiwan despite their similar levels of collectivism. Craig and Douglas (2006) stated that different practices of customers could be observed even in countries with the same cultural values.

1.3 Research questions and literature review

By consolidating the issues relating to customers' cross-buying intentions of financial products in the banking services, this book explores the topic of customers' cross-buying intentions from the view of collectivism in Korea and

Taiwan. As there seems to be a lack of studies on this topic, this book begins with research questions based on the literature gaps in the related studies on East Asian and European countries.

In response to these questions, an empirical study was required to establish a conceptual framework that enabled this book to establish theoretical relationships between cultural values, such as collectivism, and the major variables that have been previously identified in similar studies of Europe and East Asia. This book built on the above research questions to conduct a study of Taiwan and Korea – two countries that have allowed cross-buying in financial services similar to the market settings in Europe (Corbett 2007; Ghosh 2006; Laeven 2005), but have traditionally had different cultural values, such as collectivism. These differing values may cause customers to express themselves differently in regard to their cross-buying intentions for financial services. The aim of this book is to empirically evaluate whether collectivism does or does not influence customers' cross-buying intentions in the financial services industry – particularly in Korea and Taiwan – and, if it does, to understand the level of influence it has on customers in this market.

In order to achieve the objectives of this book, the literature review is required to be twofold. First, it requires a thorough understanding of the operation of the culture. Therefore, concrete cultural dimensions must be defined. The culture can be operationalized in several terms (Burton 2009; Craig and Douglas 2006; Soares *et al.* 2007), and, through these terms, a common cultural value can be identified as a cultural dimension of the nation (Hofstede *et al.* 2010; Hofstede 1984b, 2001; House *et al.* 2004; Inglehart 2006; Schwartz and Bardi 2001). However, there are continuous debates about the cultural dimensions of each nation, with some studies arguing that cultural values can be changed due to rapid changes in globalization and technology (Fang 2010; Faure and Fang 2008;

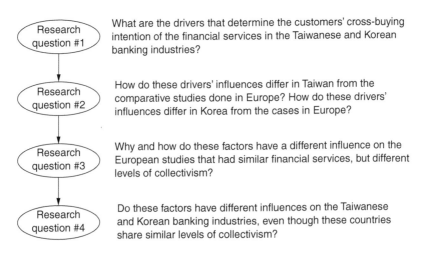

Research question #1	What are the drivers that determine the customers' cross-buying intention of the financial services in the Taiwanese and Korean banking industries?
Research question #2	How do these drivers' influences differ in Taiwan from the comparative studies done in Europe? How do these drivers' influences differ in Korea from the cases in Europe?
Research question #3	Why and how do these factors have a different influence on the European studies that had similar financial services, but different levels of collectivism?
Research question #4	Do these factors have different influences on the Taiwanese and Korean banking industries, even though these countries share similar levels of collectivism?

Figure 1.1 Research questions.

Sheth 2006; Triandis 2006), while others argue that values should be separated from the practices of the culture. They assert that the practices may change, but the values of the culture remain consistent (De Mooij and Hofstede 2002; Hofstede 2007; Hofstede *et al.* 2010; Soares *et al.* 2007; Zhang *et al.* 2008). For example, De Mooij and Hofstede (2002) confirmed that the same cultural values are still rooted strongly in each European country, even with the establishment of the European Union and the standardization of the political and social infrastructure among these countries. Zhang (2006) confirmed that there are both similarities and heterogeneities of fundamental East Asian cultural values that remain consistent, even with the different cultural dynamics in modern East Asian societies.

Among the cultural values operated throughout the years, collectivism has been the most frequently used cultural dimension for East Asian customers in recent years (Bruton and Lau 2008; Hofstede *et al.* 2010; House *et al.* 2004; Oyserman *et al.* 2002; Ozdemir and Hewett 2010; Zhang *et al.* 2008). There were concerns raised by some academics in regard to adopting the approaches developed in European countries to the East Asian context (Fang 2010; Meyer 2006; Peng *et al.* 2010). Thus, in-depth studies were required to understand what led East Asian cultural values to reflect collectivism. This book links collectivism with the common East Asian Confucian values. Confucian values are known as one of the main cultural ideas embedded in many East Asian countries, including Taiwan and Korea, which are still being presented as the evidence that East Asians still preserve a collectivistic culture (Chia *et al.* 2007; Hofstede *et al.* 2010; House *et al.* 2004; Wang 2008; Zhang *et al.* 2005).

This book applies the definition of Hofstede (1984, 2010) for its standard measurement of collectivism. For this, the literature review deals with the debates and challenges of Hofstede's (1984, 2010) cross-cultural dimensions throughout the last two decades, and through a comparison with the more recent Global Leadership and Organizational Behaviour Effectiveness (GLOBE) cultural projects (House *et al.* 2004). The review concludes with a justification of why Hofstede's cross-cultural dimensions are still valid and continue to be applied in marketing. This is supported with studies from Soares *et al.* (2007) and McCrae (2008).

Based on the definition, there are several studies that prove that collectivism plays a significant role in East Asian customers' perceived service quality (Furrer *et al.* 2000; Laroche *et al.* 2004), purchase behaviour (De Mooij and Hofstede 2002; Hofstede 2001; Zourrig *et al.* 2009), and behavioural intentions (Liu *et al.* 2001; Moon *et al.* 2008; Ozdemir and Hewett 2010). Particularly in regard to behavioural intentions, customers under a high collectivistic culture tend to react less negatively towards poor levels of service quality, compared to customers under a low collectivistic culture (Liu *et al.* 2001; Moon *et al.* 2008). They also emphasize the relationship quality more, such as through their level of trust towards the service provider (Ozdemir and Hewett 2010).

The second requirement of the literature review is to determine the common factors that affect customers' cross-buying intentions in the financial services industry. Before examining the importance of the cross-buying intentions of customers, the literature review discusses how customer management originated and evolved throughout the last three decades, and eventually created the new terminology of 'customer relationship management' (CRM) (Chen and Popovich 2003; Peelen *et al.* 2006, 2009; Peppard 2000).

The literature review examines the methodological usage of CRM in customer retention strategies, emphasizing the benefits of cross-selling. However, it also raises the concern of having a cross-selling strategy without thorough insight into customers' intentions, which leads to unfavourable outcomes of the marketing strategy. In this regard, the importance of cross-buying intention should be handled diligently, and should be examined prior to the establishment of a marketing strategy for cross-selling.

In addition to this consideration, the literature review will also address the fact that customers' cross-buying intentions in the environment of a contractual setting, such as the financial services industry, must be managed with more attention than that in a non-contractual setting, such as the traditional retail industry (Kumar *et al.* 2008; Ngobo 2004; Reinartz and Kumar 2000). This is because the characteristics of the financial industry – such as intangibility, higher customer involvement and the expertise of the service provider – will differentiate as a result of the factors that influence customer behaviour from other service industries (Maas and Graf 2008; Peppard 2000; Salazar *et al.* 2007).

Taking this into account, Verhoef and Franses (2001) and Verhoef and Donkers (2005) constructed a conceptual framework for customers' cross-buying behaviour in the financial services industry. This consisted of variables such as customer satisfaction, perceived value and trust. These variables were inherited by other academics, such as Ngobo (2004), Soureli *et al.* (2008) and Kumar *et al.* (2008), who applied them to test these factors in the cross-buying intentions of customers for financial products. However, these later studies added another variable – image.

Among these studies, the outcomes were slightly different, even though their samples were extracted from a similar service context and were based on European countries. The differences were more apparent in the studies of Korea and Taiwan. The studies of Liu and Wu (2007, 2009), Fan *et al.* (2011) and Kim and Kim (2010) – which are a few studies that have been conducted on customers' cross-buying intentions of financial products in Korea and Taiwan – show that trust and image play more important roles than the factors recognized in European studies.

The literature review uses this observation to explain the differences between cultural values and collectivism. An example of this is the studies of Verhoef *et al.* (2001) and Ngobo (2004), based in the Netherlands and France, respectively, where the cultures are considered low collectivistic (Hofstede 2001; Hofstede *et al.* 2010), compared to the study of Soureli (2008), which was based in Greece – a country considered more collectivistic than other European countries (Fang 2010; Hofstede 2001). Furthermore, the studies of Liu and Wu (2007, 2009), Fan *et al.* (2011) and Kim and Kim (2010) were conducted in Korea and Taiwan

– countries considered to have high collectivism, not only globally, but also among other East Asian countries. This observation is the main literature gap that will be filled by this book. This will be done through empirical testing of the conceptual model, which will eventually generate this book's main contribution.

This study seems to be the first empirical attempt to incorporate collectivism into a study on cross-buying. This will not only enlarge the body of knowledge for future studies of the financial services, but will also support practitioners in the related fields who are interested in exploring the rapidly growing markets of Korea and Taiwan.

1.4 Research design and methodology

In designing the conceptual model based on this literature review, this book followed the suggestions of Sekaran (1992), and categorized collectivism as the moderator. The variables – such as the bank's perceived value to the customers, the customers' trust towards the bank, the bank's image to the customers, and the customers' satisfaction towards the bank – were the independent variables that influenced the dependent variable. The dependent variable was the cross-buying intentions of customers in the Korean and Taiwanese banking services. Upon this categorization, the relationships between these variables were developed to become hypotheses that framed the conceptual model of this book. For example, to establish the theoretical assumptions between the determinants of cross-buying intentions and collectivism, this book adopted studies of customers' behavioural intentions from Zeithaml *et al.* (1996) and Ozdemir and Hewett (2010), which used the measurement criteria SERVQUAL (Cronin Jr and Taylor 1994; Curry and Sinclair 2002; Ladhari 2009). The measurements and conceptual terms for each independent variable were imported from Verhoef (2001), Ngobo (2004), Roig (2006), Liu and Wu (2007), Soureli (2008) and Bravo (2009).

This book pursued the approach of triangulation. This combined the quantitative approach of a survey with the qualitative approach of interviews with field managers in the banking services of Korea and Taiwan. This approach of triangulation followed the suggestions of Creswell and Miller (2000), and Denzin and Lincoln (2005), who stated that the combination of these two approaches – quantitative and qualitative – strengthens a study by including richer details and counterbalancing the weaknesses of each single methodology.

Both the surveys and interviews were conducted at the subjective locations of Taiwan and Korea, where two sets of samples were drawn from the surveys and interviews. From the banking service, 350 customers from each country were sampled for the survey by using the probability sampling approach – specifically the 'stratified random sampling' methodology, which complements the weaknesses of random sampling and supports greater precision in data analysis (Tharenou *et al.* 2007). To ensure the reliability of the data, the characteristics of the survey sample were compared with statistics on total populations, which were officially published by the Korean National Statistics and the Taiwanese Ministry of Finance.

The questionnaire for the survey was structured in English, and then translated into the local language, which was validated through a back-translation methodology. The back-translation methodology was guided by suggestions from Hult *et al.* (2008). This survey was prepared based on the 'TAP' (topic, applicability and perspective) procedure developed in the study of Foddy (1993), with 28 questions, consisting of four questions for each set of six variables, in five-point Likert scales.

For the interview, three field managers from each country were carefully selected based on a pre-determined qualification. The major factor in the qualifications was that the person in the financial services arena was required to have more than seven years' experience in the cross-selling of financial products, such as insurance, in the banking services of Korea and Taiwan. The standard working experience year was set at seven years because, in Korea, the cross-selling of financial products – such as the selling of insurance at a bank counter was introduced in 2003 (Chen *et al.* 2009; Teunissen 2008). The interviews were conducted in English in Taiwan, as all interviewees were fluent in English. However, in Korea, the interviews were conducted in Korean. All interviewees in the face-to-face interviews were asked for their views on the determinants of customers' cross-buying intentions, and the relationships between these determinants and collectivism as a cultural perspective.

The data collected in Korea and Taiwan were aggregated and analysed as a sample. Factor analysis was undertaken to ensure the reliability of the constructs in the survey questionnaire. Multiple regression analysis was conducted to verify the hypotheses using SPSS 17.0. Multiple regression analysis (Aguinis 1995) was selected because it allows for more than one independent variable. This meant that the independent variables of perceived value, trust, image and satisfaction could be tested against the hypotheses of customers' cross-buying intentions with respect to collectivism. By using the hierarchical regression analysis (Bennett 2000; Baron and Kenny 1986), each independent variable was measured against its relationship with customers' cross-buying intentions, and then the moderating effect of collectivism was observed based on the measurement of interaction with these variables.

Conclusions were drawn from the results of the quantitative analysis of the survey, which were complemented by the qualitative findings from the face-to-face interviews. The common findings between the quantitative analysis and the qualitative findings confirmed the validity of the conceptual model within the book, and the discrepancies between the two analyses offered topics for future discussion, including a summary of the findings' managerial implications.

1.5 Research aims and contributions

This book was initiated because the cross-buying of financial services has become a global trend as a part of the convergence of the financial services (Claessens 2009; Liu and Wu 2007; Singhal and Vij 2006; Verhoef *et al.* 2007; Yeager *et al.* 2007). This trend has recently commenced in East Asian countries, such as Taiwan and Korea, where the tremendous growth of these activities has been noticed (Chen *et al.* 2009; Ghosh 2006; Swiss Re 2007). This trend in East Asian countries requires attention, as these countries play an important role in the East Asian region (ADB 2009), and are expected to play a leading role in the global economy and financial markets (Leung 2006; Peng *et al.* 2010). Despite the importance of the cross-buying of financial services in these countries, there has previously been a limited number of empirical studies performed on this topic in these countries, except for a few studies based on Taiwan, such as the studies of Liu and Wu (2007, 2009) and Fan *et al.* (2011) and in Korea, such as the study of Kim and Kim (2010). These studies have reflected the influence of collectivism, which is the most prominent cultural value that distinguishes these countries from other countries.

Therefore, the main contribution of this book arises from the fact that it is the first attempt to reflect the role of collectivism in cross-buying activities. This is not only a milestone for studies that seek to explore the emerging activities of cross-buying in Korea and Taiwan, but is also a milestone for all cross-cultural studies and studies of cross-buying activities. With this in consideration, this book aims to achieve and deliver the following objectives and contributions.

Objective 1: Explicate the drivers of customers' cross-buying intentions in the banking services

In the contractual setting of the financial services, customers' cross-buying intentions should be scrutinized more attentively than in non-contractual settings, such as retail (Kumar *et al.* 2008). This is not only because the service environment of a contractual setting, such as the banking services industry, is formed through a more unique and sophisticated relationship with the customers and the service provider (Maas and Graf 2008; Peppard 2000; Salazar *et al.* 2007). It is also because, through various studies, it has been proven that customers' cross-buying activities will ultimately enhance a bank's profit growth, as well as the financial stability of the bank, through the improvement of customer retention (Kumar *et al.* 2008; Reinartz *et al.* 2008; Verhoef 2003; Verhoef *et al.* 2007). The importance of customers' cross-buying in banking services in East Asian countries, such as Korea and Taiwan, is more prominent because the deregulation and liberalization of financial services in these countries has taken place during the last decade (Das and Ghosh 2006; Laeven 2005). However, few studies have been conducted on this topic in Korea and Taiwan, despite the fact that they have shown tremendous growth and sustainability potential in terms of cross-buying financial products in the banking services (ADB 2009; Artikis *et al.* 2008; Claessens *et al.* 2010; Swiss Re 2007).

Therefore, the reasons behind customers' intentions to cross-buy financial products in the banking services, based on the view of theoretical reasoning, are the initial contribution of the book. There have been a number of studies on similar topics in the past; however, most of these studies focused on customer retention and relationship management, and were not purely devoted to identifying the drivers of cross-buying intentions (Ngobo 2004; Salazar *et al.* 2007; Soureli *et al.* 2008; Verhoef *et al.* 2010). To this end, this book provides an additional contribution, as it approaches the topic of cross-buying from the perspective of customers, based on their determinants towards the service quality of the bank and the antecedent value that leads them to generate these determinants.

Objective 2: Explore the relationships between the determinants of customers' cross-buying intentions and the level of collectivism

Collectivism, as a cross-cultural dimension, is one of the most frequently examined variables in cross-cultural research in terms of its link with customer services (Oyserman and Lee 2008; Schimmack *et al.* 2005; Vandello and Cohen 1999). A handful of academics have applied this dimension to the study of customer-behaviour in the financial services (Donthu and Yoo 1998; Furrer *et al.* 2000; Ladhari 2009; Lee and Kacen 2008; Liu *et al.* 2001; Schimmack *et al.* 2005; Soares *et al.* 2007). However, these studies of collectivism were limited to the customers' first purchase and repurchase behaviour of financial services, but could not sufficiently analyse relationships between cross-buying behaviour and the intentions of the customers. To a certain extent, this is understandable, given that customers' cross-buying behaviour in the financial industry is a new activity in most countries, including Korea and Taiwan. Most studies relating to customers' cross-buying behaviour have been based in European countries, such as the studies of Verhoef *et al.* (2001), Ngobo (2004) and Soureli *et al.* (2008). These studies and findings were undertaken conceptually, based on a similar level of collectivism, which is commonly lower in European countries than in East Asian countries (Brewer and Venaik 2011; Hofstede 2007; Hofstede *et al.* 2010; House *et al.* 2004, Inglehart and Oyserman 2004; Schwartz and Bardi 2001).

However, due to the rapid growth of East Asian countries, led by Korea and Taiwan, there have been a few studies of customers' cross-buying activities in the banking services of Korea and Taiwan, such as the studies of Liu and Wu (2007, 2009), Fan *et al.* (2011) and Kim and Kim (2008). However, these studies did not consider the high level of collectivism, which is a major cultural value in both these two countries (Brewer and Venaik 2011; Hofstede *et al.* 2010; House *et al.* 2004; Inglehart and Oyserman 2004), and how this might influence the outcomes of these studies compared to similar studies in Europe.

The aim of this book was to explore the relationships between the determinants of customers' cross-buying intentions in banking services and how these determinants are influenced by the cultural environment of high collectivism. By confirming the links between collectivism and customers' cross-buying intentions through empirical testing of customers in collectivistic countries, such as Korea and Taiwan, this will enable future studies to establish theoretical frameworks on similar topics – not only for these two countries, but for all countries with different cultural backgrounds.

Objective 3: Explain the influence of collectivism on customers'
cross-buying intentions in the banking services of Korea and Taiwan

Korea and Taiwan are generally recognized as the two countries that are leading the financial market of East Asia, and are active members of the World Trade Organization (WTO) (Claessens 2009; Jacobs 2007; Liu and Hsu 2006). However, these countries had not fully achieved financial liberalization and financial reform until recent years (Artikis *et al.* 2008; Claessens *et al.* 2010; Das and Ghosh 2006). These two countries underwent a similar process of industrialization during the last four decades (Jacobs 2007; Lim 2009), with the recognition of highly democratic social evolutions in the last two decades (Chia *et al.* 2007; Peng *et al.* 2010). However, as is often addressed in studies related to customers' behaviour in cross-cultural contexts, Korea and Taiwan share the same level of cultural values, such as collectivism (Hofstede 2007; Hofstede *et al.* 2010; House *et al.* 2004; Inglehart 2006; Nielsen *et al.* 2009). This is reflected in the ways in which customers behave and intend to purchase (Cunningham *et al.* 2006; De Mooij and Hofstede 2011; Kacen and Lee 2002; Kongsompong *et al.* 2009; Sternquist *et al.* 2004; Zhang *et al.* 2008).

The book's contribution arises because of its focus on Korea and Taiwan – countries that are becoming the focal interest of studies of customers' behaviour in banking services – and because it aims to explain how collectivism affects customers' behavioural intentions towards cross-buying activities, which are a new phenomenon in the local market. This explanation may be extended to test the findings of previous studies in European countries, or may be imported to test similar topics in non-bank or non-financial industries. Throughout this process, the body of knowledge in customers' cross-buying intentions will be enriched, eventually contributing to the enhancement of cross-cultural studies from the customers' behavioural perspective.

This study may also have managerial implications for the practitioners and managerial personnel who are required to investigate local customers' characteristics before introducing new marketing strategies (Pieterse 2009; Sofat and Hiro 2009). In order to consider the effect of these managerial implications on the implementation of marketing strategies, this book will also examine existing business cases from multinational financial services companies. This will be done to demonstrate how the cross-buying activities of bank customers and the understanding of cultural values of these customers have become important in the East Asian region, particularly in Korea and Taiwan.

The findings from this book will help practitioners to understand not only the marketing factors that drive customers to cross-buy, but also the cultural values that motivate customers to initiate their intentions. Furthermore, this book will provide guidance to multinational financial institutions that plan to operate, or already are operating, in East Asia. It will help these institutions understand the local customers' characteristics, and establish an optimal marketing plan in the local market (Claessens 2009).

1.6 Structure of the book

Chapter 1

This chapter highlights the significance of this study. It illustrates some major and contemporary issues regarding the subject. It maps the overall structure of the book and flags the emergent issues raised from the research.

Chapter 2: Review of literature

This chapter explores the essence of customers' cross-buying behaviours in financial products through various literatures that focus on the studies of CRM (Customer Relationship Management) in the financial services sector. This chapter identifies four key factors that are the determinants of customers' cross-buying intentions in banking services. These four factors are 'perceived value', 'trust', 'image' and 'satisfaction'. These are extracted from the studies of Verhoef *et al.* (2001, 2002, 2005), Ngobo (2004), Kumar *et al.* (2006, 2008), Reinartz *et al.* (2004, 2008) and Soureli *et al.* (2008) in the context of European countries, and from the studies of Liu and Wu (2007, 2010), Fan *et al.* (2011) and Kim and Kim (2008) in the context of Korea and Taiwan. By comparing the relationship between these four factors and customers' cross-buying intentions in these studies, this chapter demonstrates that the outcomes in the context of Korea and Taiwan differ from ones in the context of European countries.

This chapter demonstrates that this is the main research gap in the field of customers' cross-buying in banking services, which is the most rapidly growing sector in East Asia, led by Korea and Taiwan (Claessens 2009; Ghosh 2006; Swiss Re 2007). Therefore, this chapter aims to establish that this rapid growth of customers' cross-buying intentions in the banking services of Korea and Taiwan is a result of the high collectivism in these two countries. This chapter underpins this with various empirical findings from the related literature in the context of the financial services.

Chapter 3: Conceptual model and methodology

The conceptual model of this research is framed in two steps. First, it establishes the relationship between the four key determinants of customers' cross-buying – which were identified in the literature review in the previous chapter (perceived value, trust, image and satisfaction) – and the cross-buying intentions of Korean and Taiwanese customers in the banking industry. Second, it observes whether collectivism produces any moderating effect on these relationships. This chapter develops the theoretical assumptions based on this conceptual model, which eventually resulted in the hypotheses of this book. These hypotheses were tested in Korea and Taiwan with the means of the research methodology that is presented in this chapter. This chapter explicitly discusses the preparatory tasks required for designing this study, and explains how to put the conceptual model into practice.

This chapter demonstrates the requirements of the qualitative approach that the study used to conduct face-to-face interviews on ten selective practitioners from Korea and Taiwan. As for the quantitative approach, this chapter focuses on the structured survey that the study used to collect 700 sets of data from Korea and Taiwan by using the probability sampling approach. The questionnaire for the survey followed the non-experimental design of the correlational field study, which commonly requires the measurement of several independent variables; one or more dependent variables; and a control variable, such as a moderator.

Chapter 4: Data collection and analysis

Based on the conceptual model and methodologies presented in the previous chapter, the quantitative and the qualitative data collected from the two countries will be analysed. This study will apply the hierarchical multiple regression analysis on the quantitative data, from which the hypotheses in the conceptual model being verified. The findings from the qualitative analysis of face-to-face interviews will also reflect the final conclusions of this book. This chapter discusses these processes with the requisite considerations and guidelines in operationalizing the data.

In the analysis of the quantitative data, this study applies the hierarchical regression analysis, which has been proven to be most effective method used to evaluate the moderating effect of a variable on the existing relationship between the independent and dependent variable (Baron and Kenny 1986; Bennett 2000). Thus, this chapter first investigates the relationship between the four independent variables – perceived value, trust, image and satisfaction – and the dependent variable – customers' cross-buying intentions related to financial products. This relationship will be identified through multiple regression. In addition to this, collectivism will be added stepwise to observe the changes in the correlation between these relationships. Through these hierarchical steps, the hypotheses will be tested and verified. This chapter then compares the findings of the quantitative data analysis with the findings from the interviews for the qualitative analysis. This provides a more solid and subjective view on the outcomes, which will eventually serve the initial purpose of this study – to undertake a theoretical explanation of how the cultural value, collectivism, can influence customers' cross-buying intentions related to financial products – a new paradigm of the banking industry in East Asia countries.

Chapter 5: Discussion and future studies

This chapter offers a detailed discussion on the outcomes from the quantitative analysis of 700 samples and qualitative analysis of interviews with practitioners in Korea and Taiwan. The chapter also provides more insights into the management implications for practitioners, financial service companies that are operating or wish to operate internationally. This chapter also addresses the importance of the East Asian financial market by demonstrating how this service sector, particularly in the banking industry, has evolved since the Asian financial crisis of 1997. This chapter discusses the emergence of foreign companies, and the efforts of local banks to diversify the sources of their profits, which has led East Asian countries to become the most influential players in the global financial market. In particular, the chapter examines business cases from globally reputable financial institutions, such as HSBC, Citibank, BNP Paribas and the AXA Group. It discusses how these groups have expanded their global presences in the last two decades, and examines their efforts to promote customers' cross-buying activities in the banking industry in East Asia. By doing this, the chapter reviews the relationships between the cross-buying intentions of customers and each determinant that was tested in Chapter 3. This chapter compares the outcomes of these relationships with the findings from the literature reviews presented in Chapter 2. As the main theme of this book, this chapter discusses the influence of collectivism on the relationships between the key determinants and cross-buying intentions. And finally, this chapter explores the contradictory outcomes, such as the relationship of perceived value and image to cross-buying intention, and the confirmative outcomes related to trust and satisfaction.

Chapter 6: Conclusion

This final chapter summarizes and crystallizes the significance of the findings of this study and constructive recommendations.

Notes

1 The Asian Development Bank (www.adb.org) defines East Asian Countries as China (including Hong Kong), Korea, Taiwan and Mongolia. Throughout this book, the term 'East Asian Countries' will follow this definition.
2 Glass–Steagall Act, 1933.
3 The European countries referred to here are members of CEA Insurance and Reinsurance Federation, including Croatia and Turkey. Throughout this book, the term 'European Countries' will follow this definition.
4 M2. Money supply includes measures in M1, as well as time deposits and savings.
5 www.cia.org.

2 Review of literature

2.1 Introduction

Cultural values influence how people think and behave. Therefore, customers from different cultural backgrounds may react differently towards the same services from the same service providers (De Mooij and Hofstede 2011; Hansen *et al.* 2011; Ozdemir and Hewett 2010; Zhang *et al.* 2008). This chapter reviews the literature that discusses how cultural values, such as collectivism, may influence a specific financial service sector, such as the cross-buying intentions of customers in the banking industry.

This chapter indicates the critical issues in cross-cultural studies on customers' behaviour by examining the studies listed in Knight (1999) from the 1980s to the 1990s. This chapter also examines the cultural studies of international customers that were summarized by Zhang (2008) from the 1990s to the 2000s. Through these two sets of reviews, this chapter highlights the importance of the operationalization and theorization of the culture. This chapter selects the 'value and belief' approach (Criag and Douglas 2006) to confirm the invariability of cross-cultural dimensions. Hofstede's cross-cultural dimensions (1984, 2002, 2010) are recognized as one of the most widely used and adequate measurements for the study of international customer behaviour and management (Ryan *et al.* 2006; Sivakumar and Nakata 2001; Soares *et al.* 2007; Sondergaard 1994). However, it is also recognized as the measurement that has the longest history of debates and discussions in various academic arenas (Taras *et al.* 2010a). This chapter examines the debates that were cited in the studies of Trompenaars and Hampden-Turner (1995), McSweeney (2002) and House *et al.* (2004). This chapter demonstrates how Hofstede's cultural dimensions (1984, 2002, 2010) successfully responded to these challenges. This discussion mainly focuses on the debates with the GLOBE project, which was initiated by House *et al.* (2004).

In Hofstede's cultural dimension (1984, 2004, 2010), individualism-collectivism is considered the most frequent and commonly used cultural value when comparing East and Western countries (Hofstede 2007; Oyserman and Lee 2008; Schimmack *et al.* 2005; Vandello and Cohen 1999). This is because East Asian customers – particularly Korean and Taiwanese customers – are perceived to be more collectivistic than their counterparts in other countries (Hofstede 2007; House *et al.* 2004; Inglehart 2006; Ladhari 2009; Ozdemir and Hewett 2010; Zhang *et al.* 2008). This chapter addresses the fact that the collectivism of Korea and Taiwan is also influenced by historical values – namely, the Confucian value, which respects harmony, hierarchy and conservatism. This value causes individuals in these countries to appreciate the benefit of a collective group, rather than the benefit of the individual (Ueltschy *et al.* 2009; Wu 2009; Zhang *et al.* 2005). Surprisingly, this cultural value – collectivism based on the Confucian value – has not previously been considered a moderating factor in any specific financial services sector.

Therefore, this chapter explores the essence of customers' cross-buying behaviours in financial products through various literatures that focus on the studies of CRM (Kumar and Reinartz 2006; Peppard 2000; Ryals and Payne 2001) in the financial services sector. This chapter identifies four key factors that are the determinants of customers' cross-buying intentions in banking services. These four factors are 'perceived value', 'trust', 'image' and 'satisfaction'. These are extracted from the studies of Verhoef *et al.* (2001, 2002, 2005), Ngobo (2004), Kumar *et al.* (2006, 2008), Reinartz *et al.* (2004, 2008) and Soureli *et al.* (2008) in the context of European countries, and from the studies of Liu and Wu (2007, 2010), Fan *et al.* (2011) and Kim and Kim (2008) in the context of Korea and Taiwan. By comparing the relationship between these four factors and customers' cross-buying intentions in these studies, this chapter demonstrates that the outcomes in the context of Korea and Taiwan differ from ones in the context of European countries.

This chapter demonstrates that this is the main research gap in the field of customers' cross-buying in banking services, which is the most rapidly growing sector in East Asia, led by Korea and Taiwan (Claessens 2009; Ghosh 2006; Swiss Re 2007). Therefore, this chapter aims to establish that this rapid growth of customers' cross-buying intentions in the banking services of Korea and Taiwan is a result of the high collectivism in these two countries. This chapter underpins this with various empirical findings from the related literature in the context of the financial services.

However, a proper understanding and disciplinary operationalization of culture with its empirical findings are crucial tasks for this study. Without a clearly theorized framework on culture, it would be difficult to accurately determine how culture influences customers' behaviour and intentions (Featherstone 2007; Oyserman *et al.* 2002; Soares *et al.* 2007; Wedeen 2003).

2.2 Operationalization of culture: value and belief system approach

Culture is defined in various terms. The classic definition of culture is by Tylor (1924, p. 1), who referred to culture as "the complex whole, which includes knowledge, belief, art, morals, law, custom and any other capabilities and habits acquired by humans as members of society". Culture is learned, not innate; thus, it derives from one's social environment, rather than from one's genes. Trompenaars and Hampden-Turner (1995) defined culture as a series of methods and rules created by a group of people in order to help them solve problems, particularly connected to relationships, time and the environment. The most cited term in the social sciences, as well as in marketing studies, is the definition provided by Hofstede (Newburry and Yakova 2006). Hofstede (1991, p. 5) defined culture as "the values formed through collective programming of the mind acquired by growing up in a particular country, with a broad tendency to prefer certain states of affairs over others". This matches Terpstra (2006), who defined culture as an integrated pattern of behaviour and the distinctive way of life of people. In more simplified terms, culture is everything that people have, think and do as members of their society (Ferraro 2006) that has been transmitted through the process of learning and interacting with their environment (Laroche *et al.* 2004). Therefore, culture has a pervasive influence on all aspects of human behaviour, and its effect may be "subtle or pronounced, direct or oblique, enduring or ephemeral" (Craig and Douglas 2006, p. 322). Specifically in the context of customers' behaviour, several studies in psychology and sociology, as well as in marketing and management, have recognized the importance of cultural characteristics in customers' behaviour and perceptions of firms' services (Furrer *et al.* 2000; Hong *et al.* 2000; Ladhari 2009; Liu *et al.* 2001; Oyserman *et al.* 2002).

For example, studies in psychology or sociology focus on explaining the differences in customers' attitudes, including their cognitive style, attribution, self-concept and relationships (DiMaggio 1997; Donald 1991; Hong *et al.* 2000; Oyserman *et al.* 2002). However, studies in marketing and management focus on measuring the differences in customers' perception and evaluation of services from the firms, based on their diverse cultural characteristics (Donthu and Yoo 1998; Furrer *et al.* 2000; Liu *et al.* 2001; Mattila 1999; Winsted 1997). Briley (2009) summarized this phenomenon by stating that academics in psychology and sociology aim to describe societal differences in core values, norms, and characteristics of culture, while academics in marketing and management aim to explain and predict customers' behaviour based on the characteristics of cultures.

However, whether from the view of academics in psychology, sociology or marketing, there is consensus that culture is widely entwined with all aspects of human existence, and that it strongly influences customers' behaviour. Therefore, irrespective of academic field, a proper conceptualization and operationalization of culture has always been essential and crucial when conducting cross-cultural research (Featherstone 2007; Oyserman *et al.* 2002; Soares *et al.* 2007; Wedeen 2003).

Sojka and Tansuhaj (1995) are some of the few academics who have proposed a structured summary of the main streams in conceptualizing and operationalizing culture in marketing studies. Their study, which reviewed 20 years of cross-cultural customer research on various service arenas, categorized three forms of approach in conducting cross-cultural research: language and communication, material possessions and artefacts, and values and belief systems. These three approaches have been commonly used and confirmed in studies of psychology, sociology, marketing and management (Burton 2009; Craig and Douglas 2006; Soares *et al.* 2007).

The first approach is to operationalize culture through language and communication, which bind and perpetuate cultural systems. Language and communication offer an interpretative code or schema for organizing and presenting the world (Sojka and Tansuhaj 1995). Language and communication stipulate the meaning of objects and symbols for the individual. They act as a unifying force, binding the members of a specific society and culture. Therefore, language and communication play an important role in the formation of customers' cognitive processes, such as perception, judgement and choice (Zhang and Schmitt 2001), as well as brand recall, recognition and the encoding or recall of information (Tavassoli and Lee 2003).

However, although language has been proven to be an important element of culture in forming and organizing cultural content and in providing a cohesive bond among its members, it may not be a good indicator of ethnicity and cannot be used alone to explain different behaviour across subcultures and cultures (Craig and Douglas 2006; Riley 2007). Abrams and O'Connor (2002) stated that people of self-identities from different cultural backgrounds may act as impediments to effective communication and, even within cultures, different groups and communities may have their own particular modes of communication. Therefore, operationalizing culture solely based on language and communication may cause numerous issues (Gudykunst 2005).

The second approach is to operationalize culture through material possessions and artefacts. These objects make the operationalization of culture more concrete than the use of language and communication (Soares *et al.* 2007; Sojka and Tansuhaj 1995). This approach binds the rituals, artefacts, institutions and symbols of a society, and establishes rules and norms for how people should behave towards others within society, both generally and on specific occasions, such as weddings, funerals and festivals (Craig and Douglas 2006). In this approach, individual possessions, artefacts, families or social groups are important elements of material culture, as is the significance attached to gifts and gift-giving rituals (Belk and Coon 1993; Joy 2001). This approach of cultural operationalization relates to the ritual impulse of customers' perceptions (Belk and Costa 1998) and customers' intergenerational transfer of possessions (Curasi *et al.* 2004).

Brand can also serve as a cultural maker in this approach (Holt 2002), as the meaning and set of associations that surrounds a brand name or category may vary from one culture to another (Joy 2001). However, the criticism of this approach is that it is often limited to a particular site or specific cultural context. This criticism is in line with the study of Craig and Douglas (2006), which discussed the difficulty of making generalizations in a broader context, or making implicit comparisons with other cultures. It can be problematic to integrate findings related to specific sites into a broader understanding of cultural influences, and to apply these influences across multiple sites. McCracken (2005) also raised the concern that these problems may arise from the fact that this operationalization of culture depends on how the sites are selected, and what specific cultural components are studied.

Finally, there is an approach to view these values and beliefs of a society as indicated by the intangible elements of culture (Sojka and Tansuhaj 1995). This approach results from a perspective that the intangible elements of culture incorporate the dominant societal values and belief systems that characterize a society or culture and guide the patterns of behaviour within that society (Craig and Douglas 2006). This approach, which is most widely and frequently used in marketing (Craig and Douglas 2006; Newburry and Yakova 2006; Soares *et al.* 2007; Sojka and Tansuhaj 1995), examines the culture at the level of the society, specific groups or organizations within a society, and the individual. It examines the underlying differences in management practices, organizational patterns and decision-making. This approach has been used in marketing studies to characterize the national culture of different countries and as an independent variable to explain or understand cross-national differences (Hofstede 2005; Inglehart 2000; Oyserman *et al.* 2002; Schwartz and Bardi 2001; Sivakumar and Nakata 2001; Smith *et al.* 2002).

However, this approach – the value-oriented approach – is often criticized. This criticism stems from the fact that this approach constitutes too broad a societal construct, which may not reflect the process-oriented aspects of the society or the importance of contextual variables in influencing customers' behaviour and cognition (Miller 2002; Oyserman and Lee 2008). In addition to this criticism, through this approach, the differences among individuals might be ignored to the extent to which they subscribe to the dominant societal cultural orientation (Briley *et al.* 2000; Briley and Aaker 2006). Therefore, it has been argued by a dynamic constructionist that culture should be adopted by focusing on the identification of specific knowledge structures or by implicating cultural theories that mediate social behaviour in specific domains (Briley 2009; Hong and Chiu 2001).

These negative views on the value and belief-oriented approach of culture are mostly challenged by personality psychology, in which it is asserted that social-cultural training leaves people from different cultural groups with different personalities. Briley (2009) postulated that it is more practical to understand cultural influence from a dynamic perspective rooted in a social cognition theory, rather than operationalizing culture in terms of broad and domain-general values. There is also another view from this perspective that states that those values and beliefs have transformed their patterning due to the growing links between local cultures and the increasing permeability of cultural boundaries. Craig and Douglas (2006) present a case that values – typically those characterizing Western societies, such as individualism – will increasingly be adopted by collectivist East Asian societies, and that East Asian values – such as harmony – will become more evident in Western societies. In other words, individuals in a certain society or nation will embrace non-traditional values from other societies, providing evidence that the values and beliefs of the culture will change in the future.

While this criticism is valid to a certain extent, there is also a theoretical position that values and beliefs will maintain their consistency. In other words, the culture does not have to be adopted as a specific social behaviour, but will remain as it is and will be unlikely to change. For example, in Europe, even with the economic union and progress towards the standardization of political and social infrastructure, the cultural values and beliefs of nations are still strongly rooted in history and appear to remain unchanged over time (De Mooij 2000; De Mooij and Hofstede 2002). This finding aligns with the studies of Arnett (2002), who explained that new cultural values being widely embraced by people of various societies do not necessarily mean that people will entirely reject their old values to adopt new ones.

An example of this is in East Asia, where countries are influenced by the Confucian value. Modern values, such as individualism, are gaining prominence within the region and the contemporary lifestyle, and are competing with traditional values and norms (Zhang and Harwood 2004). However, these new values come to coexist with the traditional values and norms of these societies, rather than replacing them, which ensures the Confucian value is maintained (Zhang *et al.* 2005). The local culture continues to exist, as fundamental values and beliefs continue to exert an influence on the habits and traditions of the people. Even Oyserman and her colleagues (Oyserman *et al.* 2002; Oyserman and Lee 2008), who once held a perspective of cultural operationalization, admitted that the cultural dimension, such as the individualism-collectivism of Hofstede's model (Hofstede 1984b; Hofstede and Hofstede 1991), has been stable for the past 20 years, according to their meta-analysis on cross-cultural research, published in January 2005.

Therefore, despite the debates and discussion of its limitations, operationalization of culture through the value and belief systems is known to be the most adequate proposition, and has been accepted by several academics (Soares *et al.* 2007). In the context of marketing, Sojka and Tansuhaj (1995) also conclusively confirmed that the value and belief system is the most useful to understand and predict customer behaviour in a cross-cultural setting.

2.3 Cultural studies and customer behaviour: critical considerations

The influence of culture on customers' behaviour and perception of services has been a constantly challenging topic in the field of international marketing. The topic received attention because, as an increasing number of firms started to operate internationally to provide marketing services to international customers, the need to understand these customers' characteristics increased (Ueltschy *et al.* 2007; Wirtz and Lovelock 2007). Furthermore, understanding the customers' perceptions of the services and their future needs became an imperative element in the marketing arena, as it links to firms' ability to effectively compete in a globalized environment (Cunningham *et al.* 2005; Javalgi and White 2002; Ueltschy *et al.* 2009). Numerous cross-cultural studies in the marketing arena have been conducted throughout the decades to evaluate the influence of culture on the various dimensions of customers' behaviour. However, among these cross-cultural studies in the marketing arena, there are a number of critical considerations that have commonly been noted as requiring further examination.

One of the challenges is that most of the studies in the past, as well as a few in recent years, have focused on this topic from the firm's perspective, rather than from the customer's perspective. An example is the study of Knight (1999), in which he reviewed 124 international marketing studies from 31 academic journals published between the 1980s and 1990s. This study has been recognized as a milestone in the international service-marketing arena because of its comprehensive summary and consolidation of cross-cultural studies. It is also credited as the study that attempted to determine special characteristics of the services in the light of the requirements for successful international marketing (Craig and Douglas 2006). However, most of the studies listed by Knight (1999) showed biased approaches that often led these studies to poor validity in pragmatic application.

As aforementioned, these studies focus on marketing topics from a firm's perspective, rather than a customer's perspective. For example, Erramilli and Rao (1993) focused on the entry mode of firms; Bhuian (1997) explored the orientation of the banking services from the bank perspective; and Porter (1990) explained how to build a national competitive advantage based on the implications of action taken by firms. In other words, the characteristics or individual values of the customers, such as their cultural values, were not considered. This remained a limitation for the studies investigated by Knight (1999). It is undeniable that, in recent international markets, understanding the nature and extent of the difference between customers from different nations is essential in order to create effective target marketing strategies and to conduct successful business in each local market (Schiffman *et al.* 2008; Ueltschy *et al.* 2009). Therefore, the needs of the investigation from the customer's perspective and the understanding of the cognitive values that motivate customers' behaviour should have been addressed in the study of Knight (1999).

Nevertheless, the work of Knight (1999) was inherited by Zhang (2008), who summarized 40 cross-national comparative studies from 30 academic journals, covering 11 years of research, from 1996 to 2006. This study supplemented the limitations of the study from Knight (1999), as Zhang (2008) provided examples of cross-cultural studies that were conducted from the customer's perspective, not the firm's strategic perspective. This approach offered more insight into the relationship between the cultural value and the customer's behaviour and preferences. This ultimately increased the value of Zhang's (2008) study. However, among these selected cross-cultural studies, there is a lack of the conceptual framework that occasionally causes confusion in the outcomes.

For example, the study of Sultan and Simpson (2000) provided the finding that customers' expectations and perceptions of service quality are varied among different nationalities. However, they failed to include the cultural values or dimensions that measure these differences. Similar limitations are found in the studies of John (2004), Brady and Robertson (2001), Gilbert and Veloutsou (2004) and Cunningham and Young (2005), where the differences among the nations were expressed only as the differences in nationalities. All of these studies, as well as a few others listed by Zhang (2008), lacked theoretical and conceptual frameworks to distinguish between the cultures; they only evaluated the outcomes based on the historical recognition of cultural values. This generated criticism, as Gudykunst (2005) stated, because without proper theorizing and conceptualizing of cross-cultural differences, it is difficult to validate the findings and expand the knowledge gained from the findings. Therefore, it is crucial and essential that the studies related to customers' cross-cultural behaviour should first focus on developing insights and conceptualizing the cross-cultural dimensions.

Noticeably, some cross-cultural research of the past has succeeded in providing a framework that explains the cultural values of nations and their cultural groups. For example, Winsted (1997) examined how customers with different cultural values evaluated service encounters by formulating behavioural based service encounter dimensions. The study identified significant cross-cultural differences between the US and Japan – particularly the fact that many types of behaviour that were important in determining the dimensions of service encounters in the US samples were not instrumental in identifying the dimensions in the Japanese samples.

Mattila (1999) conducted a conjoint analysis to assess the differences between customers with a Western and East Asian cultural background. In this study, it was discovered that customers with Western cultural backgrounds were more likely to rely on tangible cues from the physical environment compared to the East Asian customers. Furthermore, the hedonic dimension of the consumption experience was more important for Western consumers, whose core values include fun and enjoyment, than for Asians, whose core values tend to reflect duty in life.

However, the studies of Winsted (1997) and Mattila (1999) were based on a restaurant business and a luxurious hotel, thus limiting their applicability to other service sectors. For example, in the financial services, several specific characteristics need to be considered. Characteristics such as intangibility, customer involvement and confidentiality are inherent to the products of most financial service providers (Maas and Graf 2008). Therefore, compared to other service industries, aspects such as risk, uncertainty, trust and personal relationships may represent an important role to customers' behaviour and perceptions of service quality in the financial services sector.

The study of Donthu and Yoo (1998) is an early example of cross-cultural research based on the financial services. In this study, 281 respondents were selected from Canada, Great Britain, India and the US, and were asked about their expectations of banking quality. This study adopted Hofstede's cultural dimensions (Hofstede 1984b; Hofstede and Hofstede 1991) to strengthen the hypotheses on each country's cultural values. For example, they hypothesized that individualistic customers would have a higher service quality expectation than collectivistic customers. At the same time, individualistic customers were expected to have a higher expectation of assurance from the provider than collectivistic customers in banking service sectors. Based on these assumptions, Donthu and Yoo (1998) used a specific service quality framework – SERV-QUAL (Parasuraman *et al.* 1993; Zeithaml *et al.* 1993) – to evaluate the service quality of the customers of each country, and investigate the relationship between the findings and cultural dimensions. This study was one of the first, significant empirical cross-cultural studies, particularly in the context of the financial services sector. However, this study was challenged by Furrer and Liu (2000), who claimed that Donthu and Yoo (1998) did not use an adequate number of service quality dimensions, and lacked an explanation about other possible relationships with cultural dimensions. Furrer and Liu (2000) stated that, as five cultural dimensions and five service quality frameworks were used in the study of Donthu and Yoo (1998), there should be 25 possible relationships tested, rather than only six.

In order to test a complete set of hypotheses relating all SERVQUAL scales (Parasuraman *et al.* 1993; Zeithaml *et al.* 1993) to Hofstede's cultural dimensions (Hofstede 1984a; Hofstede and Hofstede 1991), Furrer and Liu (2000, 2001) conducted a study with 302 samples from the Western and East Asian background. This study not only confirmed the fact that SERVQUAL highly correlated with Hofstede's cultural dimensions, but also explicitly mapped the relationship between service quality perceptions and cultural dimension positions. In their study, they found that individualistic customers tended to expect a high level of service quality, but wished to maintain a distance between themselves and their service providers. To a certain extent, this matched the findings of Donthu and Yoo (1998). However, in contradiction to Donthu and Yoo (1998), Furrer and Liu (2000) found that individualistic customers tended to have a negative correlation with the assurance of customers towards a service provider.

Limitations still existed in these studies. Furrer and Liu (2000, 2001) stated in their notes that these studies were based on the assumption that the interpretation of SERVQUAL was the same, even in different cultural settings. In other words, if SERVQUAL is interpreted differently in different cultures, their model is not theoretically suitable. This weakness of SERVQUAL has also been addressed in the literature of Ladhari (2009), in which he reviewed 20 years of cross-cultural studies related to SERVQUAL.

Although the SERVQUAL instrument has been widely applied and valued by academics and practitioners, some academics identified potential difficulties with the conceptual foundation and operationalization of SERVQUAL scales. Cronin and Taylor (1994) challenged this approach and established the SERVPERF scale, which captures customers' performance perceptions more directly in comparison with their expectations of the service encounter. SERVPERF has been supported by several studies undertaken by Brady (2002) and Zhou (2004) as an alternative to

SERVQUAL, while academics such as Donthu and Yoo (1998), Furrer and Liu (2000), Arasli (2005) and Gounaris (2005) adhere to the use of SERVQUAL.

Both SERVQUAL and SERVPERF's operationalizations are based on the conceptual definition that service quality is an attitude towards the service offered by a firm, resulting from a comparison of expectations with performance (Cronin Jr and Taylor 1994; Cronin Jr *et al.* 2000; Parasuraman *et al.* 1985, 1994). SERVQUAL directly measures both expectations and performance perceptions, whereas SERVPERF only measures performance perceptions. SERVPERF assumes that respondents provide their ratings by automatically comparing performance perceptions with performance expectations. Therefore, SERVPERF assumes that directly measuring performance expectations is unnecessary. This raises caution in the application of SERVPERF in studies of customer behaviour. For example, for practitioners, customers' performance expectations may be as important as performance perceptions.

In this regard, SERVQUAL is considered superior to SERVPERF in terms of the diagnostic power to pinpoint areas for managerial intervention. Jain and Gupta (2004) stated that, even though SERVPERF may be proper for assessing overall service quality due to its psychometric soundness, SERVQUAL is preferred to identify areas relating to service quality shortfalls that require a firm's reaction. As for SERVPERF, the diagnostic ability of the scales has not been explicated and empirically verified in the past. In other words, SERVQUAL provides more value to practitioners with more specific managerial implications. This is in line with the studies of Curry and Sinclair (2002), which demonstrated the usefulness and relevance of SERVQUAL to determine customers' priorities and to measure service performance.

Landrum (2007) also reported in his study that the SERVQUAL model offers a higher predictive power than other service quality scales. Moreover, SERV-QUAL has demonstrated higher validity with specific cross-cultural dimensions in a particular market sector. In the study of Carrillat (2007), it was demonstrated that the predictive validity of SERVQUAL on service quality is highest in intermediate customer processing industries, such as hotels, rental cars and banks. This group has an intermediate level of customization and judgement of service employees that generated in both the back and front offices. The result of this study is understandable, as these types of services, including the financial services industry, were one of the sectors SERVQUAL originally initiated (Parasuraman *et al.* 1985). Particularly in the retail banking services, where two way interactions are more common than any other industry (Vandermerwe and Chadwick 1989), there will be more opportunities for managerial intervention, which allows for more use of SERVQUAL.

At the same time, SERVQUAL shows high validity for a specific cross-cultural dimension. Carrillat (2007) found that one country's individualism negatively affects the predictive validity of SERVQUAL. This was found from 17 studies containing 42 effect sizes of the relationships between SERVQUAL and SERVPERF. In other words, in a country with higher collectivism, SERVQUAL has greater validity. At the same time, Carrillat (2007) also demonstrated that, compared to SERVPERF, SERVQUAL has a higher predictive validity for non-English speaking countries. These findings and suggestions are unique because SERVQUAL and SERVPERF were both developed in the US – an English-speaking country with a low level of collectivism (Hofstede 1984a, 2004). However, when replicated in other countries outside the US, the use of SERV-QUAL is preferable. In this regard, for cross-cultural studies of customer expectation and behaviour – particularly in the East Asian context, where most countries show a high level of collectivism – SERVQUAL appears to be the most frequently used.

In addition to these considerations of SERQUVAL in cross-cultural studies, there are more debates regarding the study of Furrer and Liu (2000). One of these debates argues that some terms of measurement may cause confusion due to local interpretation. The terms used in this study, such as 'assurance', might be differently interpreted by other countries. For example, of the subjective sample countries used by Furrer and Liu (2000) and Donthu and Yoo (1998), only the US was commonly selected – all the other countries were different. The two countries that were selected as counterparts were India and Japan, which have different historical origins of cultural values (Hofstede 2007; Hofstede *et al.* 2010), and different levels of operating financial services (Berger 2007). Therefore, even in the same segments defined as 'Asian customers' by Furrer and Liu (2000) and Donthu and Yoo (1998), there could have been different interpretations of the term 'assurance'.

In fact, India and Japan are considered the most individualistic countries among their East Asian peers, according to the individualism-collectivism scores of Hofstede's dimensions (2010). India is 48 and Japan is 46, which are the two highest scores of Asian countries. Therefore, the findings based on these two studies might not be applicable to other East Asian countries, such as Korea and Taiwan, which are considered highly collectivistic (Hofstede *et al.* 2010). A similar example is noted in the findings of Cunningham (2005), who stated that, for customers in the US, convenience is highly correlated with the ease of changing providers, with discrete service delivery and with no formal relationship. However, Korean and Taiwanese customers may have a completely different concept of convenience. Even Korea and Taiwan – two countries known to share similar cultural and historical values – might have different views of the same classified terms, based on their cultural values. The practice of terms is not exclusively the same, even in the same region (Craig and Douglas 2006).

There are other arguments in addition to this debate on the terms of measurement. Furrer and Liu (2000) used a sample of students with different cultural backgrounds, whereas Donthu and Yoo (1998) used an actual customer base. This may also have influenced the outcomes, as the sample of students might have had different preferences of service quality to actual customers with a wider range of ages. In cross-cultural studies, it is crucial to consider the factual effects of specific characteristics in the services setting, cultural background and even in testing samples (Ember and Ember 2009). Therefore, it is preferable to use a sample of end customers, rather than an abstract sample of students.

However, in the latter study of Furrer and Liu (2000), it was mentioned that the sample for the survey of their study was based on MBA students, who had working experience in the financial services industries in their local countries. This partially justifies the eligibility of the samples that were used by Furrer and Liu (2000, 2001), but still leaves room for debate.

Furrer and Liu (2001) reached the conclusion that customers from high individualistic cultures, mostly in Western countries, tend to focus more on their own interests and benefits, meaning that their expectations of service quality are higher than customers from collectivistic cultures. Laroche (2004) also explained that, since East Asian cultures are traditional service cultures, which are based on collectivistic and long-term oriented cultures, East Asian customers have lower expectations of service quality. However, commitment and trust are considered necessary for a good relationship between East Asian customers and service firms. Based on the study of Laroche (2004), among the samples of Canada, the US and Japan, Japanese customers were recognized as more conservative in the evaluation of superior services, but less critical of inferior services. Moreover, there is other research that assumes that customers from East Asian countries, as collectivistic societies, will place more value on the relationship, rather than the individual's interest (Hofstede 2007; Ueltschy *et al.* 2009; Zhang *et al.* 2008).

Furrer and Liu (2000) also found that customers from more individualistic cultures exhibited a higher likelihood to switch to other service providers. However, this may differ among different service industries in terms of customers' behavioural intentions (Kumar *et al.* 2008; Reinartz and Kumar 2000; Verhoef 2003). For example, the meaning and intention of switching, or the continuation of a relationship, can be different in the financial services industry, where the relationship is built upon a contractual setting, as opposed to the traditional retail industry, which has a relatively non-contractual setting (Ngobo 2004; Verhoef 2003). Specifically, in the context of the financial services industry, there are several characteristics that must be considered, including intangibility, customer involvement and confidentiality (Salazar *et al.* 2007). Therefore, in the financial industry, compared to other service industries, values such as risk, uncertainty, trust and personal relationships may represent a more important role in customers' behaviour (Maas and Graf 2008). These characteristics of financial service require more attention, as the financial services industry has undergone dynamic changes due to the consolidation of the industry, globalization of the market and the convergence of financial services (Ghosh 2006; Laeven 2005). These changes are more noticeable in East Asian countries, where deregulation and liberalization occurred relatively late, as the local regulators allowed cross-selling activities of financial institutions only in recent years (Corbett 2007).

When reconciling these considerations into approaches and measurements in cross-cultural studies related to customer behaviour, it is essential that these studies are approached from the perspective of customers, and that the measurements are based on rigorous operationalization of cultural values. These are key conclusions that were found in the studies of Craig and Douglas (2006), Featherstone (2007), Zang *et al.* (2008) and Ueltschy *et al.* (2009). Furthermore, in cross-cultural studies, particularly in studies related to customers' behaviour, it is crucial to rigorously assess the difference between the service industry and the specific cultural value of the country or region (Cunningham *et al.* 2005; Kumar *et al.* 2008; Reinartz and Kumar 2000; Verhoef 2003). For example, East Asian customers are often defined as cherishing Confucian values that appreciate interpersonal harmony, relational hierarchy and traditional conservatism (Ueltschy *et al.* 2009; Zhang *et al.* 2005). This is an important factor that may influence East Asian customers to be collectivistic; however, this cannot alone be conceptualized as the cultural value. Neither can the practices that resulted from these different cultural values be considered as the cultural value itself. These assertions are in line with the conclusions of several studies, such as those of White (2002), Tsui (2004) and Meyer (2006), which commonly emphasized the danger of plainly adopting the findings of Western countries to the East Asian context, without these findings being tested and modified to improve their validation in East Asia.

Therefore, in order to ensure a reliable cross-cultural study, it is essential to scrutinise the cultural values that represent customers with different cultural backgrounds, and operationalize these into theoretical dimensions. Once these cultural values are operationalized, practical validation of these values for a specific culture may be required. For example, collectivism, which is one of the most commonly and frequently operationalized cultural values in cross-cultural studies (Hofstede 2005; Oyserman *et al.* 2002; Triandis and Gelfand 1998; Vandello and Cohen 1999), is often recognized as a representative value of East Asian culture (Hofstede 2007; Ueltschy *et al.* 2009; Watchravesringkan *et al.* 2008). However, to validate and confirm this assumption, a detailed study of the nature of the East Asian culture and its core culture is necessary.

Cross-cultural research is relatively new and has tremendous potential for developing insights into the services marketing arena (Zhang *et al.* 2005). At the same time, cross-buying and customer value management is comparatively new to marketing, particularly in the Korean and Taiwanese financial services markets, which are expected to become increasingly important (Appiah-Kubi and Doku 2010; Lin *et al.* 2009; Liu and Wu 2009; Sofat and Hiro 2009). In fact, from cross-cultural studies in the financial services arena, it can be seen that collectivism influences customers' perceptions of service quality and behavioural intentions (Furrer *et al.*, 2000; Liu *et al.*, 2001; Zhang *et al.*, 2008). Customers with a collectivistic cultural background tend to be more tolerant towards poor quality of service, and more likely to complain less (Liu *et al.*, 2001). This is because their culture encourages them to appreciate a relationship with the financial service provider more than their individualistic needs. Concurrently, Donthu and Yoo (1998) demonstrated that banking customers in a collectivistic culture have less expectation of service quality, but rely on aspects of their relationship with their bank, such as trust. Unfortunately, these are the only empirical studies that have been undertaken on cultural influences in the East Asian financial services.

Through an exhaustive summary of cross-cultural customer research from 1996 to 2006, Zhang (2008) found that, out of 40 selected cross-cultural researches, 27 used Hofstede's cross-cultural dimension (Hofstede 1984b; Hofstede and Hofstede 1991) to test the cross-cultural effect associated with the customers' intentions, service expectations and behaviour in the local market. Hofstede's dimension and theories are one of the most widely used measurements among global customer studies and management (Ryan *et al.* 2006; Sivakumar and Nakata 2001; Soares *et al.* 2007; Sondergaard 1994). However, it is also the dimension that has the longest history of debates and discussions in various academic arenas (Taras *et al.* 2010a).

2.4 Hofstede's cultural dimensions: debates and beyond

During his period of publication, from the 1980s to 2010, the cross-cultural dimension established by Hofstede inspired numerous academics, not only in psychology and sociology (Gelfand *et al.* 2007), but also in the marketing fields (Soares *et al.* 2007) and the management fields (Tsui and Nifadkar 2007). From his first study of 40 different countries in the 1980s (Hofstede 1984a) to his most recent publication (Hofstede *et al.* 2010), Hofstede (2010) adhered to cultural scores from five cultural dimensions to measure the differences between countries. Initially, he derived four dimensions: 'power distance', 'uncertainty avoidance', 'individualism-collectivism' and 'masculinity-femininity' (Hofstede 1984a). Later, he added a fifth dimension: 'long-term versus short-term orientation' (Hofstede and Hofstede 1991). This work was undertaken with the contribution of Bond (1987), who sampled a different domain of values derived from Chinese culture and reached an ecological factor analysis that yielded four factors: 'integration', 'Confucian dynamism', 'human-heartiness' and 'moral discipline'.

These dimensions of Hofstede (1991) were challenged and compared with various studies. One of the first studies that challenged Hofstede's dimensions was the seven dimensional model of Trompenaars and Hampden-Turner (1995). This model was composed of time orientation, relation to nature, universalism versus particularism, individualism versus collectivism, affectivity versus neutrality, specificity versus diffuseness, and achievement versus ascription. By expanding the model to include more cultural values, Trompenaars and Hampden-Turner (1995) claimed that this would resolve the weaknesses of Hofstede's study, which used Aristotelian categories of 'A' and 'Non-A', which implied the study was too linear and exclusive.

However, Hofstede (1997) responded to this criticism by stating that Trompenaars and Hampden-Turner's model simply borrowed conceptual distinctions from previous studies of Parsons and Shils (1951) and Kluckhohn (1961), and that it did not provide an empirical analysis. The only empirical analysis of this model was made by Smith and Dugan (1996), who surveyed 8,841 managers in 43 countries on the cultural values of organizational employees. In this survey, only two independent dimensions confirmed it to be valid – one correlated with Hofstede's individualism-collectivism; the other correlated primarily with power distance, and secondarily with individualism-collectivism. These findings were criticized by Gustafsson (2009), who stated that Trompennars and Hampden-Turner's (1995) study of individualism versus collectivism was very similar to Hofstede's individualism versus collectivism dimension. Gustafsson (2009) also stated that their research approach was too involved in the process of cultural creation, whereas the approach of Hofstede (1984b, 1991) was more focused on analysis of the variables of national culture, which provides a higher validity.

Hofstede's study was also challenged by McSweeney (2002), who had a different perspective on Hofstede's five methodological assumptions. McSweeney stated that the notion of culture should have multiple and inclusive definitions, whereas Hofstede described culture as mental programming, or as subjective values represented by scores. McSweeney (2002) also disagreed with Hofstede's approach because the values of dimensions cannot be strong, absolute causality cannot be associated with the national culture, and the national culture cannot be theorized as the only culture within a nation. This claim was extended by recent criticisms from Fang (2003, 2010), who also stated that Hofstede's dimensions offered little insight into the dynamic process of cross-cultural evolutions, characterized by changes, such as knowledge transfer (Holden 2002), multiple cultural identity (Sackmann and Phillips 2004) and cultural dialectics and paradox (Fang 2005).

In response to McSweeney (2002) and Fang (2003, 2010), Hofstede (2002, 2010) stated that different replications confirm different dimensions, and that the validations of dimension scores do not imply assumptions about the causality, but only point to causes, effects or associations based on circular causation or on hidden third factors. For this reason, the culture within a nation can be theorized, and could culturally distinguish the members of one nation from another. As for the dynamic process of cross-cultural evolution, Hofstede (2010) confirmed that values related to cultural dimensions are reluctant to change, and prefer to stay stable. This means that, regardless of the evolution of other practices, such as knowledge transfer and changes of cultural identity or dialectics, cultural values will remain the same because the members of the society will maintain the same beliefs from the collective programming of their minds, acquired through the learning process of a particular society.

This assertion derives from two major cross-cultural projects that were undertaken during the 1990s and 2000s. The first major project was by Inglehart (2006), who also indicated that cultural changes were occurring, but that a society's religious tradition, colonial history and other major historical factors give rise to distinctive cultural traditions accumulated through historical processes. He stated that these factors continue to influence a society's value system, despite the speed of the changes occurring in the contemporary world. Based on the World Values Survey carried out between 1981 and 2001, Inglehart (2000, 2006) concluded that cross-cultural variation is coherent, and that the world's societies cluster into relatively homogenous cultural zones that persist robustly over time. This is in line with the statement of the second major cross-cultural project, Survey of Values, completed by Schwartz and Bardi (2001). This study of Schwartz and Bardi (2001) details the derivations of the ten basic values – Self direction, Stimulation, Hedonism, Achievement, Power, Security, Conformity, Tradition, Benevolence and Universalism – that build the values theory, which defines values as desirable, trans-situational goals, varying in importance that serves as guiding principles in individual's lives. These ten basic values of individuals are then incorporated into cross-cultural values, which generate a different standard in cultural dimensional distance (Tung and Verbeke, 2010). In this regard, cross-cultural research based on the value-oriented approach has been appreciated for its appealing attributes – particularly the work of Hofstede (1984b, 1991), which has been the most influential. Recent research, such as the GLOBE project (House *et al.* 2004), has brought a more contemporary approach to the study of culture on an international scale (Mearns and Yule 2009).

The GLOBE project (House *et al.* 2004) was based on 170 collaborators' collected data from 17,000 managers in 951 organizations. These organizations belonged to the industries of food processing, financial services and telecommunication services, in 62 societies, worldwide. Hofstede (2006) recognized GLOBE as one of the most significant cross-cultural research projects, in addition to the World Value Survey (Inglehart *et al.* 2000) and the Survey of Values (Schwartz and Bardi 2001). However, Hofstede criticized GLOBE's theory-driven approach because of its main reliance on statistical pre-tests by previous studies. Hofstede's work and the other two major cross-cultural studies were genuinely action-driven. Hofstede (2006) confirmed this criticism by presenting the fact that he designed his survey questionnaires as a management tool that was developed through an open-ended pilot interview with managers in nine countries. As a result of this, his surveys could deal with issues that practitioners from different categories considered relevant in their work situation; GLOBE could not have fully achieved this with its theory-driven approach.

In response to this criticism, Javidan and House (2006) argued that, since the GLOBE project purports to establish an integrated theory developed from the central proposition and to define a specified culture are predictive of leadership styles and organizational practices in that culture, it has to be theory-driven. The essence of the GLOBE project was to predict selected aspects of cultural practices that account for the economic competitiveness of nations, as well as the physical and psychological well-being of their members, based on the theory built by this approach (House *et al.* 2004). However, there need to be more empirical studies that apply the conceptual model of the GLOBE project, in order to validate this project's approach. As Hofstede's model has been used for more than 20 years, and still is being used by several academics in various cross-cultural research areas (Gelfand *et al.* 2007; Soares *et al.* 2007; Tsui and Nifadkar 2007), the GLOBE project also needs to expand its scope of applications to marketing, psychology and sociology in order to justify its theory-based approach, which is currently criticized as being a barrier.

In addition to its different approaches to research methodology, main differences can be noticed between the GLOBE project and Hofstede's studies in terms of the separation of practices and values. The GLOBE used the term 'practices' to refer to culture 'as it is', and 'values' to refer to culture 'as it should be' (House *et al.* 2004). Hofstede (1984b, 1991) only focused on the values of culture. He stated that 'practices' are for symbols, heroes and rituals that are visible to the outside observer, but 'values' refer to things that respondents prefer, often unconsciously (Hofstede 2001). Hofstede (2006) offered an example: when questions from the GLOBE project are asked, respondents will not be able to describe practices in any other way than by applying their values.

Javidan and House (2006) responded that the GLOBE project has taken the position of Schein (2004), who referred to culture as the product of a collective's attempts to address two sets of groups: external adaptation and internal integration. This is the reason that GLOBE asked respondents to express their views regarding what was desirable in their societal cultural dynamics, rather than what was desirable to them as individuals. GLOBE asserted that its approach to understanding and measuring national cultures by separating values and practices is a more rigorous approach than that of Hofstede (Javidan *et al.* 2006).

However, it can be argued that practices and values can coincide and that most academic studies have value in terms of the individual respondent's own preferred end states, not their preferable ones. If the respondent wishes to be something, it does not follow that the respondent wishes others to be something else. Smith (2006) stated that the values measured by GLOBE have a lack of logical linkage with the measures of values in previous studies, such as those by Schwartz (2001) or by Inglehart (2000). Smith stated that GLOBE's values give the impression that GLOBE simply adopted Hofstede's dimensions. For instance, the nine dimensions of GLOBE seem to have simply expanded Hofstede's dimension for conceptual reasons – they maintain power distance and uncertainty avoidance, but split collectivism into 'institutional collectivism' and 'in-group collectivism', while masculinity-femininity is split into 'assertiveness' and 'gender' (Hofstede 2006; Leung *et al.* 2005). McCrae (2008) also argued that the GLOBE project was heavily influenced by Hofstede's work in its choice of variables assessment. Even the participants of the GLOBE project admitted that they found inspiration from Hofstede's exploratory analysis to support their scales on cultures (House *et al.* 2004).

Most recently, Hofstede's model was challenged for its possible limitations to the evolution of technology. With advances in technology, culture is increasingly affected by the global exchange of ideas, products and images (Craig and Douglas 2006). However, Hofstede (2006) asserted that the values of culture are resilient against technology. It is true that technology affects culture generally – not on the basic level of values, but on the more superficial level of practices. Practices change according to the needs of available resources, but this does not necessarily affect the underlying values. For example, practices depend on a person using computer programs, but the purposes for which these programs will be used depend on the values of the people, who are influenced by their culture (Hofstede *et al.* 2010). This interpretation is formulated in Hofstede's onion model (Hofstede 2001). This model demonstrates that the outer layers of the onion diagram, labelled 'practices', are subject to change quickly, while the core of the onion, labelled 'values', changes extremely slowly.

To summarize, according to Hofstede's cultural dimension model, which is undoubtedly the most frequently used model in cross-cultural research arenas, symbols, heroes and rituals, which are subsumed under the term 'practices' may change periodically. However, 'values', which are the broad tendencies of culture, may become stable over time. These values, which Hofstede segmented into five dimensions, have influenced several academics in cross-cultural research, as various studies have replicated or extended to test and explain their findings. These have included studies relating to customers' behaviour and behavioural intentions. Indeed, this raises the importance of having a thorough understanding of each cultural value; however, at the same time, it invites the need for an investigation of the contingent variable that may have affected the cultural value.

Among these five cultural dimensions, Hofstede (2007) emphasized that the most significant difference between Western and East Asian countries relates to individualism-collectivism. There are other cultural dimensions, such as Power distance and Uncertainty Avoidance, are mentioned also as the dimensions that display the difference between Western and Eat Asian countries (Mattila 1999; Voss *et al.* 2004). However, in his contribution to Asia Pacific Journal of Management's 25th anniversary special issue (2007, p. 6) and throughout his recent publication (2010), Hofstede reconfirms that *the most evident difference between Asian countries on the one side and Western European and Anglo countries on the other relates to the dimension of Individualism versus Collectivism*. In fact, from Hofstede's first study (1984), Western countries all scored above average on individualism-collectivism, with the US and Australia being the most individualistic countries. On the other hand, Asian countries, particularly East Asian countries, all scored below average in the same category. This means that these countries are highly collectivistic. Korea and Taiwan received the lowest score for individualism (Hofstede *et al.* 2010). This theoretical assumption has been used in several cross-cultural studies related to Asian customers' behaviour and perceptions towards service quality (Hofstede 2007; Ueltschy *et al.* 2009; Zhang *et al.* 2008). Numerous empirical studies have linked individualism-collectivism to explain how culture influences Asian customers' behaviour and intentions in international marketing (Donthu and Yoo 1998; Furrer *et al.* 2000; Ladhari 2009; Lee and Kacen 2008; Liu *et al.* 2001; Schimmack *et al.* 2005; Soares *et al.* 2007).

However, there are concerns relating to the categorization of Asians, particularly East Asians, under one simplified term, such as collectivism, without supporting this categorization with legitimate reasons or historical explanations (Zhang *et al.* 2005). This concern was supported by several studies that argued that the conceptual models developed in Western countries must be tested and modified before they can be applied in an Asian context (Tsui 2004; White 2002). In addition, the studies conducted by Asians should be more confident in challenging these models, based on analysing and considering local particularities

(Fang 2010; Meyer 2006). Therefore, in advance of defining Asian countries as collectivism-oriented nations, there must be an in-depth review of the reasons that these countries are labelled with this orientation. At the same time, particularly in Korea and Taiwan, which, in recent decades, have experienced rapid economic growth (Chia *et al.* 2007; Watchravesringkan *et al.* 2008) and social development (Jacobs 2007; Zhang *et al.* 2005), there should be a theoretical confirmation of the fact that these cultural values remain valid for academics to use in future studies.

2.5 Asian cultures and collectivism: Confucian values

The topic of East Asian countries and their markets has received keen attention in several studies due to the rapid transition of market economies following their recovery from the Asian financial crisis of 1997. This recovery made these countries lucrative and promising for many global firms that were seeking ways to geographically diversify their profit generation (Johnson *et al.* 2000). A decade later, markets around the world suffered from a much larger and more severe economic crisis. Asia was the first region to rebound from the devastation of the global financial crisis and has now risen to lead the world towards economic recovery (Peng *et al.* 2010). During the worst months of 2008 to 2009, Asian markets were weakened; however, for the past two decades, they have maintained an average positive growth of 8 per cent annually (*The Economist* 2009). This has mainly been led by the rapid economic expansion of China and India (Kim *et al.* 2006; Schramm 2006), but has also been propelled by the significant economic performance of Korea and Taiwan (Chia *et al.* 2007; Watchravesringkan *et al.* 2008).

Due to these rapid changes during the past two decades, it is often questioned whether the culture of these countries is going through a more dynamic process than countries in other regions (Briley 2009; Craig and Douglas 2006; Fang 2010; Leung *et al.* 2005; Ueltschy *et al.* 2009). For example, in China, while relational hierarchy and traditional conservatism are commonly regarded as the core values of the nation (Xu 1998), it is no longer uncommon for a son or daughter to pay the bill when a family dines at a restaurant, as they earn a salary ten or even 20 times higher than their father (Faure and Fang 2008). These phenomena are also observed in Korea and Taiwan, where there has similarly been tremendous economic growth in a short period of time, which has affected their cultural hierarchical structures (Lee 2008; Zhang *et al.* 2005). Another example is that, in China, as well as in other countries in East Asia, such as Taiwan and Korea, the hero and ritual were historically led or manipulated by governments during earlier periods of modernization. In China, from the 1950s to 1970s, Mao Zedong and Maoist rhetoric were the only hero and ritual to the Chinese people, regardless of these people's age. However, since the 1980s, it has become common for younger Chinese people to talk about money, market, Mercedes and MTV through their mobile phones (Fang 2010, p. 162). This is largely due to China's open door policy, which was adopted by Deng Xiaoping in the late 1970s following the death of Mao Zedong (Faure and Fang 2008).

However, these changes in the family hierarchy and the perceptions of young people cannot justify the cultural values that have changed through the dynamic process of culture. Economic growth may demolish the traditional hierarchy of an East Asian family and shift the capital control from the elders to the juniors of the family. However, the important factual outcome is that the family still goes dining together, and one member of the family is taking the financial burden for the other members. This can be referred to as an action that originated from a cultural value, such as collectivism, or as part of a nation's heritage of the Confucian value, in which one family member takes responsibility for the other family members (Hofstede 2001; Oyserman and Lee 2008; Triandis and Gelfand 1998). The act of a younger family member paying bills or taking financial burden should be considered as a practice that has changed. However, this does not necessarily mean that the cultural values have changed. The same explanation can be applied to younger generations' adaptation of Western technologies, trends and trademarks. Those elements, such as mobile phones, MTV and Mercedes, are considered rituals, heroes or symbols, which were categorized as practices by Hofstede (Hofstede 2001, 2007; Hofstede *et al.* 2010). These practices can change over time; however, the level of young Asians' collectivistic action towards these new practices will remain stable.

New practices can be created by the dynamic process of culture, mainly due to cultural interpenetration and de-territorialization (Craig and Douglas 2006; Fang 2005). However, the value underlying these practices will remain unchanged or will only be changed after a very long period. This assertion supports the findings of De Mooij (2002) and Hofstede (2010), who stated that Roman cultural values still influence and are rooted in the behaviour of a certain part of European countries. Inglehart and Welzel (2009) also held a similar view regarding the changes of cultural values. They stated that, although economic development tends to bring predictable changes to people's views, a value of society leaves a lasting imprint on its viewer. A society's value system usually reflects an interaction between the driving forces of modernization and the persisting influence of traditional culture, from which these traditional values have proven to be highly resilient and remarkably enduring.

The cultural value of East Asian countries traditionally refers to the studies of two well-respected academics: Hall (1997) and Hofstede (2001). Hall (1997) classified East Asian cultures as high-context cultures that place important meanings on relationships and collective harmony. Hofstede (2001) expressed East Asian cultures as collectivist in nature, exhibiting long-term orientation and high power distance, where hierarchy and status are important. From these two studies, which are respected as the major literature representing East Asian cultures (Ueltschy *et al.* 2009), collectivism has been commonly identified as a characteristic value to describe the cultural values of East Asian countries.

Collectivism refers to a society in which people from birth onwards are integrated into strong, cohesive in-groups that, throughout their lifetime, continue to protect them, in exchange for unquestioning loyalty (Hofstede and Hofstede 1991). People in collectivistic cultures learn to think in terms of 'we' – harmony and consensus are the ultimate goals. People in low collectivistic cultures indicate that individuality and individual rights are paramount within a society. Individuals in societies with low collectivistic cultures tend to form protective relationships and learn to think in terms of 'I' – self-actualization by each individual is the ultimate goal (Hofstede 2001).

From a psychological perspective, collectivism is viewed as a construct that summarizes fundamental differences in how the relationship between individuals and society is construed (Oyserman *et al.* 2002). This perspective arises from the determination of whether individuals or groups are seen as the basic unit of the analyses. Within collectivism, the core unit is the group or society within which an individual must fit. Individuals are seen as fundamentally connected and related through relationships and group memberships (Oyserman *et al.* 2002; Oyserman and Lee 2008). By using the definitions of collectivism from previous studies by Hofstede (1991, 2001) and Oyserman (2002, 2008), which are widely used by a number of academics in the marketing arena (Ladhari 2009; Schimmack *et al.* 2005; Zhang *et al.* 2008), there are theoretical links to be found between collectivism and the core cultural heritage of East Asia – namely, the Confucian value.

The Confucian value relates to interpersonal harmony, relational hierarchy and traditional conservatism. These values are generally emphasized in East Asian cultures (Xu 1998). These values spread geographically to the countries of mainland China, Korea and Japan for thousands of years during the process of civilization. They are still observed as the main promoters of cultural values in these countries (Ueltschy *et al.* 2009). Through following these values, East Asians are taught in school, in the media and through praise from officials to seek harmonious relationships with others (Wei-Ming 1996). These relationships are considered the precondition for social integration and stability, and individuals are taught to respect and follow tradition and social hierarchy (Zhang *et al.* 2005).

In Taiwan – a country directly influenced by China – the people strongly value harmony and hierarchy, and dislike open displays of aggression. Family and connections are extremely important, with the Chinese people being loyal and generous to their families and close friends, yet indifferent towards people outside the group (Xu *et al.* 2007). Chinese people also have fundamental polarities at the heart of their personalities, and have contradictory tendencies. They believe in fate, as opposed to an individual's effort (Davin 1999).

In Korea, which is generally designated as a Taoist culture, with foundations of Confucianism, Buddhism and Taoism, the traditional culture is represented by both shame and reputation (Lee 1999). People are proud of having good educations and decent jobs, and are ashamed of working in what are perceived to be lower ranked jobs. To preserve one's reputation, one must not only safeguard one's own reputation, but also that of one's competitors. This is necessary in order to maintain harmony (Shim *et al.* 2008). These values are known to influence Korean people's hesitation to express their dissatisfaction, and causes them to show more tolerance towards poor services (Ueltschy *et al.* 2009).

These characteristics of the Confucian value have placed Taiwan and Korea as collectivistic countries, compared to their Western counterparts. The behaviour of countries that have Confucian influences, where people place great emphasis on protecting family members and relationships, are similar to the behaviour of countries with high collectivism (Hofstede 2001; Hofstede and Hofstede 1991). This assertion supports the findings of Yoo and Rao (2006), who conducted a comparative study on cultural differences and quality practices in four countries, including Korea and Taiwan. Yoo and Rao (2006) confirmed that high collectivistic cultures typify societies with close ties between individuals. They also reinforce collectives in which everyone has responsibility for fellow members of the group.

Another interesting characteristic commonly found in Korea and Taiwan is people's behaviour of 'face-saving', which refers to a person's reputation before their peers. This behaviour is believed to be initiated by people's desire to maintain positive social images as being reliable, capable and intelligent, in order to gain prestige and recognition within their group (Oetzel and Ting-Toomey 2003). Chung and Pysarchik (2000) demonstrated that Chinese and Korean people sacrifice themselves for benefits that largely accrue to a particular social unit, or even to the whole society. This encourages most Chinese and Korean people to feel a strong social pressure to comply with group norms, regardless of their own private views. Yoo and Rao (2006) related this to East Asians' strong emphasis on the desire to be united as a group, which, once again, can refer to a strong collective cultural value.

Therefore, the cultural value of East Asians, specifically of Korean and Taiwanese people, is highly collectivistic and is rooted in their traditional heritage of Confucian values. In Hofstede's cross-cultural dimensions (Hofstede 1984, 2001, 2010), Korea and Taiwan remain the most collectivistic nations, with the lowest scores of individualism. At the same time, these two countries persistently pursue the Confucian value as their nation's heritage, despite their rapid growth and industrialization of recent decades. For example, Zhang and Lin (Zhang *et al.* 2005) argued that even the young generations in Korea and Taiwan accept a certain level of harmony and social hierarchy with traditional conservatism. This confirms that these two countries remain influenced by Confucian values. Jacobs (2007) indicated that Korea and Taiwan have undergone similar processes of modernization through becoming Japanese colonies in the early 1900s, and through being governed by authoritarian governments thereafter. As a result of this process, even with the rapid liberalization of their societies, both countries still have an overlay of Confucian values, as both regimes promote high levels of education, which is partly owed to the official Confucian values. At the same time, the authoritarian leaders in both Korea and Taiwan promoted the policy in order to maintain discipline in their societies. Therefore, Confucian values have mixed implications for authoritarian rule, while encouraging education and proto-democratic ideas for their social foundation (Jacobs 2007).

In this regard, collectivism is the most essential variable in cross-cultural studies concerning Korea or Taiwan. This is also because of the fact that collectivism has been considered the most important dimension of cultural differences in social behaviour (Triandis and Gelfand 1998; Triandis 2006), and is one of the most useful and actively employed constructs in studies of psychology and sociology (Schimmack *et al.* 2005; Vandello and Cohen 1999). Collectivism has also frequently been used in a variety of international marketing literature for various industries to identify customers' behaviour and perceptions towards the quality of services (Ladhari 2009; Zhang *et al.* 2008).

According to Oyserman (2002, 2008), people in a collectivistic culture are more likely to emphasize relationships instead of their individual needs. Therefore, collectivist customers are expected to place a greater value on relationships than on other issues because collectivism has been suggested to be predominantly important for relational behaviour among individuals. This characteristic of collectivism can influence not only the customers themselves, but also the relationship between customers and service providers. De Mooij and Hofstede (2002) stated that customers under collectivistic cultures will be more receptive to a social bonding mechanism, which means that service providers can encourage them to repeat purchase through the relationship. However, less focus is placed on service quality as a motivation to continue this purchasing.

On the other hand, Bagozzi and Lee (2002) stated that people from a more collectivistic culture were more strongly influenced by identification processes, such as the value expressive influence, while people from a more individualistic culture were more influenced by internalization process. This supports the findings of Mourali (2005), who undertook a study via a comparison of French Canadian and English Canadian customers. Mourali (2005) found that customers from a collectivistic culture were more susceptible to value an expressive social influence than those from an individualistic culture. In other words, the information will have less influence on the individualistic customer's satisfaction with the purchase decision, whereas the customers in a collectivistic culture will have stronger influence over information received by others, as they use the group to enhance or support their self-concepts.

Considering these findings, the customers of Korea and Taiwan, as part of collectivistic nations, will place high importance on the relationship quality, but low importance on service quality. Furthermore, these customers may be inclined to be influenced by the information they receive from others, which may affect their satisfaction. This could also be explained from the perspective of both countries' Confucian value, which persistently promotes harmony, hierarchy and conservatism. The Korean and Taiwanese customers, who still maintain the Confucian value, will appreciate the opinion given by members of the group with which they associate, and will willingly accept the opinion of people superior to themselves.

These findings of Korean and Taiwanese customers' cultural characteristics became the basis of topics in studies of customers' behaviour in various service areas. For example, the studies of Kim *et al.* (2002), Choi and Miracle (2004), Yoo *et al.* (2006), Davis *et al.* (2008), Watchravesringkan *et al.* (2008) and Lee *et al.* (2009) were a few of the studies that explored the influence of cultural values on customers' behaviour towards consumer products. In these studies, Korea and Taiwan were included as one of several countries, but were not specifically targeted. Furthermore, these studies were mostly focused on consumer products and non-financial services, rather than specifically focused on financial services (Maas and Graf 2008; Salazar *et al.* 2007).

In addition to this, surprisingly, it appears that there is limited literature with empirical findings on the relationship between cultural values and financial services in Korea and Taiwan. The studies of Furrer and Liu (2000, 2001) are the only acknowledged literature concerning this topic in financial services. These studies compared the service perception and behavioural intentions of banking customers with Western and East Asian backgrounds. However, they did not segregate the Korean and Taiwanese sample, but integrated them into the 129 total Asian samples in the study. In addition, these samples were taken from students in the US, which meant they had less empirical validation than studies undertaken with real samples surveyed in the field.

This highlights the need to explore the influence of collectivism on customers' behavioural intentions in the financial services arena. This is particularly the case for new financial services, such as cross-buying, which have only recently developed in East Asian countries (Corbett 2007; Ghosh 2006). It seems like there are a lack of studies that have explored the cultural influences of this phenomenon, yet the expansion of these activities in the local markets is remarkable (Artikis *et al.* 2008; Chen *et al.* 2009; Swiss Re 2007).

2.6 Customer behaviour: relationship management and customers' cross-buying intentions

For more than a decade, marketing services have sought to understand the key factors that influence customers' behaviour when purchasing products from the same firms. The desire to understand these factors has been driven by the fact that firms, regardless of the industry in which they are engaged, have started to shift their interest from new customers to existing customers by measuring their potential profit based on the value of each customer and the level of relationship with them (Verhoef *et al.* 2007).

Until the 1980s, the focus of marketing was on the purchase behaviour of new customers. Most service firms relied on the satisfaction of new customers and quality ratings from customer surveys to understand the influence of customers' purchase behaviour and decision-making processes (Oliver 1980). Firms used these measurements to monitor customers' performance, to compensate employees and to allocate resources (Bearden and Teel 1983). However, these phenomena were challenged by various studies as firms started to embrace the concept of the relationship with the customer as one of their marketing strategies.

Berry (1983) expressed this in his early literature as firms started to change their focus from attracting customers to maintaining and enhancing customer relationships. This was clearly a cornerstone in the marketing literature of that period. Berry (1983) stated that the 'new customer only' approach to marketing is wasteful because it may cost more to acquire new customers than to retain or build existing relationships. This statement was verified by other studies in the late 1980s. For example, Fornell and Wernerfelt (1987) demonstrated that small increases in retention rates can have a dramatic effect on the profits of a firm because the cost of retaining an existing customer is less than the cost of acquiring a new customer. At the same time, existing customers tend to purchase more than new customers, and there are more efficiencies in dealing with existing customers than with new customers (Fornell and Wernerfelt 1988). However, in this study, there was no clear empirical evidence regarding how the relationship between customers and the service company affected the performance or profitability of the service company.

Berry (1983) also predicted that the combined effect of low growth rates in many service industries, as well as rapid deregulation, which is centred on service industries, would result in 'everyone getting into everyone else's business'. A similar statement was made in the studies of several other academics as they began to pragmatically implement the concept of the customer relationship into their studies (Garbarino and Johnson 1999; Reichheld 1996; Reichheld and Sasser Jr 1990). Still, there remained a lack of practical direction of service companies on how to retain customers or build the tools to further the relationship with existing customers. Nevertheless, the contribution of the study of Berry (1983) was significant in the sense that it led existing customers and their relationship with the service company to become a prominent topic to academics in the 1990s. It caused service companies to become increasingly concerned with customer retention.

Several studies began addressing the fact that a higher level of customer satisfaction would increase customer retention and ultimately lead to a better profit for firms (Bolton 1998; Gale 1997; Garbarino and Johnson 1999). The case study in Gale's (1997) paper demonstrated that retail banks, with many branches or locations, found that branches with higher retention rates performed better in the key criteria of customer value, such as satisfaction and perceived quality, than branches with lower retention rates. Eventually, those branches that underperformed lost more customers to competitors. Bolton (1998) supported this finding in her study of 650 samples from mobile telephone companies. She established a model that explained how satisfaction and perceived quality influenced customer retention. She concluded that prior cumulative satisfaction influences the retention of customers indirectly, as well as directly. Her study showed that the strength of the relationship between customer retention and satisfaction levels depended on the length of customers' prior experience with the firm, even though there was considerable heterogeneity across customers.

However, these findings should be challenged because they neglect to examine other factors that may influence customer retention, other than customer satisfaction. This was also found in Gale's (1997) study, in which he claimed that satisfaction cannot be the only driver in increasing customer retention. This supported the argument raised by Reichheld (1996), who warned that many firms had fallen into a 'satisfaction trap'. Reichheld (1996) stated that firms should not only focus on the level of satisfaction, but also on understanding customer retention and lifetime purchase. In this study, he presented a case study of a bank that implemented a loyalty bonus programme, but failed to retain existing customers. This demonstrated that high satisfaction does not always translate into customer retention, nor does it necessarily lead to an increase in the profit of the firm. Later, Bolton and Lemon (1999) demonstrated that customers' repurchase behaviour or usage of two services in sequence depends not only on their prior satisfaction levels, but also on their assessments of payment levels and prices.

Despite these attempts, in the 1990s, to understand the various factors that influence customers' behaviour, there was still insufficient evidence from academic studies to provide a clear direction for service companies in the rapidly evolving market fields. These studies were not yet empirically conducted to provide a theoretical framework that could flexibly fulfil the needs of practitioners. Palmer (2002) also pointed out that these studies may be lacking or even absent from the theoretical positioning of their studies, meaning that practitioners fail to find tangible benefits from implementing these studies in the practical market environment. Moreover, most of these studies focused on the topic of customer retention, rather than distinctly evaluating the effect of customers' values and relationships with the firm.

In the 2000s, customer relationships became a dominant concept in marketing, particularly in the service industry. When revisiting his paper of 1983, Berry (2002) stated that the concept of the customer relationship had only been investigated by academics since the mid-1990s. He stated that the development of information technology (IT), which was a significant evolution in business environments, enabled firms to identify and anticipate customer relationships more efficiently and profitably. Palmer (2002) explained that this phenomenon was also driven by the reduction in power imbalances between the customer and firms through the development of a customer focused approach. He also provided a retrospective analysis of four elements, under the overlapping labels of 'technological', 'social', 'economic' and 'political'. This facilitated the changes of the marketing environment in the 1990s. Through this analysis, Palmer projected that future studies of customer relationships would require a more comprehensive and pragmatic approach, rather than being limited to certain factors or measurements that influence customers' relationships with the firm. This projection is in accordance with various academics who expanded the concept of customer relationship and purchase intention by creating the aforementioned CRM (Kumar and Reinartz 2006; Payne and Frow 2005; Peppard 2000; Swift 2000; Reinartz *et al.* 2004; Ryals and Payne 2001).

The definitions and descriptions of CRM differ, depending on various terms. For example, CRM can be known as the term that emerged in the IT industry as 'information-enabled relationship marketing', which is commonly interchangeable with the solution to relationship marketing (Peppard 2000; Ryals and Payne 2001). However, CRM is not limited to IT solutions. It can be extended to customer relationship marketing, and should be a contribution to the outcome of customers' values. Swift (2000, p. 12) defines CRM as 'an enterprise approach to understanding and influencing customer behaviour through meaningful communication to improve customer acquisition, customer retention, customer loyalty and profitability'. One of the comprehensive syntheses on the definition of CRM is the study of Payne and Frow (2005). In this study, 12 definitions and descriptions were listed and categorized into three broad perspectives: 'narrowly and tactical as a particular technology solution'; 'wide-ranging technology'; and 'customer-centric'. Among these perspectives, it was concluded that CRM should be positioned in the strategic context of 'customer-centric'.

These interpretations of CRM from the academic viewpoint were often criticized, as it is views CRM as too narrow that it may cause the organizations to realize that their efforts to implement CRM are in vain. It is crucial to understand that CRM is not only a common technical application for marketing, but that, when fully and successfully implemented, CRM requires a cross-functional, customer-driven, technology-integrated business process management strategy, which maximizes relationships and encompasses the entire organization (Cooil *et al.* 2007; Goldenberg *et al.* 2003). This is in line with Musalem and Joshi's (2009) statement that CRM should be a philosophy translated into a business strategy, supported by a system and technology.

In due course, Peelen and Van Montfort (2006, 2009) suggested the following practical strategies in order to effectively implement CRM from a relationship strategy perspective. Relationship strategy is based on the concept that individual customer information must be used to develop a long-lasting relationship between the customer and supplier. The purpose of this relationship should be to target and retain customers within the organization, and engage them in continuous communication with the service company. There are four common strategies that were identified from the related studies.

The first strategy was to employ loyalty programmes. Ibáñez (2006) argued that most service industries heavily rely on loyalty programmes in these areas – that service companies try to mitigate negative effects by rewarding customer loyalty. For example, Bolton *et al.* (2000) stated that the aim of loyalty programmes is to establish greater customer retention in the profitable segments. Epstein *et al.* (2008) stated that this could be achieved through increasing satisfaction and value to certain customers. For this proposition, Morgan *et al.* (2009) offered a wider range of motives for establishing loyalty programmes, such as building lasting relationships by rewarding customer loyalty, gathering customer data and developing it into useful information, and reinforcing brand image by differentiating the company from competitors.

With the extension of these strategies, some studies stated the use of membership loyalty cards as evidence of the advancement of relationships in the services industry (Hoffman and Lowitt 2008). However, while features such as loyalty cards may have a part to play in relationship maintenance, they cannot realistically be considered the panacea of marketing activities. Malthouse and Mulhern (2008) defined loyalty programmes as nothing more than sophisticated sales promotions in which costs frequently outweigh advantages. Barry *et al.* (2008)

suggested that loyalty programmes should be conducted as reinforcing mechanisms, as it appears that they reward those customers who already have higher levels of loyalty than other customers. This is in line with Bolton *et al.*'s (2000) finding that loyalty programmes have a minor effect on the intention of customers in terms of affective commitment and the likelihood of account retention.

The second strategy is to increase existing barriers. This strategy involves making an arduous situation or difficult arrangement for customers who decide to switch relationships. Commonly, high switching costs are known to be the most effective exit barrier for service companies from a customer's perspective (Michalski and Helmig 2008). Bruhn (2003) stated that switching cost barriers increase customer retention, which will eventually ensure that the customer is dependent on the firm, and that the related turnover and profits are secured over the specific time period. There are several ways to implement these barriers. One of the common types is referred to as a 'contractual switching barrier' (Jones *et al.* 2007), through which the customer is contractually bound to the service company. The other type of barrier is an 'economic switching barrier', which implies that an early defection would be non-advantageous for the customer.

Customers can also create their own exit barriers. Chen and Wang (2009) stated that these are the products of mutually recognized satisfaction, which is created by the service company adding value to the relationship. This type of barrier exists because of the relationship. It might not be created by the service company directly, but it is in the services company's best interests to illustrate the potential cost to the customer.

In terms of the specific categorization of switching costs, Bolton *et al.* (2004) stated that there are one-time costs that customers must bear when switching from one service company to another. Those costs may be created by the service company, by the consumer, or by the relationship itself. These costs include search costs, learning costs, inertial costs, risk, social costs, financial costs, legal barriers and emotional costs.

However, although each of these interaction strategies is recognized as a powerful tool to strengthen the exit barrier, it is noted that these tactics are not insurmountable (Augusto de Matos *et al.* 2009). For example, having too strong exit barriers for customers might result in inactivate customers, with a high maintenance cost involved. Moreover, these strategies may transmit the message to the customer to seek the best economic offer, independent of the other elements of the value propositions.

The third CRM strategy is customer customization. The service company will gain a better knowledge of their customers' requirements and needs through various retention programmes (Berry 1995). This knowledge, combined with a social rapport, can build a number of service encounters to tailor and customise the service to the customer's specifications (Little and Marandi 2003). Eventually, this leads to the importance of CRM in the customization of products and communication with each customer. Minami and Dawson (2008) proposed four approaches to customization. The first is called 'collaborative customization', which is commonly represented as a dialogue between the company and the customer in the design of new products for each customer. The second approach of customization is 'adaptive', which consists of offering customers a standard product that the customer can alter or customise. The third is 'cosmetic customization', which consists of an external customization of the packaging of a standard offering. The final strategy is 'transparent customization', which consists of offering unique goods or services to customers without informing them that the item has been customized (Minami and Dawson 2008).

In conjunction with this strategy of customization, there is an alternative strategy, which is to persuade customers to reactivate their relationship with service companies. This strategy, namely, 'customer stimulation' (Bruhn 2003), is applied over the short term, and the aim is to reactivate the relationship with the service company. However, in this strategy, issues occur when the service company offers extraordinary discounts or economic value to customers to the extent that this may generate the opposite effect. The customers can become opportunistic players who only expect and show interest in these kinds of benefits, and who will become disappointed when they do not receive these benefits on a regular basis. This is also in line with the fact that any retention strategy solely focusing on discounts or economic values will be questioned, as it may not be based on the emotional boundaries that should be developed between service companies and their customers (Salazar *et al.* 2007).

The last customer retention strategy for CRM is the 'cross-selling' strategy. The cross-selling strategy consists of horizontal growth of products and services (Kamakura 2008; Salazar *et al.* 2007). In relationship management, it is proven that a one-time transactional relationship with customers may not generate sufficient profitability for traditional service companies, unless the individual customer holds a number of other products purchased by the service company during a certain period (Farquhar 2005). Therefore, cross-selling is considered one of the main tools for relationship marketing and CRM that can strengthen the relationship with customers and induce them to acquire additional products or enlarge the ownership of those already purchased from the service company (Kamakura *et al.* 2003; Li *et al.* 2011). This may increase the number of contact points between the customer and service company, generating a higher switching cost to the customer.

Previous marketing studies, such as that of Felvey (1982), have proven that it is more efficient and easier for a service company to grow their relationship with existing customers by cross-selling, than to attract new customers. By having a proper cross-selling strategy in place, the service company can aim to achieve two main goals: increasing the switching cost to the customer, and reinforcing customer loyalty (Salazar *et al.* 2007). These are the other two main customer retention strategies previously explained in this study. Furthermore, as the customers remain with a company for a longer period, the service companies can understand more from the customers' buying behaviour and their preferences in terms of products and timing. This will allow them to satisfy their customers' needs more effectively.

There can be a cause for concern when cross-selling attempts are executed without a supporting strategy, as this may result in unfavourable consequences.

If customers are continuously contacted with senseless offerings, they can become less willing to repurchase, and more likely to switch companies (Kamakura *et al.* 2003; Li *et al.* 2011; Ngobo 2004; Verhoef *et al.* 2010). Therefore, in order for service companies to establish a proper cross-selling strategy, they need to develop the proper customer customization, which will then be part of their cross-selling strategy. Having a proper cross-selling strategy will serve the purpose of the other three relationship marketing strategies introduced in this literature review, which again indicates the importance of cross-selling strategies in the contemporary service-marketing arena.

As was discussed in the first chapter of this book, one of the critical issues of service companies, particularly the financial services industry, is that marketing strategies are mostly derived from companies' internal policies, and are not sufficiently based on their customers' behaviour and needs (Fan *et al.* 2011; Güneş *et al.* 2010; Ngobo 2004; Soureli *et al.* 2008; Verhoef *et al.* 2010). This leads to the basis of this book that, despite the bank seeking to cross-sell different categories of financial products with the purpose of customer retention and securing a future stream of revenue, this effort will be in vain if the bank has not fully identified the actual drivers of their customers' cross-buying intentions.

For example, Güneş *et al.* (2010) warned that too many sales attempts may cause customers to respond negatively. Eventually, cross-selling may backfire if not implemented cautiously. In this sense, Verhoef *et al.* (2010) stated that, despite the rhetoric and numerous studies on CRM and customer management, it is becoming more important to understand customer engagement as a new perspective in customer management. As part of customer engagement, Verhoef *et al.* (2010) discussed an example from the study of Bijmolt *et al.* (2010), which examined past accomplishments in the modelling of customer transactional behaviour, such as cross-buying. If service companies cannot identify an effective strategy to motivate the intentions of their customers to cross-buy, it is not efficient to seek to engage in a relationship with this customer. In the financial services industry, such as the banking industry, the issue of identifying the customer's intention to cross-buy can be more crucial. This is because the relationship between the customer and the bank is based on a contractual setting (Ngobo 2004), and in a contractual setting, that customer lifetime value has great importance. Therefore, the bank has to fully use every opportunity to closely engage with their customers (Fader and Hardie 2010). Essentially, the bank cannot cross-sell if its customers do not have the intention to cross-buy.

Therefore, measuring customers' value through examining the relationship between the customer and the service provider has been a frequently studied subject in the field of marketing (Blattberg *et al.* 2009; Bolton *et al.* 2000; Cronin Jr *et al.* 2000; Jain and Singh 2002; Maas and Graf 2008; Puccinelli *et al.* 2009; Verhoef *et al.* 2007; Woodruff 1997). The length of a customer's relationship with a service provider is linked to the duration of customer retention (Bolton 1998; Bolton *et al.* 2000; Kamakura *et al.* 2003; Liu and Wu 2007), while the breadth of a customer's relationship relates to the number of services that a customer uses, or to the product that they repurchase from the same financial service provider (Bolton and Lemon 1999; Mittal and Kamakura 2001; Salazar *et al.* 2007; Verhoef *et al.* 2001).

Increasing customer retention and expanding customer repurchase behaviour from the same service provider will increase the value of the customer, which will eventually lead to more potential profit for the service provider. In their efforts to increase the value of each customer, most service providers have facilitated the customer relationship length and depth, particularly focusing on cross-selling (Kamakura *et al.* 2003; Li *et al.* 2005; Salazar *et al.* 2007), which is based on a strategy to encourage customers to cross-buy products or services from the same service provider.

Therefore, understanding the drivers of customers' cross-buying intentions is becoming more important to academics, as well as practitioners in the marketing arena (Kumar *et al.* 2008; Liu and Wu 2007; Ngobo 2004; Soureli *et al.* 2008; Reinartz *et al.* 2005, 2008; Verhoef *et al.* 2007). In fact, this should be given more importance than cross-selling, itself, as the benefits of cross-selling can only be achieved if customers are willing to cross-buy (Kumar *et al.* 2008; Ngobo 2004). Without identifying the customers' intentions to cross-buy, cross-selling can be a threat to customer relationships and can even weaken the firm's relationship with the customer, as frequent attempts to cross-sell can render the customer non-responsive or can even motivate them to switch to a competitor (Kamakura *et al.* 2003).

Despite the importance of cross-buying, the academic literature published regarding this topic is scarce (Kumar *et al.* 2008; Liu and Wu 2007; Ngobo 2004; Reinartz *et al.* 2008; Soureli *et al.* 2008; Verhoef and Donkers 2005). Within this limited literature on cross-buying, most studies discuss the relationship's depth and length, but have little focus on the factors that actually affect the relationship and the motivations behind cross-buying (Soureli *et al.* 2008). In other words, most of previous studies exhibited cross-buying as a variable to test their model for customer retention and customer expansion (Bolton *et al.* 2006; Liu and Wu 2007; Verhoef *et al.* 2007), but did not empirically investigate what causes or motivates customers to be engaged in cross-buying. Kumar and George (2008) criticized a number of studies on customers' cross-buying intentions. They stated that, with the limited resources available within firms for the allocation of different marketing activities, it is not possible to assume that all existing customers will cross-buy. Therefore, identifying the customers who are most likely to cross-buy is the first and most important step in developing a marketing strategy for the service provider.

When studying customers' cross-buying intentions, there should be different approaches based on the service setting of the customer with the service provider. For example, when cross-buying in a non-contractual setting, such as retailing, the switching cost is often insignificant and the natural sequence of product purchase is less apparent. However, in a contractual setting, such as the financial industry, customers purchase products and services in a natural sequence, with barriers relating to switching cost and complexity (Reinartz and Kumar 2000). Furthermore, relationships in the financial industry are usually long-term. For example, in terms of the customer relationship in the financial services industry, cross-buying refers to buying additional products or services from the existing service provider in addition to or based on a previous contractual setting (Ngobo 2004). Therefore, when the contractual setting is terminated, the level of cross-buying reduces compared to the previous period (Kumar *et al.* 2008; Verhoef 2003), but in a non-contractual setting, such as in other retail businesses, there is nothing equivalent to a service termination.

This is in line with the study of Reinartz and Kumar (2000), in which it was asserted that some of the findings observed in a non-contractual setting might not be applicable in a contractual setting. At the same time, in the financial services industry, several characteristics must be considered. Certain characteristics, such as intangibility, customer involvement and confidentiality, are inherent to the products of most financial service providers. Therefore, risk, uncertainty, trust and personal relationships are more critical drivers of a customer's behaviour in the financial services industry than in other service industries (Maas and Graf 2008).

At the same time, the financial industry can be considered a growing sector with large competition between traditional players and other non-traditional providers, such as retailers, telecommunication companies and convenience stores (Laforet 2008; Salazar *et al.* 2007). All these companies follow multi-product and multi-channel strategies aimed to offer a comprehensive solution to the needs that customers might expect from financial products and services. In this regard, the retail strategy, traditionally based on offering branch services, has been updated and complemented with a direct marketing centre, agents and internet services, to provide a competitive response to customers' needs (Elsas *et al.* 2010; Wagner 2010).

In addition to this, customers in the financial services industry are moving away from generic formulas, and require a unique response to their specific problems. A strategy is required to understand customers' needs beforehand in order to identify the right financial segment of customers (Koderisch *et al.* 2007; Sunikka *et al.* 2010). This also increases the importance of each customer as a crucial asset for financial value in the financial industry compared to other industries (Wood 2007).

In this regard, studying the drivers of cross-buying behaviour or the cross-buying intentions of the customer in the financial services industry must be undertaken in a more attentive manner. Verhoef (2001) is one of the few pioneers who undertook early research of the financial services industry to explore how satisfaction and payment equity affect cross-buying, in consideration of competitors' performance in relation to these factors. According to the findings of this study, satisfaction has a positive effect on cross-buying, as it is increased by the length of the relationship. Meanwhile, high satisfaction in the beginning of customer relationships may have a negative effect on customers. This is because high satisfaction scores in the early phases of the relationship generate high expectations that are difficult to meet. Payment equity, which is defined as the perceived fairness of the price, will influence a customer's decision to cross-buy, as the customer may compare the difference between payment equity of the focal supplier with that of a competing supplier. Verhoef (2001) stated that payment equity may negatively affect a customer's cross-buying of financial products; however, this is only the case when there is a long-term relationship between the customer and the financial services provider. Verhoef (2002) expanded these findings by adding the effect of trust on cross-buying. However, interestingly, this study found that trust was less important with respect to cross-buying.

Ngobo (2004) is one of the recent academics who magnify customers' cross-buying intentions in the financial services industry. Ngobo asked 280 customers of a global retailer – which is a multi-service firm that also provides financial services – for their evaluations of service experiences to facilitate cross-buying. The questions were designed to examine the customers' cross-buying intentions, rather than their actual cross-buying behaviour. This study shows that the determinants of cross-buying intentions are mostly affected by customers' perceptions of the provider's capability to offer different types of services.

The results of this book indicate that the images of a service provider's ability to present different services of equally high quality, and the perceived convenience of purchase, were the key factors that influenced customers' cross-buying intentions. A customer's satisfaction with the service provider has a weaker or marginal effect on their cross-buying intentions. This supports the findings of Verhoef and his colleagues (Verhoef *et al.* 2001, 2002, 2003) in which it was concluded that the state of the current relationship between the customer and the provider is not an accurate indicator of the customer's potential for cross-buying.

Synthesizing these research propositions of cross-buying behaviour and intentions, Soureli (2008) established four determinants of cross-buying intention: satisfaction, image, perceived value and trust. She stated that customers' cross-buying intentions were generated from a combination of the interrelationships among these determinants, which should effectively interact simultaneously. In other words, not only should the correlation between independent variables and cross-buying intentions be tested, but the interrelationship among independent variables should also be tested. For example, customers' trust and favourable image of a bank directly influence their cross-buying intentions, whereas satisfaction and perceived value have an indirect influence. Overall, the major influence results from satisfaction, which has the greatest effect in determining cross-buying intentions. These findings from Soureli (2008) are contrary to the findings of previous studies. Several previous studies stated that satisfaction has a weaker or less important effect on customers' cross-buying behaviour and intentions (Ngobo 2004; Verhoef 2003; Verhoef *et al.* 2001).

Soureli (2008) argued that this difference is because Verhoef (2001) and Ngobo (2004) did not consider the effect of interrelationships between the constructs on cross-buying; they only focused on the effect of each separate construct. However, from the conceptual framework of Ngobo (2004), it can be seen that he did consider switching costs and repurchase intentions as mediators to cross-buying consideration, and identified the interrelationships between service quality, perceived value and satisfaction as part of the assessment of the existing relationship with the provider. Verhoef (2001) did not clearly indicate the interrelationships in his early studies. However, in his studies (Verhoef *et al.* 2002, 2007; Verhoef 2003; Verhoef and Donkers 2005) he consistently used satisfaction as one of the main variables, and each time he added a new variable to his conceptual framework. The interrelationship between satisfaction and the new variable were indirectly tested.

Therefore, the above interpretation of Soureli (2008) on the differences between the findings does not provide sufficient explanation. A more fundamental analysis is required to enable greater understanding, particularly in terms of cross-cultural values. Previous studies, such as the studies of Verhoef (2001, 2003), Ngobo (2004) and Soureli (2008), all took place with customer samples with different nationalities and different cultural backgrounds. Verhoef (2001) extracted samples from the Netherlands, Ngobo (2004) from France, and Soureli (2008) from Greece. According to Hofstede's cultural dimension (Hofstede *et al.* 2010; Hofstede and Hofstede 1991; Hofstede 1984b), the Netherlands and France are considered high individualistic countries, with higher scores in individualism, while Greece is considered a collectivistic country, with a score in individualism that is lower than the average European country. However, this fact has not been addressed in the literature or by academics. This is probably because each study was based in one country, separately, and there might have been a conventional belief that these countries would have similar cultural values, as they are all located in Europe and have similar financial service environments. There is clearly a need to have an empirical study that fills this study gap in order to establish a more concrete and theorized framework, and to test customers' cross-buying intentions in the financial services industry.

2.7 Cross-buying intentions in the financial services: Europe and Asia

Since the proposition of marketing globalization (Levitt 1983), some studies predicted that globalization would progressively create a more homogenized world market, with a growing number of consumers from diverse cultural backgrounds sharing the same preferences (Alden *et al.* 1999; Hannerz 1990; Jain 1989; Robertson 1992). These studies asserted that firms would move from the emphasis of customizing items to offering globally standardized products that were advanced, functional, reliable, and had a low price. While these studies are appreciated for their effort to expand the scope of the marketing research arena from the local to the global market, they have often been challenged by academics. This is because the assumptions and propositions in these studies still remain at testing a hypothesized relationship between the theoretical framework and other variables employed from cross-sectional data (Mittelman 2004; Ritzer 2003). They also, unrealistically, place customers outside the cultural context (McCracken 1990). Furthermore, most of these studies are extensively focused on how firms can reduce their costs by customizing their products and services. However, they do not diligently examine customers' intentions to purchase or receive services from these firms, nor do they examine how customers' cultures may affect this behaviour.

The critics of these studies are in line with De Mooij and Hofstede's (2002) statement that there are many purchase differences across countries because customers are often irrational and do not make purchase decisions that maximize utility. This statement is supported by several academics, who have developed a new idea in relation to 'globalocalization' (Featherstone *et al.* 1995; Kjeldgaard and Askegaard 2006; Robertson 1992; Turner 2003). This emphasizes that local cultures remain a powerful influence for customers (Alden *et al.* 2006).

However, these studies and findings do not provide empirical evidence to identify the cause of customer behaviour, but rather focus on explanatory investigation based on a sociological or ideological argument (Beyer 2007; Ritzer 2007). In other words, these studies were insufficient in providing validated measurements for individual customer behaviour linked to cross-cultural dimensions – they did not fulfil the needs of academics in global customer studies. Therefore, it is important to establish a proper theoretical framework in order to measure the effect of cross-cultural dimensions on customers' behaviour and intentions.

Understanding the relationship between the local customer and their cultural influences has always been an important topic for academics. This is becoming particularly important in the East Asian region in this era in which multinational companies are expanding their services globally, particularly to new territories (Cummins and Venard 2008; Sofat and Hiro 2009; Ueltschy *et al.* 2007; Wirtz and Lovelock 2007) where financial services related to cross-buying have only recently been introduced (Chen *et al.* 2009; Ghosh 2006, Gopalan and Rajan 2009; Liu and Wu 2007; Teunissen 2008; Wu *et al.* 2008).

The request for studies of customers' cross-buying intentions in the financial services industry is more crucial and is an imperative task in the East Asian context. There have been few studies based in Taiwan and Korea that have dealt with this topic. The study of Liu and Wu (2007) was the first study that dealt with this topic in Taiwan. Liu and Wu (2007) conducted a survey of 470 customers who had banking accounts in Taiwan. They tested their preferences of seven different banking services for:

• Cross-buying and the four customer values, mediated by satisfaction and trust;
• Locational and one-stop shopping convenience, mediated by satisfaction;
• The bank's reputation and expertise, mediated by trust.

Location convenience did not have an effect on cross-buying; one-stop shopping convenience showed strong correlations; and satisfaction played a critical mediating role only between one-stop shopping convenience and cross-buying. As for the bank's reputation and expertise, these were totally substituted by the direct effects of trust. This meant that, even though these values had an effect on cross-buying, this was mainly because the customers' trust in the bank was strong.

Another study on customers' cross-buying of financial products in Taiwan is the study of Jeng (2008). This study demonstrated how customers' cross-buying intentions are influenced by corporate reputation in the insurance industry. This study showed that customers' cross-buying intentions rely intensively on an insurance company's reputation and the interpersonal relationships between salespeople and customers. The competing service provider's price and product variety negatively affect customers' cross-buying intentions. However, this study was conducted on customers who were cross-buying insurance products from insurance companies, not from banks. Therefore, the definition of customers' behaviour in this cannot be purely defined as cross-buying, but rather as 'up-selling', by the definitions of such studies as Gupta and Zeithaml (2006), Salazar *et al.* (2007) and Verhoef *et al.* (2010). Moreover, the behaviour of customers in the insurance industry may differ from those in the banking industry, as each customer has different financial needs and criteria in their selection of financial institutions, as is mentioned in the study of Ennew *et al.* (2007).

The most recent study on cross-buying intention in the Taiwanese banking industry is the study of Fan *et al.* (2011). In this study, Fan *et al.* (2011) conducted interviews with 23 financial advisers, who were engaged in customers' cross-buying activities over the bank counter. These advisers were selected through a purposive sampling technique. The results showed that the payment equity and experience of the bank staff were less important than image, interpersonal relationships and trust. Furthermore, the importance of pricing and product variety were considered less influential than the above factors. This aligns with previous studies in Taiwan, such as those of Liu (2007) and Jeng (2008), in which interpersonal relationships, image and trust were commonly found to be the most influential factors in the cross-buying of financial products.

In Korea, surprisingly, there has been only one empirical study related to cross-buying intentions in banking services. This was published in a local marketing journal by Kim and Kim (2010). This study was based on survey of 484 banking customers in Korea. These customers were surveyed about their cross-buying intentions of financial products in their main bank. This study concluded that customers' satisfaction, trust and emotional bonding had a positive influence on customers' cross-buying intentions. This was similar to the findings from the studies in Taiwan (Fan *et al.* 2011; Jeng 2008; Liu and Wu 2007). Furthermore, Kim and Kim (2010) stated that Korean customers' cross-buying intentions were influenced by the convenience of the services, such as direct marketing. However, due to local regulation, insurance products are not allowed to be sold as direct marketing, and investment products require the customer's written consent, which also makes it particularly difficult to sell through direct marketing.[1] Therefore, it is not practically feasible to examine the relationship between direct marketing and customers' cross-buying intentions from this study, from a managerial perspective.

Importantly, the studies in the context of Korea and Taiwan, such as the study of Liu and Wu (2007), Kim and Kim (2010) and Fan *et al.* (2011), highlight a manifest research gap when compared to studies in the European context. For example, Verhoef (2002) and Ngobo (2004) confirmed that trust and customers' perceptions towards the financial service providers were not important for their cross-buying intentions. However, all the studies based in Korea and Taiwan found that trust was the most critical driver of cross-buying for Korean and Taiwanese banking customers (Fan *et al.* 2011; Kim and Kim 2010; Liu and Wu 2007). There were also slight differences noticed between the studies in Korea and Taiwan. Soureli (2008) indicated that the image of the bank has a positive effect for cross-buying intentions. However, in the studies of Liu (2007) and Fan *et al.* (2011), which were based in Taiwan, these values – which were referred to as the bank's reputation and expertise – were mediated by other variables, such as trust. The findings from the studies in Korea and Taiwan were more similar to the findings of Soureli (2008) than the findings of Verhoef (2002) and Ngobo (2004).

These differences can be interpreted from a cross-cultural perspective. Taiwan is one of the most collectivistic nations in Hofstede's individualism-collectivism, with a score of 17. It has traditional cultural characteristics that emphasize relationships within the group, and it encourages tolerance towards inconvenient services that are within the group in which the Taiwanese people are engaged. Therefore, Taiwanese people do not focus on location convenience, but focus on trust for their banks and other aspects that reflect the bank's reputation and expertise. Meanwhile, the Netherlands and France, where Verhoef (2002) and Ngobo (2004) conducted their research, have Hofstede's individualism-collectivism scores of 80 and 71, respectively, and are considered highly individualistic nations. In these countries, customers are highly sensitive towards the quality and convenience of services, and are less influenced by trust or other factors built during the relationship. However, Greece, where Soureli (2008) conducted the most recent empirical study, has Hofstede's score of 36, which is lower than other countries in Europe. Even within the same region in Europe, according to the level of individualism-collectivism, the outcomes of customers' cross-buying intentions in the financial services are different. The outcomes from the study of Soureli (2008) are similar to those of Liu and Wu (2007, 2010), Fan *et al.* (2011) and Kim and Kim (2010). This could be because Greece, Korea and Taiwan are all considered to have relatively low individualism-collectivism scores compared to other peer countries. There could be a debate that the study of Soureli (2008) purported to identify the drivers of cross-buying intentions, whereas the study of Liu and Wu (2007) focused on cross-buying, which is the outcome of customer behaviour.

However, as cross-buying intentions are the antecedents of cross-buying behaviours (Verhoef 2001, 2010) and there is a lack of studies that investigate the topic of customers' cross-buying behaviours in the financial services sector, it is not accurate to take these studies – the studies of Soureli (2008) and Liu and Wu (2007) – as a reference to one another.

2.8 Significance of literature review

During the last two decades, as services and markets have evolved and become more sophisticated with continuous globalization, various types of cross-cultural studies have emerged (Knight 1999; Zhang *et al.* 2005). In these numerous cross-cultural studies, there have been many concerns identified, particularly in the context of customers' behaviour. First, most cross-cultural studies in marketing focused more on the firms' perspective, rather than the customers' perspective. Examples of these studies include Porter (1990), Erramilli and Rao (1993) and Bhuian (1997). Second, some of these studies neglected to build a strong conceptual framework based on an empirical study; they merely relied on the generic assumptions of a nation's characteristics. The studies of Gilbert *et al.* (2004), Johns *et al.* (2004) and Cunningham *et al.* (2005) are examples. Lastly, these studies of cross-cultural customer behaviour did not fully consider the effect of customers' specific characteristics by service segment. The topic of customers' behaviour in financial services should be examined differently to the behaviour of customers in non-financial services (Liu *et al.* 2001; Maas and Graf 2008).

Prior to commencing cultural studies, this chapter reviewed the operationalization of culture. This procedure is essential, as the cultural values of a nation must be segregated from the other practices of the nation, such as its symbols, rituals and heroes (Hofstede *et al.* 2010; Soares *et al.* 2007). This chapter confirmed that, despite the recent globalization and standardization of the international market (Newburry and Yakova 2006; Pieterse 2009), the cultural values of a nation remain consistent, while other practices can be changed. In other words, the cultural dimensions of a nation pertain to the behaviour of customers within that nation. This confirms that the cultural dimensions and scores, which have been identified and verified throughout previous studies, are still valid for use in cross-cultural studies on customers' buying behaviours. The representative studies of cultural dimensions are the World Value Survey from Inglehart (2006, 2000), the Survey of Values by Schwartz and Bardi (2001), the GLOBE project by House *et al.* (2004), and the studies of Hofstede (1984, 1991, 2010).

Among the various cultural dimensions that have been used in numerous cross-cultural studies, Hofstede's cultural dimensions (1984, 2010) are recognized as the most suitable theories. This is because Hofstede's dimensions have a long history of use in various studies (Fang 2003; Javidan *et al.* 2006), including Trompenaars and Hampden-Turner (1995), McSweeney (2002) and House *et al.* (2004), who established the GLOBE project, which had a larger scale and extended a number of dimensions. For each criticism of his work, Hofstede (1997, 2002, 2010) has answered with the fact that his cultural dimensions were based on an action-driven approach, and, throughout the years, these dimensions have remained stable, regardless of the evolution of other practices, such as knowledge transfer and changes in cultural identity or dialectics. Hofstede (2010) readdressed this assertion with his initial definition of culture as a collective programming of mind acquired by the learning processes in a particular society. He reconfirmed that culture is reluctant to change. Even in the GLOBE project (House *et al.* 2004), which was the most recent contestant to Hofstede's (1997, 2002, 2010) studies, it was confirmed that some of the cross-cultural scales used in GLOBE were derived from the cultural dimensions of Hofstede (Javidan *et al.* 2006).

In Hofstede's cultural dimensions, individualism-collectivism was the most frequent and commonly used cultural value, particularly when comparing East Asian and Western customers (Oyserman and Lee 2008; Schimmack *et al.* 2005; Vandello and Cohen 1999). Asian customers – specifically, customers in East Asian countries, such as Korea and Taiwan – are perceived to be more collectivistic in customer behaviour than their counterpart European customers (Hofstede *et al.* 2010; Hofstede 2001; House *et al.* 2004; Inglehart 2000; Ladhari 2009; Ozdemir and Hewett 2010; Zhang *et al.* 2008). This is often stated as being because the collectivistic culture of Korea and Taiwan is derived from the Confucian value that is part of their culture and history (Chung and Pysarchik 2000; Wang 2008; Wei-Ming 1996; Zhang *et al.* 2005).

The Confucian value respects harmony, hierarchy and conservatism. This leads individuals to appreciate the benefit of a collective group, rather than the benefit of the individual (Ueltschy *et al.* 2009; Wu 2009; Zhang *et al.* 2005). Previous empirical studies identified customers in these countries as being less sensitive to the quality of services. Rather, these customers emphasized the importance of their relationship with service providers (De Mooij and Hofstede 2002; Furrer *et al.* 2000; Liu *et al.* 2001; Oyserman *et al.* 2002; Zhang *et al.* 2005). Therefore, customers from collectivistic cultural backgrounds, such as in Korea and Taiwan, behave differently and are motivated by different factors than the individualistic customers of European countries. Trandis (2006) stated that, for this reason, collectivism has been one of the most useful and actively researched constructs in psychology and sociology. Subsequently, in the context of international marketing, collectivism has been frequently used as the most important variable in cross-cultural studies that seek to identify customers' behaviour and perceptions towards quality of services (Ladhari 2009; Zhang *et al.* 2008).

Therefore, customers in Korea and Taiwan – nations that share a high level of collectivism (Hofstede *et al.* 2010; Hofstede 2001; House *et al.* 2004; Inglehart 2000; Ladhari 2009; Ozdemir and Hewett 2010; Zhang *et al.* 2008) – are expected to react differently from their counterparts who share a low level of collectivism. This knowledge should be applied to the new types of financial services, such as the cross-buying of financial products in the banking services, which is recognized as an emerging paradigm in East Asian countries (Claessens *et al.* 2010; Corbett 2007; Ghosh 2006). Moreover, the fact that Korea and Taiwan are two countries that are leading this paradigm of cross-buying activities in East Asia (Artikis *et al.* 2008; Chen *et al.* 2009), means that it is important to explore the influence of collectivism on Korean and Taiwanese customers' cross-buying of financial products in the banking services.

2.9 Summary

This chapter reviewed studies related to the cross-buying of financial products. It examined how the management of a firm's relationship with its customers has previously been undertaken in the financial services industry. It examined how, in due course, the strategies of financial services providers' cross-selling and their customers' cross-buying intentions have played an important role in CRM.

CRM is a term that became increasingly popular in the early 2000s as increasing importance was placed on the financial value of the existing customer base (Kumar and Reinartz 2006; Payne and Frow 2005; Peppard 2000; Reinartz *et al.* 2004; Ryals and Payne 2001; Swift 2000). This chapter introduced the strategies of CRM, including the four customer retention methodologies of loyalty programmes, increased exit barriers, customer customization and cross-selling. Among these four methodologies, this chapter addressed the fact that a proper cross-selling strategy could fulfil the demands of the other three methodologies (Salazar *et al.* 2007). However, it was also noted that cross-selling can become meaningless if it has no supporting strategies (Kamakura 2008) – it can even result in negative outcomes (Güneş *et al.* 2010). Ultimately, if customers do not have the intention to cross-buy, firms cannot cross-sell their financial products (Ngobo 2004).

A number of studies were published on the topic of cross-buying, among which few have succeeded in offering empirical findings with pragmatic implications. For example, the studies of Bolton *et al.* (2006) and Kumar *et al.* (2008) examined the importance of customers' cross-buying in relation to customer retention and expansion. However, their studies lacked any identification of the behavioural intentions and motivations behind customers' engagement in cross-buying products from the same service provider. There have been a few studies that have dealt thoroughly with the topic of customers' cross-buying behaviour, and the causes for this behaviour.

Verhoef's (2001) study was one of the pioneering studies. This study identified that perceived value and satisfaction are factors that influence customers to cross-buy. Verhoef (2002) added the factor of trust to test its influence on the cross-buying of customers in the financial services. Ngobo (2004) also included the factor of the image of the financial services provider to these three factors to see how this influenced customers' cross-buying behaviour and cross-buying intentions. Soureli (2008) tested all these factors – perceived value, trust, image and satisfaction – in an empirical model. This enabled an examination of the interrelationships between these factors, as well as a thorough examination of customers' cross-buying intentions in the banking services.

This chapter reviewed studies in Korea and Taiwan in the context of customers' cross-buying intentions of financial products. Liu and Wu (2007) confirmed that perceived values, such as locational convenience, do not influence cross-buying, while satisfaction plays a critical mediating role between perceived value – this included things such as one-stop shopping convenience and cross-buying. Meanwhile, the effect of a bank's image, such as reputation and expertise, were surpassed by the direct effects of trust in cross-buying. This was verified by the study of Jeng (2008); however, this study was not based on cross-buying in the banking industry, but in the insurance industry. The studies of Fan *et al.* (2011) in Taiwan, and Kim and Kim (2010) in Korea confirmed that Taiwanese and Korean banking customers' cross-buying intentions are driven by trust, image and satisfaction, and are less influenced by competitive pricing or the convenience of the product variety.

Through these reviews of studies in European countries, as well as in Korea and Taiwan, it was identified that there is a research gap regarding the outcomes of the relationships between the factors that affect cross-buying, and the cross-buying intentions of customers. Verhoef (2002) and Ngobo (2004) stated that trust and customers' perceptions of financial service providers are not important for their cross-buying intentions. However, all the studies related to Korean and Taiwanese banking customers (Fan *et al.* 2011; Kim and Kim 2010; Liu and Wu 2007) confirmed that trust is the most critical driver of cross-buying intentions. There were also slight differences noted between the study of Liu and Wu (2007) and the study of Soureli (2008). Soureli (2008) identified that the image of the bank has a positive effect on cross-buying intentions. However, Liu and Wu (2007) stated that these values, which are referred to as a bank's reputation and expertise, only have an effect when they are mediated by other variables, such as trust. Nevertheless, the findings of Liu (2007) and Fan *et al.* (2011) are more similar to those of Soureli (2008), than to those of Verhoef (2002) or Ngobo (2004).

The discovery of this research gap inevitably provides the theoretical assumption that the high collectivism in Korea and Taiwan may have caused this outcome. The studies of Verhoef (2002) and Ngobo (2004) were conducted in the Netherlands and France, where Hofstede's (2010) individualism-collectivism scores are 80 and 71, respectively. This means that these studies were conducted on highly individualistic customers. However, the similar context of studies from Liu (2007) and Fan *et al.* (2011) were conducted in Taiwan, where Hofstede's (2010) individualism score is 17. The study of Kim and Kim (2010), which showed a similar outcome to the study from Taiwan, was conducted in Korea, where the score is 18 – a similar level of collectivism to Taiwan. Interestingly, the outcomes from Taiwan and Korea, which are considered highly collectivistic countries, were similar to the study of Soureli (2008), which was conducted in Greece – a location with Hofstede's (2010) individualism-collectivism score of 36. The outcomes from the study of Soureli (2008) were similar to the studies of Korea and Taiwan because Greece is less individualistic than the Netherlands or France, and more collectivistic, in the manner of Korea and Taiwan.

Based on the reviews of literature relating to cross-cultural studies and marketing studies of customers' cross-buying of financial products, it can be theoretically assumed that collectivism can influence the relationship between the factors that determine customers' cross-buying intentions of financial products, and customers' cross-buying intentions, in Korea and Taiwan. These theoretical assumptions have not been tested in any previous studies, making this study the first to attempt to apply cultural values to a study of cross-buying activities. The conceptual model that will underpin these assumptions will be tested in the two countries: Korea and Taiwan. These countries were chosen because they are the areas in which the most active and significant cross-buying activities have been observed (Artikis *et al.* 2008; Swiss Re 2007). This study will contribute to the body of knowledge in the literature of both cultural studies and marketing studies in the financial services area.

Note

1 As outlined in the sales guideline in bancassurance business, announced by Korean Financial Supervisory Services in 2003.

3 Conceptual model and methodology

3.1 Introduction

The conceptual model of this book was framed in two steps. First, it established the relationship between the four key determinants of customers' cross-buying – which were identified in the literature review in the previous chapter – and the cross-buying intentions of Korean and Taiwanese customers in the banking industry. Second, it observed whether collectivism produces any moderating effect on these relationships. This chapter develops the theoretical assumptions based on this conceptual model, which eventually resulted in the hypotheses of this book. These hypotheses were tested in Korea and Taiwan with the means of the research methodology that is presented in this chapter. This chapter explicitly discusses the preparatory tasks required for designing this book, and explains how to put the conceptual model into practice.

This chapter begins with an explanation of each variable of the conceptual model by categorizing these variables according to the instructions of conceptual modelling established by Sekaran (1992). The four key determinants of customers' cross-buying intentions – perceived value, trust, image and satisfaction – were categorized as the independent variables in the conceptual model. Customers' cross-buying intentions became the dependent variable to these independent variables, and collectivism acted as the moderate variable for the relationships between these independent variables and the dependent variable. This chapter delineates the source of conceptual terms for each variable, adopting the definitions indicated in the studies of Reinartz and Kumar (2000), Salazar *et al.* (2007), Maas and Graf (2008), Verhoef (2001; 2002), Ngobo (2004), Roig (2006), Liu and Wu (2007), Soureli *et al.* (2008) and Bravo (2009).

Based on these definitions, this chapter demonstrates how the interrelationships between these variables were formulated. Specifically, in terms of formulating the relationship between collectivism and each independent variable, this chapter applies a theoretical framework to customers' behavioural intentions (Hewett 2010; Liu *et al.* 2001; Ozdemir and Gounaris *et al.* 2007; Zeithaml *et al.* 1996) and cultural values (Hofstede 1984a; Hofstede 2001; Hofstede *et al.* 2010). This leads to the ten hypotheses that construct the conceptual model of this book.

To use this conceptual model with ten hypotheses, this book implemented the research design of triangulation, which combined the qualitative approach of survey questionnaires with the qualitative evidence of interviews and observations of the local market (Denzin 1989). This chapter discusses the reasons for using this methodology, and explains how this methodology ensured this book's outcomes had concrete validation. This not only enabled this study to offer empirical findings, but also to sufficiently receive the perspectives of practitioners in the field. This chapter also discusses why this book required unique consideration due to its specific research topic. As the cross-buying of financial products is a relatively new phenomenon for customers in Korea and Taiwan (Claessens 2009; Ghosh 2006), and as no previous studies have been conducted in the view of the collectivistic cultural background, this study required careful design to ensure it avoided operational misconduct in the data collection approaches. This design process is described in this chapter.

This chapter demonstrates the requirements of the qualitative approach that the study used to conduct face-to-face interviews on six selective practitioners from Korea and Taiwan. As for the quantitative approach, this chapter focuses on the structured survey that the study used to collect 700 sets of data from Korea and Taiwan by using the probability sampling approach. The questionnaire for the survey followed the non-experimental design of the correlational field study, which commonly requires the measurement of several independent variables; one or more dependent variables; and a control variable, such as a moderator (Tharenou *et al.* 2007). In constructing the survey questions, this study referred to the TAP procedure, which was recommended by Foddy (1993).

This chapter also deals with the importance of ethical considerations and the procedures that were undertaken to ensure this study adhered to these considerations. This study was submitted to and approved by the Human Resource Ethics Committee of the University of South Australia.

3.2 Conceptual model

Through the review of literature in the previous chapter, the factors that influence customers' cross-buying intentions of financial products in the banking industry have been tentatively identified. It has also been identified that the relationships between these factors and customers' cross-buying intentions could be influenced by collectivism, as has been noticed in cross-cultural studies of customers' behaviours in other sectors. These findings raise theoretical assumptions that the factors of customers' cross-buying intentions in the banking industry can be influenced by collectivism. However, prior to confirming these theoretical assumptions, the factors in these relationships must be operationalized as variables in the conceptual modelling (Cavana *et al.* 2001).

In order to build a strong conceptual model that can underpin the outcomes of the research, the methodology of this book follows the below properties, as proposed by Sekaran(1992):

- The variables in the conceptual model that are considered relevant to the study must be clearly identified and labelled for discussion. These include dependent, independent and moderator variables;
- The way in which the two or more variables relate to each other must be stated for the important relationships to be hypothesized between the variables;
- If the nature and direction of the relationships can be theorized, an indication must be given based on theoretical assumptions;
- A clear explanation must be given regarding why the outcomes of the relationships between these variables are expected to be as outlined by the theoretical assumptions, which are represented as hypotheses.

Based on the proposals above, the variables for the conceptual model of this book are initially operationalized based on the concepts noted from the literature review. In this process, each of the variables is defined based on the theoretical concepts. The definition of collectivism was mainly based on the concept of Hofstede's cross-cultural dimensions (Hofstede 1984a, 2001; Hofstede *et al.* 2010). Cross-buying and cross-buying intentions were referred to as the terms of the studies of Ngobo (2004) and Soureli (2008). These are the most dominant terms in other related studies on financial services. For other variables, the study has referred to the definitions from related studies of European countries, including the studies of Verhoef (2001, 2002, 2005), Ngobo (2004), Reinartz *et al.* (2008) and Soureli *et al.* (2008); and the studies related specifically to Korea and Taiwan, such as the studies of Liu and Wu (2009, 2007), Kim and Kim (2010) and Fan *et al.* (2011). These adopted variables include the bank's perceived value to the customers, the customers' trust towards the bank, the bank's image to the customers, and the customers' satisfaction with the bank. These variables were chosen from the most frequently reviewed studies on the financial services sectors.

Through the operationalization of these variables, the relationships between each variable becomes the phenomenon of theoretical interest, meaning that each variable is categorized in the conceptual model with its major task in the relationship as independent, dependent or moderating. Independent variables are hypothesized to influence others, as they are the presumed cause of the determinant or antecedent (Tharenou *et al.* 2007). In this book, the factors that have been identified as the drivers of cross-buying intentions, such as perceived value, trust, image and satisfaction, become the independent variables. These variables, as addressed by Soureli (2008), generate a combination of interrelationships which impacts the dependent variable. However, these variables can be also taken as single-dimensional constructs in other studies, such as the study of Ngobo (2004), Verhoef (2001, 2002, 2005), Reinartz *et al.* (2008) and Liu *et al.* (2010), therefore, for the conceptual model of this book, a separate relationship between the independent variables and dependent variable will be only explored.

The dependent variable in the conceptual model, which is presumed to be affected by another variable, is the cross-buying intention.

The moderator is the variable that influences the strength and direction of the relationship between the independent and dependent variable (Tharenou *et al.* 2007). It has a strong contingent effect on the influence of the independent variable on the dependent variable, as the presence of this variable modifies the original relationship between the independent and dependent variable (Cavana *et al.* 2001). In this conceptual model, the moderator variable is collectivism. The main objective of categorizing these variables in the conceptual model of this book is to establish a comprehensive theoretical framework to measure the moderating effect of collectivism on the interrelationships between the independent variables (perceived value, trust, image and satisfaction) and customers' cross-buying intentions of financial products in banking industry. Based on this main objective, the conceptual terms of variables and the relationships between these variables that build the conceptual model with theoretical hypotheses are summarized in the following sections.

Collectivism and cross-buying

The definition of collectivism is based on Hofstede's cultural dimension of individualism-collectivism (1984a), which has had its validity confirmed by several other studies (Hofstede *et al.* 2010; Hofstede 2007; Oyserman and Lee 2008; Soares *et al.* 2007). Korea and Taiwan are acknowledged as the most collectivistic countries in East Asia, not only by Hofstede's (2010) cultural dimensions, but also by Triandis (Triandis 2006; Triandis and Gelfand 1998) and Inglehart (Inglehart 2006; Inglehart and Oyserman 2004; Inglehart 2000), who have justified the high collectivism of these two countries by using different dimensions.

Other studies have also confirmed that Korea and Taiwan show relatively high collectivism, mainly due to their cultural background of Confucian values (Zhang *et al.* 2005; Wang 2008). Therefore, Taiwanese and Korean customers, similar to other collectivistic customers, appreciate harmony, group-orientation and relationships. This means that they tend to place greater value on the relationship quality with their service provider, rather than on the service quality (Ozdemir and Hewett 2010; Oyserman *et al.* 2002; Zhang *et al.* 2008). Ozdemir and Hewett (2010) stated that collectivism has been accepted to be predominantly important for the relational behaviour among individuals, and those members of collectivist cultures are inclined to reciprocate with cooperative behaviour in general.

The cross-buying intentions of customers in financial services were defined with Ngobo's (2004) definition, which was later elaborated by Soureli (2008). The conceptual terms of cross-buying mentioned in the studies of Verhoef (2002, 2005, 2001) were not considered when defining the cross-buying intentions of customers for this book, even though the studies of Verhoef (2001, 2002, 2005, 2010) are considered one of the most vital achievements in the studies of cross-buying. This was done because Verhoef (2001, 2002, 2005) used cross-buying as the variable that resulted from the outcome of customers' actions, whereas the conceptual model in this book focuses more on the customers' intentions in cross-buying. Verhoef (2001, 2002, 2005) also tended to generalize the conceptual terms of cross-buying in order to expand its usage for other sectors of service industries, while Ngobo (2004) and Soureli *et al.* (2008) limited the conceptual term of cross-buying intentions to financial products specific to the banking industry.

In terms of the identification process of the four key drivers in customers' cross-buying intentions, the studies of Verhoef (2002, 2005, 2001) were considered, given these studies' importance and influence over other empirical studies, such as those of Ngobo (2004), Reinartz *et al.* (2008) and Soureli *et al.* (2008). Verhoef (2001) stated that perceived value is a key driver in cross-buying, as perceived payment equity with the focal service provider has a positive effect on cross-buying. Meanwhile, satisfaction has no effect, except for those customers with lengthy relationships with the service provider. Ngobo (2004) agreed with the findings of Verhoef (2001), but added the factors of trust and image of the financial service provider as additional key drivers for customers' cross-buying intentions in France. Soureli (2008) aggregated these findings and also tested the relationships among these four variables, confirming that perceived value, satisfaction, trust and image are key drivers of customers' cross-buying intentions in the banking services. Soureli (2008) found that trust and image have a more direct influence than perceived value or satisfaction. These variables were also used in the conceptual model of the studies conducted on Korea and Taiwan (Fane *et al.* 2011; Kim and Kim 2010; Liu and Wu 2007).

In understanding the relationships between these four key drivers of customers' cross-buying intentions with collectivism, as there is a lack of studies on the cross-buying intentions of financial products in the view of cultural values, such as collectivism, this book rationalizes a new theoretical framework from similar cross-cultural studies on the financial services industry (Gounaris *et al.* 2007; Liu *et al.* 2001; Ozdemir and Hewett 2010; Zeithaml *et al.* 1996). The behavioural intentions of customers can be expressed by their loyalty, willingness to pay more, switching intentions, external responses, and internal responses (Gupta and Zeithaml 2006; Zeithaml *et al.* 1996).

These constructs of behavioural intentions are theoretically linked to the four key drivers of cross-buying intentions, which can delineate the relationship between collectivism and the four key drivers of cross-buying intentions. For example, Colgate and Tong (2007) stated that in a collectivistic culture, such as in Chinese societies, loyalty is highly regarded and is often an underlying reason for customers staying with their service provider, including those customers within the banking sector. Loyalty in financial services can be evaluated as the length and width of the relationship between the customer and financial service provider – a relationship that directly correlates with image, trust and satisfaction (Lewis and Soureli 2006). Therefore, customers in countries with high levels of collectivism will have relatively high levels of loyalty towards their service providers, with an emphasis on trust, image and satisfaction.

In terms of their switching intentions, individualistic customers tend to be more self-responsible and demand more efficiency than collectivistic customers (Furrer *et al.* 2000). Individualistic customers have a higher propensity to switch when they encounter a problem with their financial service provider than customers from a collectivistic culture (Liu *et al.* 2001). Switching intentions are considered an unfavourable behavioural intention. They are generally expressed through negative word-of-mouth and complaints (Antón *et al.* 2007), which are linked to the perceived value and satisfaction variables of this book. This provides the basis for the assumption of a correlation between collectivism and perceived value and satisfaction.

A customer's willingness to pay more positively relates to their loyalty and switching intentions. This is because this is a part of a customer's willingness to expand their relationship with their service provider (Liu *et al.* 2001). Ozdemir and Hewett (2010) also conceptualized this as a component of behavioural intentions in a higher-order construct that links to positive word-of-mouth, and a customer's intentions to continue buying from a particular service provider. Collectivistic customers, who engage more in positive word-of-mouth with service providers, will have a higher acceptance towards a willingness to pay more. In other words, collectivistic customers will be more willing to cross-buy than individualistic customers. This generates the main assumption of the research question of this book.

Based on these theoretical assumptions of collectivism and the four key drivers of customers' cross-buying intentions – perceived value, trust, image and satisfaction – the following ten hypotheses are formulated to build this book's conceptual model, as illustrated in Figure 3.1.

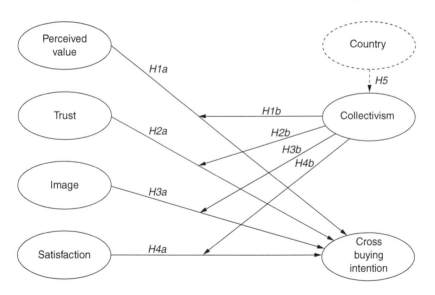

Figure 3.1 Conceptual model with hypotheses.

3.3 Variables and hypotheses

Perceived value

'Perceived value' is defined as the quality that customers receive for the price they pay (Lichtenstein *et al.* 1993). This was traditionally measured in terms of quality regarding the price, and price regarding the quality. This definition has recently been expanded to include various functional values of the establishment, employee professionalism, and social and emotional values (Roig *et al.* 2006). In fact, Gouanris *et al.* (2007) have broaden the scope of perceived value to a personnel value, such as service personnel skills and capabilities, and a procedural value, which refers to the delivery procedure and operation time of services.

Perceived value has been noted as a key driver of cross-buying behaviour (Bolton *et al.* 2004; Verhoef 2003). Specifically in the study of Verhoef *et al.* (2001), it is confirmed that the payment equity, which represents perceived value to the bank customer, impacts on customers' cross-buying activities. However, in the context of cross-buying intentions, there are varied perspectives. Ngobo (2004) indicated that, among French banking customers, cross-buying intention is positively associated with the perceived convenience of cross-buying from the same bank. However, Soureli (2008) stated that, based on customers of Greek banks, the effect of perceived value on cross-buying intention is not significant, as customers would not cross-buy from their main bank simply because the bank offered the most competitive terms or convenience. Jeng's (2008) study of Taiwan found that customers' perceived product variety and the price of a product are not the only considerations in customers' decisions related to the cross-buying of insurance products. These customers made decisions mostly based on the professionalism and image of the financial institution. Although Jeng's (2008) report is not solely based on banking services, his study provides valuable insight to customers' cross-buying intentions, as there are currently few studies in the context of Korea and Taiwan. It can be seen from the studies of Liu and Wu (2007, 2009), Kim and Kim (2010) and Fan *et al.* (2011) – which are the studies that measure the effect of perceived value on customers' cross-buying intentions in the Korean and Taiwanese banking industry – that perceived value, to a certain extent, motivates Korean and Taiwanese banking customers to cross-buy. Therefore, the following hypothesis can be established:

> *H1a: Customers' perceived value of their banks influences their cross-buying intentions in their banking service.*

However, the perceived value from a collectivistic perspective is considered a less favourable driver for purchase intentions. Jin and Sternquist (Jin and Sternquist 2003; (Sternquist *et al.* 2004) found that collectivistic customers, such as those from China and Korea, show less value awareness in their purchase intentions for retail services. Specifically in the banking and financial services, Furrer and Liu (Furrer *et al.* 2000; Liu *et al.* 2001) confirmed that banking customers from collectivistic cultures tend to tolerate poor services from their banks, as opposed to their counterparts from individualistic cultures. This aligns with the fact that individualism refers to the value of the individual's rights, characteristics and identity over those of the group (De Mooij and Hofstede 2002; Hofstede and Hofstede 1991; Hofstede *et al.* 2010). This was theoretically confirmed in the perspective of the behavioural intentions (Brady *et al.* 2001; Gounaris *et al.* 2007; Ozdemir and Hewett 2010; Zeithaml *et al.* 1996) of collectivistic customers who tend to have less propensity to switch service providers than their individualistic customers when they encounter a problem in the quality of services from their financial service provider. Therefore, customers in a collectivistic culture, such as in Korea and Taiwan, will be less influenced by perceived value in their cross-buying intentions of financial products in the banking industry. As a result, the following hypothesis can be established:

> *H1b: Collectivism of customers will not moderate the influence of their perceived value of their banks on their cross-buying intentions in their banking service.*

Trust

Trust is viewed as a customer's confidence in the reliability and integrity of their service provider (Morgan and Hunt 1994) – it is the basis for stable relationships (Garbarino and Johnson 1999). In banking services, the trust that customers have towards their bank strongly relates to their loyalty; it is even regarded as a prerequisite for loyalty (Lewis and Soureli 2006). More specifically, trust is believed to positively affect loyalty when a significant level of uncertainty and risk is present. In other words, a customer's trust in a financial service provider may help reduce the uncertainty and risk that dissimilar extensions might encounter (Lymberopoulos *et al.* 2004). Keh and Xie (2009) define customer trust in a more complex manner. They define customer trust as, not only the customer's overall willingness to take the other party's interests into account, but also an integrity of service provider as the truster's belief is that the trustee is honest and fulfils its promises.

In the context of customers' cross-buying intentions in the banking services, a customer's trust in the bank or financial service provider is displayed via different outcomes. Verhoef (2002) found that trust does not affect the number of banking products purchased by customers in the insurance industry in the Netherlands. Ngobo (2004) also indirectly confirmed that trust, which is an antecedent of the repurchase intention, is negatively associated with cross-buying intentions in French banking services. However, different outcomes have been noticed in other countries. In Greek banking services, Soureli (2008) found that trust directly influences customers' cross-buying intentions. Results also differ in the studies of Liu and Wu (2007, 2009), Fan *et al.* (2011) and Kim and Kim (2010), which are studies of customers' cross-buying intentions of financial products in Korea and Taiwan. In these studies, specifically focusing on Korea and Taiwan, it was stated that trust plays an important mediating role in customers' cross-buying of dissimilar product categories in the banking industry. Therefore, despite the incongruities between different countries, this book asserts to conclude with the hypothesis as follows:

> *H2a: Customers' trust towards their banks influences their cross-buying intentions in their banking service.*

Trust is an important concept that is associated with collectivism. One of the key concepts recognized in individualism is self-confidence. Individualistic customers, who have high self-confidence, expect to have a lower degree of assurance with the banking service provider (Furrer *et al.* 2000). In other words, collectivistic customers are more prone to have a higher degree of assurance with the banking service provider. As assurance is knowledge and a courtesy of service providers who have the ability to inspire their customers' trust and confidence (Parasuraman *et al.*,1993), a high degree of assurance represents a high level of trust, which has been conspicuously noticed among collectivistic customers (Furrer *et al.* 2000; Tsoukatos and Rand 2007). In the perspective of behavioural intention (Brady *et al.* 2001; Gounaris *et al.* 2007; Ozdemir and Hewett 2010; Zeithaml *et al.* 1996), trust correlates directly with loyalty of customers in financial services, which strongly influences collectivistic customers' willingness to pay more or to purchase additional products. This explains the fact that trust plays an important role in the cross-buying behaviour in the banking service in high collectivistic countries, such as Greece (Soureli *et al.* 2008) and Taiwan (Liu and Wu 2009), compared to more individualistic countries, such as the Netherlands (Verhoef *et al.* 2002) and France (Ngobo 2004). This allows the following hypothesis to be developed:

> *H2b: Collectivism of customers moderates the influence of their trust towards their banks on their cross-buying intentions in their banking service.*

Image

Image represents customers' total impression of a service provider. It relates to corporate reputation and can create a sustainable competitive advantage (Dowling 1993; Fombrun and van Riel 1997). In the financial services industry, image is an important determinant of customer patronage, and it executes a crucial role in retaining customers. Image influences customers' preconceptions and loyalty towards a banking service provider, which eventually leads to purchase intentions (Hansen and Sand 2008; Lewis and Soureli 2006). Bravo and Montaner (2009) emphasize that a dynamic approach of the corporate image, such as social responsibility, is also becoming one of the important images to be managed by banks.

Cross-buying intentions in the banking service industry are known to be influenced by the image of the bank. Ngobo (2004) stated that if there is a negative image of the bank's capabilities to meet their customers' needs, it lowers the propensity for those customers to cross-buy. This aligns with Soureli's (2008) findings that customers place great importance on the image of their bank, and intend to buy additional products from their main bank only if they accept the positive image. Similar empirical findings have been reported in the context of the Taiwanese banking industry. These findings state that customers' cross-buying intentions of financial products are strongly influenced by the image of financial institutions, and also by the reputation and size of the service provider (Jeng 2008; Liu and Wu 2009). The cross-buying intention of customers may also be caused by the image of initial product provider to the bank. For instance, the image of insurance company may influence the customer's cross-buying intention instead of the image of the bank. However, as it was noted in other literature of cross-buying in financial services, the focal subjective of the study is the financial institution that provides cross-buying services – the banks – and not the initial product provider – the insurance company, this book will adopt the definitions of image of the bank which engages in cross-buying activities. Thus, the hypothesis of image and the cross-buying intentions is as follows:

H3a: Customers' image of their banks influences their cross-buying intentions in their banking service.

Collectivistic customers are known to appreciate and be driven by relationships within society more than individualistic customers (Oyserman and Lee 2008; Oyserman *et al.* 2002). They are strongly influenced by the identification process (Bagozzi and Lee 2002). Collectivistic customers are more expressively and socially influenced, which tends to mean they are more influenced by the information they receive from others (Mourali *et al.* 2005). Walsh and Mitchell (2009) stated that corporate reputation, which highly correlates with corporate image, has a strong relationship with word-of-mouth among their customers. Therefore, collectivistic customers who have the aptitude to follow word-of-mouth will be inclined to place more emphasis on the image of the service provider when making a decision to cross-buy.

This is also linked to the fact that, in terms of customers' behavioural intentions (Brady *et al.* 2001; Gounaris *et al.* 2007; Ozdemir and Hewett 2010;

Zeithaml *et al.* 1996), collectivistic customers will place higher value on the image of the financial service provider to justify their loyalty towards this service provider. Particularly in Korea and Taiwan, where the Confucian value is known to generate face-saving behaviour with others (Oetzel and Ting-Toomey 2003; Shim *et al.* 2008), the image of the bank will affect customers' purchase intentions more than in other countries. Therefore, the hypothesis of image and collectivism on cross-buying intentions is as follows:

H3b: Collectivism of customers moderates the influence of the image of their banks on their cross-buying intentions in their banking service.

Satisfaction

Satisfaction is an emotional state that results from a customer's interaction with a service provider (Crosby *et al.* 1990). Satisfaction is known to be the antecedent of affective commitment, and a factor to lengthen the duration of the relationship between the customer and the financial service provider (Verhoef 2003; Verhoef *et al.* 2001). Hansen and Sand (2008) stated that satisfaction also affects various behaviours moderated by the characteristics and personality differences between customers.

In terms of customers' cross-buying intentions in the financial services, the effect of satisfaction has been considered negligble. Ngobo (2004) stated that satisfaction is positively associated with repurchase intentions, but that repurchase intentions are not positively associated with cross-buying intentions in the bank. Soureli (2008) also confirmed that the effect of satisfaction on the cross-buying intentions of Greek banking customers is not significant unless it plays a mediating role in the other key factors of cross-buying intentions.

From studies in the context of Korea and Taiwan, the direct role of satisfaction is not clearly identified; however, it is noted that customers' satisfaction indirectly influences the customer to cross-buy. For example, Liu and Wu (2007, 2009) stated that satisfaction with trust mediates the influence of perceived value in customers' cross-buying intentions. Kim and Kim (2010) stated that satisfaction has an overall positive influence on customers' cross-buying intentions, with emotional bonding occurring among the customers. Therefore, although satisfaction was not expressed to have a significant influence on the cross-buying intentions of customers in Europe, in the context of East Asia, particularly for Korea and Taiwan, the following hypothesis can be formed:

H4a: Customers' satisfaction towards their banks influences their cross-buying intentions in their banking service.

Satisfaction is related to perceived service quality and loyalty to the bank (Lewis and Soureli 2006; Moutinho and Smith 2000). Previous studies have confirmed that there is a significant positive relationship between overall customer satisfaction and loyalty with positive word-of-mouth (Cronin Jr and Taylor 1994; Ladhari 2009). When customers from a collectivistic culture are satisfied, they tend to praise the service quality and offer positive word-of-mouth (Furrer *et al.* 2000; Liu *et al.* 2001). Furthermore, collectivistic customers express more loyalty towards service providers than individualistic customers, as they consider the relationship one of the most important factors to consider in regard to their service provider (Oyserman and Lee 2008; Ozdemir and Hewett 2010). From the perspective of behavioural intention (Brady *et al.* 2001; Gounaris *et al.* 2007; Ozdemir and Hewett 2010; Zeithaml *et al.* 1996), a customer's satisfaction strongly correlates with their loyalty, switching intentions and external response. The customers from collectivistic cultures are highly driven by these factors in terms of evaluating the quality of services from financial service providers. Therefore, the following hypothesis can be formulated:

> *H4b: Collectivism of customers moderates the influence of their satisfaction towards their banks on their cross-buying intentions in the banking services.*

Collectivism: Korea and Taiwan

Korea and Taiwan are considered two of the most collectivistic countries reflected on the scale of Hofstede (2010). This has been unwaveringly accepted by Triandis (Triandis 2006; Triandis and Gelfand 1998) and Inglehart (Inglehart 2000, 2006; Inglehart and Oyserman 2004), who have proven that Korea and Taiwan are countries with high levels of collectivism, with their own conceptualized cultural dimensional scales.

Despite these similarities in Korea and Taiwan, there could also be some differences in customers' cross-buying intentions in the banking services. Sternquist and Byun (2004) stated that Korean customers and Chinese customers express different levels of price perception in their purchase habits in their general shopping behaviour. Watchravesringkan and Yan (2008) also confirmed that, even in the same region, such as East Asia, different patterns of customer behaviour exist in general items. This is in line with the assertion made by Craig and Douglas (2006), in which it was stated that a particular culture is no longer defined exclusively in terms of a specific geographic location.

However, the reason for Korea and Taiwan being collectivistic countries is rooted in the historical influence of the Confucian value, which is still embedded in these countries' contemporary cultures (Ueltschy *et al.* 2009; Wei-Ming 1996; Zhang *et al.* 2005).

In addition, Korea and Taiwan have experienced similar paths of change in terms of modernization through political liberalization, as well as robust growth in the national economy. This may also have been caused by this similarity in cultural values (Chia *et al.* 2007; Inglehart and Oyserman 2004; Jacobs 2007). Therefore, the relationship of collectivism to Korea and Taiwan can be hypothesized as follows:

> *H5: The moderating effect of collectivism on customers' cross-buying intentions in their banking services will be the same in Korea and Taiwan.*

To summarize, a total number of ten hypotheses were formulated from the four independent variables, the one dependent variable, and the one moderating variable in the conceptual model. The relationships among each variable were operationalized based on the theoretical framework of customers' behavioural intentions and Hofstede's cross-cultural dimension. By establishing this conceptual model, the study in this book tested and verified these hypotheses in the conceptual model by implementing the following direction of research design and methodology.

3.4 Research design and methodology

The research design is a plan for research that converts the research decisions from broad assumptions to detailed methods of data collection and analysis (Creswell 2009). Typically, the research design is represented in three methodological approaches: quantitative, qualitative, and mixed, which is commonly called 'triangulation' (Creswell and Miller 2000). However, these three approaches are not discrete and should not be viewed as polar opposites or dichotomies; instead, they represent different ends of a continuum (Newman and Benz 1998). In other words, particularly for the quantitative and qualitative approaches, they are designed to reach the same outcomes of the research through different methodological procedures and perspectives. For example, the quantitative approach is based on post-positivist assumptions that verify the theory through determination and reductionism. On the other hand, the qualitative approach builds the theory from the view of a constructivist, through understanding and meanings that form a multiple participant, which is also known as an ethnographic design (Creswell 2009). Through these two approaches, the study compensates for the weaknesses of each single methodology through the counterbalancing strengths of the other (Creswell and Miller 2000).

This book employs the mixed approach, known as triangulation. Triangulation is the validity procedure that seeks convergence of multiple and different sources of information, and seeks to structure themes or categories in a study (Creswell and Miller 2000). It was first theoretically inaugurated to research methodology by Denzin (1989), who identified four types of triangulation across data sources, theories and methods, and among different investigators. Lincoln and Guba (1994) discussed the importance of triangulation in their studies as a means of improving the rigour of the analysis by assessing the integrity of the inferences that are drawn from more than one vantage point. Occasionally, triangulation involves the use of multiple data sources, researchers, theoretical perspectives and methods (Denzin and Lincoln 2005). In particular, triangulation was viewed as involving the use of multiple data collection tools (Oliver-Hoyo and Allen 2006).

Through applying the concept of triangulation, this book combined the quantitative approach of a structured survey randomly given to bank customers in Korea and Taiwan, with the qualitative approach of carrying out selective personal interviews with local field managers. The structured survey of the bank customers was executed with closed-ended questions that were based on the view of determination from a post-positivist perspective. The interviews with local sales and marketing managers in the field were conducted with open-ended questions to represents the view of constructivism. By mixing these two approaches, the triangulation approach in this book provided more pragmatic knowledge based on a more valid procedure. This was in line with the direction of Creswell and Miller (2000), who stated that, as a validity procedure, triangulation is a systematic process of sorting through the data to find common themes or categories by eliminating overlapping areas.

The importance of the systematic process of triangulation to the book can be verified for the following three reasons. First, the dependent variable – the customers' intention to cross-buy a financial product – is not a commonly established concept in Korea and Taiwan, due to its short history in the market and the local regulatory framework (Adams 2008; Laeven 2005; Swati 2006). Thus, there was concern that the survey questionnaire – which was based on the theoretical reasoning of the European context, in which cross-buying a financial service is a common practice with a relatively longer history (Artikis *et al.* 2008; Teunissen 2008) – might be unclear to survey participants. This concern about the survey questionnaire, particularly in terms of the cross-cultural studies, was also addressed in the study of Ember (2009). Ember (2009) argued that cross-cultural surveys require an additional qualitative procedure to ensure a rigorous validation of the research outcomes.

The second reason is that only a qualitative interview with local professionals in the related fields could allow an understanding of customers' intentions to cross-buy financial products. This is one of the critical issues that was raised in the previous review of the literature because most existing studies focused on cross-buying from the perspective of the service provider, not from the perspective of the customer (Kumar *et al.* 2008; Reinartz *et al.* 2008). Specifically in the context of cross-buying financial products in Korea and Taiwan, more caution is required with interviewees. This is because, despite their field experience in the local market, there is a lack of empirical research and theoretical frameworks on this topic comparing these to other markets, such as those in European countries. Therefore, it is essential to execute the quantitative approach in a parallel manner to the qualitative approach of face-to-face interviews.

Last, this book aimed to analyse the influence of the cross-cultural factor in the relationship between the independent variables and dependent variables of customers' cross-buying intentions in two countries. Therefore, it was more beneficial to adopt a multiple methodological procedure in order to validate these findings. Creswell and Miller (2000) stated that using qualitative inquirers to provide corroborating evidence to the data collected by the survey questionnaire will offer a more narrative account of the outcome, as it passes through this process and relies on the multiple forms of evidence, rather than a single incident or data point in the study. Most previous cross-cultural studies were based on the quantitative approach of a group of a nationality, such as the studies of Furrer *et al.* (2001, 2000). However, none have yet succeeded in conducting additional data collection with a qualitative approach. Therefore, obtaining additional data from qualitative interviews of actual professionals in the local field provided more practical insights, from a seller's perspective, into customers' cross-buying intentions. This ultimately served the main purpose of triangulation, which is to support richer details and initiate new lines of thinking to reach a conclusion (Denzin and Lincoln 2005).

In terms of implementing triangulation, this book pursued the direction of Leech and Onwuegbuzie (2007), who contended that triangulation should be extended and focused through data analysis tools, rather than theoretical reasoning. There are two major rationales for the use of multiple data analysis tools in research: representation and legitimation. 'Representation' refers to the ability to extract adequate meaning from the underlying data. Using multiple data analyses, such as triangulation, allowed this study to use the strengths of each qualitative data analysis tool to understand better the phenomenon of cross-buying activities, thereby enhancing the quality of interferences (Leech and Onwuegbuzie 2007). Therefore, using multiple qualitative data analysis tools can supplement the crisis of representation and the difficulty in capturing lived experiences via text (Denzin and Lincoln 2005).

'Legitimation' refers to the trustworthiness, credibility, dependability, conformability and/or transferability of the inferences made (Guba and Lincoln 1994; Leech and Onwuegbuzie 2007). As noted by Onwuegbuzie and Leech (2007), lack of legitimation means that the extent to which the data has been captured has not been adequately assessed, or that any such assessment has not provided support for legitimation. Therefore, using multiple qualitative data analysis tools can support the study to address the crisis of legitimacy – namely, the difficulty in assessing qualitative findings (Denzin and Lincoln 2005).

Both these rationales of triangulation – representation and legitimation – as data analysis tools, meet the needs of systemic procedures. This justifies the above reasons for using triangulation in this book. The data from the questionnaire survey will resolve the risk of representation by compensating with data from the interview, and the interview approach will support the questionnaire survey in terms of assessing qualitative findings to resolve the crisis of legitimation.

3.5 Qualitative approach: interview design

As a part of the qualitative approach, interviews with selective professionals in each country were conducted. In terms of formatting the interview, the book followed the guideline of Tharenou *et al.* (2007), which categorized interviews into three categories: structured, unstructured and semi-structured. This book implemented semi-structured interviews, which were a combination of structured and unstructured interviews.

In a structured interview, the researcher measures specific variables, and the interviews provide the technique to measure those variables. Seidman (2006) defined structured interviews as a composition of completely pre-set standardized questions that are normally closed-ended. This is in line with the statement of Crabtree and Miller (1992), who conceived structured interviews as being analogous to spoken questionnaires, with a rigidly structured interview schedule directing the interview. Creswell (2009) also described structured interviews as being essentially questionnaires that are administered verbally with immutable response options.

Unstructured interviews are typically naturalistic, interpretive and inductive. With this type of interviewing, the questions are open-ended and the interview is conducted in a manner that is similar to a friendly conversation (Seidman 2006). This follows the argument given by Crabtree and Miller (1992), who stated that, in an unstructured interview, the interview has one or more topics to explore. The data gathered from unstructured interviews are usually qualitative. King (1994) mentioned that this is why the data gathered from unstructured interviews are suited to research questions in which a descriptive account is required, without formal hypothesis testing.

By combining these two types of interviews, Tharenoun *et al.* (2007) suggested the semi-structured interview. Semi-structured interviews are more flexible than structured interviews in terms of pre-set questionnaires, but they have more focus on the topics than unstructured interviews. Crabtree and Miller (1992) stated that semi-structured interviews are guided, concentrated and focused, but have open-ended communication. The questions, probes and prompts are written in the format of a flexible interview guide or schedule.

Due to this book's specific topic, and to benefit from the advantages of the flexibility of the procedure, this book used semi-structured interviews instead of structured interviews. For structured interviews, as the book adopted the triangulation approach with parallel closed-ended questionnaires, there was less necessity to deploy this in the data collection process of the interview. The interview topics included collectivism, which was difficult for the practitioners to theoretically define and quantify. Therefore, an unstructured interview was found to be more valid than straightforward closed-ended questionnaires. This was in line with the suggestion of King (1994), who proposed to use unstructured interviews in cases in which the nature and range of the participants' likely opinions about the research topic are unknown and are difficult to quantify.

However, simultaneously, the interview required a preparatory format in order to efficiently relay the research questions to the interviewees. It is because, even for the interviewees, who had a sufficient local experience in the field, were not accustomed to this topic of cross-buying. Furthermore, the variables that were identified as the drivers of closed-end cross-buying of financial products were not theoretically conceptualized by the interviewees. Basic conceptualizations of the four variables (perceived value, trust, image and satisfaction) had to be explained and presented in fixed scenarios. Therefore, in the sense of pre-set scenarios with prepared questions on conceptualized variables, the questionnaire partially adopted the format of a structured interview to meet both the needs and complexity of the two concepts – collectivism and cross-buying. The research used the format of a semi-structured interview.

Conducting a semi-structured interview requires the same level of skills and techniques as an unstructured interview. Therefore, under the topic of semi-structured interviews, Crabtree and Miller (1992) included in-depth and focused interviews that intensively explore a particular topic, life histories, critical incidents techniques and free listing. Hickman and Longman (1994) also addressed the fact that some interviewees can subsequently become reticent and tired, for which the interviewers must be able to reframe the questions and use various probing questions. Therefore, Creswell (2009) also suggested that the interviewer begins with four or five questions. These are typically 'ice-breaking' questions that are followed by a concluding statement, or questions that directly lead to a prepared closed-ended statement.

Based on these formats and guidelines, the interviews were conducted with six participants from Korea and Taiwan. The interviewees were selected or referred through the personal networks of the interviewer, who had been working in the financial service-marketing arena for more than ten years in Korea and Taiwan. The interviewees went through the selection process, with the criteria being their working experience in financial institutions, which included retail banking or other financial services in each local market. The invited interviewees were required to have been engaged in the cross-selling of financial products for more than seven years, including through planning and monitoring sales campaigns. This minimum of seven years was chosen because cross-buying activities in the banking industry, particularly bancassurance, were officially allowed in Korea from 2003, and Taiwan from 1998.

In terms of the interview procedure, the interviewees were first asked open questions about the determinants of customers' cross-buying intentions in banking services. The researcher then explained the four key factors that were identified in the academic research, and, together with the interviewees, the researcher categorized the interviewees' answers relating to these factors. Second, the interviewer explained the characteristic of collectivism, and enquired as to the level of consensus from interviewees on each measurement. Finally, the interviewees were asked to determine the level of collectivism that influenced customers' cross-buying intentions, moderated with the factors that the interviewee mentioned. At the end of each interview, the findings were paraphrased. All interviews were recorded with the interviewees' permission.

In Taiwan, the interviewees included a general manager of a bank and an insurance joint-venture company, a senior executive of a foreign insurance company, and a senior manager of a marketing department of a major bank in Taiwan. An average of 60 minutes was spent on each interview, and all interviews were conducted in English, as all interviewees were fluent in this language.

In Korea, the researcher selected two marketing and sales managers from an insurance company, who were in charge of developing products and training their sales staff on the cross-selling activities within the bank. Another interviewee was a senior manager responsible for the cross-selling of insurance products in one of the largest foreign banks in Korea. As the researcher was Korean, all interviews were executed and recorded in the Korean language.

3.6 Quantitative approach: survey design

As the data collection was conducted in two countries – Korea and Taiwan – the key factor in designing a quantitative surveying approach was the sampling. The sampling is the process of selecting a sufficient number of elements from the population in order to generalize the properties or characteristics of the population elements (Cavana *et al.* 2001). Therefore, designing an optimal size of sample through an appropriate sampling methodology is the basis for achieving accurate outcomes in the research.

Determining an optimal sample size for a study is a crucial item in the research design. This is because if the sample size is too low, it lacks precision in providing reliable answers to the research questions being investigated. However, if the sample size is too large, time and resources may be wasted, with minimal gain (Salant and Dillman 1994). In addition, the sample drawn from the population must be representative, so that it allows the study to make inferences or generalizations from the sample statistics about the population being studied (Maleske 1995).

Therefore, in terms of determining the sample size, this book followed the most common methodology, which was determined by Krejcie and Morgan (1970). In their studies, which are inherited by most empirical researchers, they identified factors for the sample size calculation, such as population size, confidence level and interval, and the estimation of the smallest subgroup within the sample for which estimates are required. By incorporating these understandings, the following formula was used:

$$s = X^2 NP (1-P) \div d2 (N-1) + X^2 P (1-P)$$

s = the required sample size
X^2 = the table value of chi-square for one degree of freedom at the desired confidence level

N=the population size
P=the population proportion (assumed to be 0.50, as this would provide the maximum sample size)
d=the degree of accuracy expressed as a proportion (0.05)

However, according to the table value of chi-square, it is noted that, after the total population of 9,000, the sample size increases at a diminishing rate, with the sample size remaining constant from 368 to 385.

With this finding and its application in several sample size determinations, Roscoe (1975) proposed the following rule when determining the adequate sample size:

• Sample sizes larger than 30 and smaller than 500 are appropriate for most research;
• If samples are to be broken into sub samples, a minimum sample size of 30 for each category is usually required;
• In multivariate research, the sample size should be several times larger than the number of variables in the study.

Therefore, in this book, the total sample size of 700, with 350 samples collected from both Korea and Taiwan, was adequate for the research design.

Probability sampling was used in this study. Cavana *et al.* (2001) explained that probability sampling is more applicable when the sample is required to be used for wider generalization. As this book was a cross-cultural study that took place in two different countries, the ability to generalize the samples was crucial. Therefore, probability sampling was selected as the sampling method. Ember (2009) confirmed from the findings of eight major cross-cultural samples used in the dominant cross-cultural studies that the probability sampling procedure – particularly random sampling – was most frequently used. This is in line with Cavana *et al.* (2001), who stated that, particularly for sampling in cross-cultural research, apart from ensuring the functional equivalence of the concepts investigated for the population concerned, using matched samples, such as probability sampling, is better than using non-probability sampling.

In probability sampling, there are five types of sampling in terms of the methodological approach: simple random sampling, systematic sampling, cluster sampling, area sampling, double sampling and stratified random sampling. For this book, stratified random sampling was adopted, with a consideration of area sampling. Stratified random sampling is a probability sampling design that first divides the population into meaningful, non-overlapping subsets, and then randomly chooses subjects from each subset (Cavana *et al.* 2001). Stratified sampling is most appropriate when subjects within each stratum are homogeneous, but are different from the subjects in other strata (Tharenou *et al.* 2007). Ember (2009) stated that, because of the aforementioned reasons, particularly in cross-cultural studies, in which every case requires an equal chance of being chosen in order to ensure higher generalizability, a proportionate stratified sampling is in favour. Therefore, among the different types of probability sampling, stratified random sampling was selected for the local execution of sampling.

The samples were randomly collected from the capital city and county of Korea and Taiwan, where the economic populations are mostly situated.[1] This took into account that most of the banking and financial service activities are vigorous and concentrated in these areas.[2] This was also done to ensure similar social settings were used in this study, which ensured that appropriate area sampling was used in the methodological approach. In addition, the gender proportion based on the age band was considered to serve as guidance of stratified random sampling. These stratifications were shown to be clear and meaningful with each stratum, and were essential to enable further studies on the initial outcomes of the research. For example, after achieving the goal of this book – to identify the influence of collectivism on customers' intentions to cross-buy financial products – there could be a more segmented analysis into the study's details, by examining age band or gender. This would provide more insight into the outcomes and opportunities and would allow for further topics for future research.

3.7 Questionnaire and measurements design

The questionnaire represents a vital part of the survey process. A written questionnaire does not exist in a vacuum, but is an integral part of the survey process (Brace 2008). Particularly in cross-cultural research, one of the main challenges relates to issues of the instrumentation of communication (Brislin 1970). Potential risk can be encountered, such as idiomatic equivalence, for which certain idioms unique to one language do not lend themselves to translation into another language. Conceptual issues may also arise from the fact that certain words have different meanings in different cultures (Cavana *et al.* 2001).

To avoid such risks and to ensure accuracy in communication, three steps of back-translations were used in this procedure. First, the English survey questionnaire was translated into Korean by the researcher, who was born and studied in Korea for 16 years. This Korean translated the survey questionnaire, which was then translated into Chinese traditional characters by a Korean-Taiwanese professional who majored in Korean Literature in a Chinese cultural university in Taiwan.[3] Finally, this Chinese translated survey questionnaire was translated back into English by a professor at the Shih Chien University.[4] The researcher of this book monitored each step of the translation, and the final version was reviewed by one of the interviewees, who had more than 10 years' experience in the cross-selling of bank products in Taiwan.

The 'TAP' procedure was referred to when structuring the questionnaire (Foddy 1993) – 'TAP' refers to 'topic', 'applicability' and 'perspective'. The topic of the research – the influence of collectivism on customers' cross-buying intentions – was indicated at the top of the questionnaire, with a brief explanation about the purpose of the research. In regard to applicability, most of the questions were simple and easy to answer, as they were based on the participants' daily experience. The data of customers who indicated that they did not have a main bank was excluded from the data analysis. In regard to perspective, the questions were reviewed by local translators to ensure they were written in plain local language, which was then confirmed by the researcher through the back-translation.

The questionnaire was structured in five-point Likert scales, with the responses to the questions relating to a particular concept or measurement. In terms of the contents of the questions, each question was built around a theoretical measurement that had been used in similar previous empirical studies with similar contexts. The questions could be assorted into six main categories: the four key drivers of customers' cross-buying intentions in the banking services, cross-buying intentions, and collectivism. Each category consisted of four measurements that were sourced and adopted from the knowledge gained from the literature review.

In regard to cross-buying intentions, measurements were imported from the study of Soureli (2008), which synthesized and used all of the above four key variables to measure customers' cross-buying intentions in banking services in Greece. Of the four measurements tested by Soureli (2008), two were used in this book. Another two were adopted from the constructs of Ngobo (2004), who also used these four variables to identify the drivers of customers' cross-buying intentions towards the financial services in France. These four items are also commonly found in other studies of cross-buying intentions, such as the study of Verhoef *et al.* (2001, 2005, 2008), Reinartz *et al.* (2008) and Liu *et al.* (2009). Therefore, the final measurements were as follows:

*   CB1: I have the intention of increasing the volume of business with my main bank;
*   CB2: I have the intention to buy more products from my main bank besides banking products;
*   CB3: I will take the opportunity to cross-buy if my main bank offers this;
*   CB4: I will seriously consider this offer if it is from my main bank.

In terms of measuring collectivism, the definitions were from Hofstede's (2010) most recent cross-cultural dimensions. This was to reconfirm the fact that Korea and Taiwan are still one of the most collectivistic countries in East Asia by Hofstede's scales of cross-cultural dimensions (Hofstede *et al.* 2010; Hofstede and Hofstede 1991; Hofstede 1984a). The two measurements were selected from Hofstede's (2010) 12 items of general norms of collectivistic societies, and two measurements were selected from nine items of language, personality and behaviour of people with high collectivism on the same report. This was to confirm the balanced approach of defining collectivism from both social and personal perspectives. These items were also selected in consideration of the fact that they were strongly associated with the Confucian value of Korea and Taiwan, as discussed in the literature review. For instance, in the study of Chung *et al.* (2000) and Zhang *et al.* (2005), the measurements used for Confucian values are similar to these four defined measurements of collectivism. Therefore, the measurements for the question-naire were as follows:

- CL1: Harmony should always be maintained and direct confrontations should be avoided;
- CL2: Value standards differ for in-groups and out-groups – exclusionism exists;
- CL3: Social networking is a primary source of information – purchase pat-terns depend on others;
- CL4: My consumption patterns show dependence on others.

The measurements of perceived value were based on the study of Roig (2006). Roig (2006) used 14 measurements to identify customers' perceived functional values, including establishment, contact personnel, services purchased and price. Out of these measurements, the four with the highest factor loadings were chosen for this book. These measurements were similar in definition to measure-ments used by Verhoef (2002, 2001), Ngobo (2004), Soureli (2008) and Liu (2009, 2007). The measurements that were used in the questionnaires were as follows:

- PV1: My main bank branch is easy to find and access compared to other banks;
- PV2: The personnel at my main bank know their job well;
- PV3: My main bank provides valuable information to me;
- PV4: I am happy with the expense my main bank causes me.

Figure 3.2 shows the relationship between the measurements of perceived value with collectivism and the cross-buying intentions of customers.

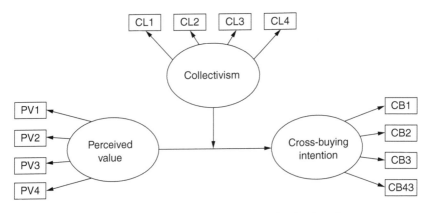

Figure 3.2 Perceived value with collectivism and cross-buying intention.

The measurement of trust was adopted from the study of Liu (2007). Out of the five measurements used by Liu (2007), the four measurements with the highest factor loadings were selected (Liu and Wu 2009). Liu (2007) developed these measurements based on studies from Morgan and Hunt (1994), Verhoef (2002) and Ngobo (2004). This development of measurements was in line with the definition of trust used in the study of Soureli (2008), as both studies shared the same concept of trust from the study of Morgan and Hunt (1994). The measurements for the questionnaire were as follows:

- TR1: My main bank is honest and has high integrity;
- TR2: My main bank keeps the promises it makes me;
- TR3: My main bank is trustworthy;
- TR4: My main bank can be trusted at any time.

Figure 3.3 demonstrates the relationship between these measurements of trust with collectivism and the cross-buying intentions of customers.

The measurement of image was adopted from the study of Bravo and Montaner (Bravo *et al.* 2009), who studied the role of bank image for the customer segment and the non-customer segment. Since this book was focused on cross-buying, which is more eligible for existing bank customers, only the measurements from the customer segment were taken into account. Of the 32 measurements used in the study of Bravo and Montaner (Bravo *et al.* 2009), the four items with the highest t-value were selected. These measurements were similar to a definition used by Liu (2009, 2007), which was expressed mainly in terms of the firm's reputation. This was in line with the measurement indicated in the studies of Lewis and Soureli (Lewis and Soureli 2006; Soureli *et al.* 2008), in which image was one of the variables related to customers' cross-buying intentions in the banking services. Therefore, the measurements of image are as follows:

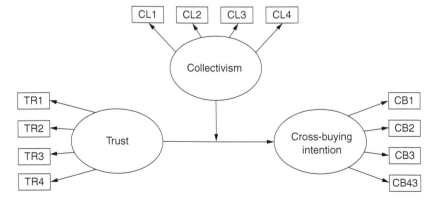

Figure 3.3 Trust with collectivism and cross-buying intention.

- IM1: My main bank has a good reputation and image compared to other banks;
- IM2: My main bank makes a good impression on me;
- IM3: My main bank is highly committed and contributes to society;
- IM4: The staff of my main bank, in general, are friendly and warm.

The relationship between these measurements of image with collectivism and the cross-buying intentions of customers is shown in Figure 3.4.

As for satisfaction, the measurements with the most general and frequently used items were adopted. In fact, satisfaction was a composition of other key drivers of customers' cross-buying intentions with strong correlations. Ngobo (2004) and Liu (2007) confirmed that perceived value positively affects the satisfaction of customers' cross-buying intentions. Soureli (2008) stated that satisfaction has significant influences on the trust and image of a bank in customers' cross-buying intentions. These findings were in line with Verhoef's (Verhoef 2003; Verhoef *et al.* 2001, 2002) studies, which used similar terms for satisfaction. Therefore, to avoid any overlap or conflict between these constructs, only one measurement with general terms expressed on satisfaction was adopted from each of these studies. These were as follows:

- ST1: My main bank always meets my expectations;
- ST2: I am happy with the quality of service from my main bank;
- ST3: I am satisfied with my relationship with my main bank;
- ST4: Overall, I am very satisfied with my main bank.

The relationship between these measurements of satisfaction with collectivism and the cross-buying intentions of customers is shown in Figure 3.5.

To summarize, there were a total of 28 questions, consisting of four questions each of the six sets of variables – perceived value, trust, image, satisfaction,

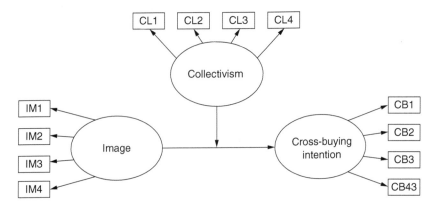

Figure 3.4 Image with collectivism and cross-buying intention.

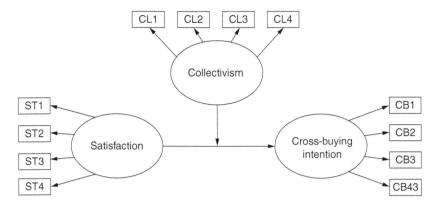

Figure 3.5 Satisfaction with collectivism and cross-buying intention.

cross-buying intention and collectivism – with four more questions added for the purpose of data classification. The summary of the measurements for each variable and section were as shown in Table 3.1.

3.8 Summary

The conceptual model of the book was twofold. It was based on the relationship between the determinants of customers' cross-buying intentions of financial products, and the influence of collectivism on these relationships. The determinants of customers' cross-buying intentions were identified in the previous chapter. These were the perceived value of the bank to the customer, the customer's trust towards the bank, the image of the bank to the customer, and the customer's satisfaction with the bank. These determinants were operationalized as the independent variables of the conceptual model as the book developed the theoretical assumptions of how these independent variables influenced the dependent variable of customers' cross-buying intentions. In the second step, collectivism was added to each relationship of these independent variables in order to measure collectivism's moderating effect on customers' intentions to cross-buy financial products in the Korean and Taiwanese banking industry.

In the operationalization of each variable, the conceptual terms and definitions were adopted from previous related literature. For example, the operationalized concept of cross-buying in this book adopts its definition from the study of Ngobo (2004), which evolved into the definition of cross-buying intention used in the study of Soureli (2008). The same definitions of cross-buying and cross-buying intentions were also employed in the studies of Liu and Wu (2007, 2009), Fan *et al.* (2011) and Kim and Kim (2010), which were studies conducted specifically in the banking industries of Korea and Taiwan.

Table 3.1 Measurements and survey questions

Perceived value	Reference	Questions
PV1	My main bank branch is easy to find and access compared to other banks.	(Roig 2006)	Q3
PV2	The personnel in my main bank know their job well.	(Roig 2006)	Q4
PV3	My main bank provides valuable information to me.	(Roig 2006)	Q5
PV4	I am happy with the expense caused to me by my bank.	(Roig 2006)	Q6
Trust		
TR1	My main bank is honest and has high integrity.	(Liu 2007)	Q7
TR2	My main bank keeps promises it makes to me.	(Liu 2007)	Q8
TR3	My main bank is trustworthy.	(Liu 2007)	Q9
TR4	My main bank can be trusted any time.	(Liu 2007)	Q10
Image		
IM1	My main bank has a better reputation and image than other banks.	(Bravo 2009)	Q11
IM2	I have a good impression of my bank.	(Bravo 2009)	Q12
IM3	My main bank is highly committed and contributes to society.	(Bravo 2009)	Q13
IM4	The staff of my main bank, in general, are friendly and warm.	(Bravo 2009)	Q14
Satisfaction		
ST1	My main bank always meets my expectations.	(Ngobo 2004)	Q15
ST2	I am happy with the quality of service from my main bank.	(Verhoef 2001)	Q16
ST3	I am satisfied with my relationship with my main bank.	(Liu 2007)	Q17
ST4	Overall, I am very satisfied with my main bank.	(Soureli 2008)	Q18

Cross-buying intentions		
CB1	I have intention to increase the volume of business with my main bank.	(Soureli 2008) Q19
CB2	I have intention to buy more products from my main bank besides banking products.	(Soureli 2008) Q20
CB3	I will take an opportunity to cross-buy if my main bank offers.	(Ngobo 2004) Q21
CB4	I will seriously consider any offer if it is from my main bank.	(Ngobo 2004) Q22
Collectivism		
CL1	Harmony should always be maintained and direct confrontations should be avoided.	(Hofstede 2010) Q23
CL2	Value standards differ for in-groups and out-groups: exclusionism exists.	(Hofstede 2010) Q24
CL3	Social network is primary source of information: purchase patterns depend on others.	(Hofstede 2010) Q25
CL4	My consumption patterns show dependence on others.	(Hofstede 2010) Q26
Data classification		
DC1	Do you have a main bank and main bank account?	Q1
DC2	How long have you been a customer of this main bank?	Q2
DC3	What is your gender?	Q27
DC4	What is your age band?	Q28

Perceived value was rationalized under the definition of Roig (2006), who enlisted various measurements for the perceived functional values of financial products. This definition was verified through its historical applications in the studies of Verhoef (2001, 2002, 2005) and Ngobo (2004). As for trust, the definition followed the studies of Liu and Wu (2009), who measured this concept based on findings from Morgan and Hunt (1994), Verhoef (2002) and Ngobo (2004). Image was defined by the terms from Bravo and Montaner (2009), who distinguished the role of the bank's image between the customers and non-customers of the bank. These terms were previously used by Lewis and Soureli (2006) and Soureli *et al.* (2008), and were also applied in the studies of Liu and Wu (2009). As for satisfaction – taking into account its comprehensive terminologies in various types of consumer studies – this book adopted the conceptual terms from the studies of Verhoef (2001), Ngobo (2004), Liu and Wu (2007) and Soureli *et al.* (2008). Finally, for collectivism, this book adopted the conceptual terms of the studies of Hofstede (Hofstede *et al.* 2010; Hofstede 2001; Hofstede 1984a), which were known as the most commonly used cross-cultural dimensions for comparison of Asian and Western consumers (Hofstede *et al.* 2010; Ozdemir and Hewett 2010; Zhang *et al.* 2008).

The conceptual model was initially constructed based on the relationship between dependent variables, customers' cross-buying intentions, and each independent variable of perceived value, trust, image and satisfaction. From the operationalization and rationalization of these relationships, all independent variables were assumed to have a positive influence over the dependent variable. This generated a set of fundamental hypotheses in the conceptual model. These hypotheses were labelled H1a, H2a, H3a and H4a. Subsequently, collectivism, which acted as the moderator variable, was added to these relationships between the independent variables and dependent variable to generate another set of hypotheses.

In this second set of hypotheses, it was assumed that collectivism would have a moderating effect on all the relationships between the independent variables and dependent variable, except the relationship between perceived value and cross-buying intention. This was because collectivistic customers show less consciousness in purchase intention (Jin and Sternquist 2003) and fewer propensities to switch service providers when they encounter poor perceived value (Furrer *et al.* 2001). This formulates the hypotheses H1b, H2b, H3b and H4b.

The correlations of moderator variable and cross-buying intentions, to the relationships between independent and dependent variables were based on the theoretical framework of behavioural intentions (Cronin Jr *et al.* 2000; Liu *et al.* 2001; Ozdemir and Hewett 2010; Zeithaml *et al.* 1996) and the customers' cultural backgrounds. For example, Cronin *et al.* (2000) stated that behavioural intention is an outcome of service evaluation, which is often described as a set of customers' multiple responses. Responses may be different in terms of the evaluation on service quality under the different context of cultural background (Liu *et al.* 2001; Ozdemir and Hewett 2010). In this book, customers' responses of behavioural intention were represented as loyalty, willingness to pay more, switching intention, external response and internal response. These offered theoretical reasoning to the independent variables, which were the determinants of the customers' cross-buying intentions.

After testing the conceptual model in both Korea and Taiwan, the book tested the same conceptual model separately in Korea and Taiwan. This was to observe if the results from each country led to different outcomes. Theoretically, given that Korea and Taiwan are two countries that share similar levels of high collectivism (Hofstede 1984, 2007, 2010), the result of the conceptual model should be the same. However, even with their similar cultural values, there existed different responses to the subject due to cultural de-territorialization (Craig and Douglas 2006). Therefore, there may be contradictory results between the outcomes from Korea and Taiwan. This argument led to the hypotheses H5.

In practising the conceptual model, this book was designed based on the mixed research approach of triangulation. This was done by combining a qualitative approach of interviews with professionals in the local field, and confirming the evidence with a quantitative approach of questionnaire surveys. This approach was selected to serve the complexity of this book because cross-buying was a relatively new concept for the survey participants, and the data collections were undertaken in two different countries. The qualitative approach of interviews resolved the risk of legitimation, and the quantitative approach of a questionnaire survey resolved the risk of representation. These were two critical considerations raised by Leech and Onwuegbuzie (2007) when applying triangulation.

The format of the interview was semi-structured. This was to increase the efficiency in cross-cultural interviews (Ember and Ember 2009) and to assist the interviewees in understanding the topics clearly during the interview process (Creswell 2009). In each country – Korea and Taiwan – three selective interview participants were selected based on their personal profiling and current job positioning. These six interview participants had been engaged in the financial services industry for more than ten years and had been specifically involved in cross-buying financial products in the banking industries of Korea and Taiwan for more than seven years. On average, 60 minutes was spent interviewing each participant. The interviews consisted of open questionnaires, followed up with continuously probing questions that were undertaken by reframing examples. This followed the guidelines of Hickman and Longman (1994).

The questionnaire surveys were conducted with 700 samples from Korea and Taiwan. In terms of the sampling method, stratified random sampling of probability sampling was implemented to increase the ability to generalize these findings and better compare the subgroups, as the samples were adequately proportioned with the pre-determined categories (Cavana *et al.* 2001). The actual data was identified from the official statistics published by the governments of each country, based on which sample proportions were set for the data collection.

In terms of sample size, this book followed the most frequently used methodology of Krejcie and Morgan (1970), in which it was confirmed that, for a total population of over 9,000, a sample size of 368 to 385 is adequate. Roscoe (1975) also stated that a sample size of 30 to 500 is appropriate for most studies with the fact that as for the sub samples, it has to be more than 30. Therefore, the total sample size of 700 – 350 from Korea and 350 from Taiwan – was suitable for this research design.

The questionnaire for this survey was prepared with reference to the TAP procedure from the study of Foddy (1993), in which it was mentioned that each questionnaire should include topic, applicability and perspective. The questionnaires were first prepared in English and then translated to the languages of Korean and Mandarin. They were then back-translated to verify the accuracy of the meanings and wording. The total number of questions was 28, consisting of four questions for each of six sets of variables, in five-point Likert scales.

Lastly, ethical issues were considered prior to conducting the research project. These covered any conflicts of interest, from establishing research questions, to the methods of receiving informed consent, to preserving the confidentiality of the research outcomes. These considerations, with counter-plans, were presented to and approved by the Human Research Ethics Committee of the University of South Australia.

Notes

1 www.kostat.go.kr.
2 www.moi.gov.tw/stat.
3 In Taiwan, the people use traditional Chinese characters, which are different from those used in mainland China.
4 Doctor Jin-Lung Peng, Associate Professor of the Department of Risk Management and Insurance in Shih Chien University, Taiwan. This professor has also been a director of the Bancassurance Research Centre in Shih Chien University since 2006.

4 Data collection and analysis

4.1 Introduction

Based on the conceptual model and methodologies presented in the previous chapter, the quantitative and the qualitative data were collected for analysis. These collected data were analysed separately and then mutually compared to strengthen the outcome from the conceptual model. This book applied the hierarchical multiple regression analysis on the quantitative data, from which the 10 hypotheses in the conceptual model were verified. The findings from the qualitative analysis of face-to-face interviews were reflected to support the final conclusions of this book. This chapter discusses these processes with the requisite considerations and guidelines in operationalizing the data.

This chapter begins by examining the various types of data collection and the advantages and disadvantages of each method. This chapter views these methodologies specifically from a cross-cultural research perspective, following the suggestions from the study of Cavana *et al.* (2001) and the practical guidelines in international data collection from the study of Ember (2009). The data collection was conducted using two approaches: qualitative and quantitative. This chapter first explains how the participants of the qualitative data collection were selected and profiled prior to commencing the interviews. There were six interviewees – three interviewees from each country who shared similar backgrounds and profiles. The face-to-face interviews were conducted in two cities – Taipei and Seoul – and had a semi-structured form (Creswell 2009).

This chapter also explains how 700 quantitative data were collected in Korea and Taiwan. The data were collected with stratified random sampling in order to confirm that the samples were proportionally selected based on the given stratum (Cavana *et al.* 2001). This chapter indicates the characteristics of these samples with a comparison of the official stratum of the age band and gender proportion published by the governmental authorities of Korea and Taiwan. In terms of the questionnaire, a personally administered questionnaire, consisting of 28 questions on six variables and four profiling indicators, was distributed to these samples. This chapter describes how this questionnaire was structured and prepared for use in the two countries, particularly in terms of its translation and back-translation for the verification of the questionnaire used in Taipei.

For the quantitative data analysis, this chapter validates the appropriateness of using factor analysis on data by deploying the Kaiser–Meyer–Olkin (KMO) measure of sampling adequacy and Bartlett's test of sphericity (Dziuban and Shirkey 1974; Kaiser 1970). Based on this testing, exploratory factor analysis (EFA) (Thompson 2004; Tucker and MacCallum 1997) was performed with principal axis factoring and varimax rotation, from which some constructs of questions with lower factoring loading were eliminated for the analysis. Confirmatory factor analysis (CFA) (Fornell and Larcker 1981; Marsh *et al.* 1988) was also conducted, from which the overall fitness of the model was confirmed to be adoptable. In addition, this chapter presents the terminology of cross-checking the validity of the data with the average variance extracted, in which all data were above the adoptable level.

In the analysis of the quantitative data, this study applied the hierarchical regression analysis, which has been proven to be the most effective method of evaluating the moderating effect of a variable on the existing relationship between the independent and dependent variable (Baron and Kenny 1986; Bennett 2000). Thus, this chapter first investigates the relationship between the four independent variables – perceived value, trust, image and satisfaction – and the dependent variable – customers' cross-buying intentions related to financial products. This relationship was identified through multiple regression. In addition to this, collectivism was added stepwise to observe the changes in the correlation between these relationships. Through these hierarchical steps, the hypotheses H1a, H2a, H3a and H4a were verified in the first step, and H1b, H2b, H3b and H4b were verified in the second step. As for the hypotheses H5, the same procedure of hierarchical regression analysis was performed on the separate quantitative data of Korea and Taiwan.

This chapter then compares the findings of the quantitative data analysis with the findings from the interviews for the qualitative analysis. This provides a more solid and subjective view on the outcomes, which will eventually serve the initial purpose of the book – to undertake a theoretical explanation of how the cultural value, collectivism, can influence customers' cross-buying intentions related to financial products – a new paradigm of the banking industry in East Asia countries.

4.2 Data collection and cross-cultural studies

The appropriate data collection method was determined by various factors, such as accessibility to the data source, sample controllability and types of communication tools (Yang *et al.* 2006). For studies on cross-cultural customer behaviour, this is imperative because the inadequate use of data collection may cause the study to encounter statistical obstacles when manipulating cultural treatment and when changing subjects from one cultural treatment to another. In such cases, the samples are not controllable and, consequently, any inference drawn from the results can be purely inaccurate (Sin *et al.* 1999). Particularly in methodological terms, the failure to establish data equivalence is a potential source of measurement error, which can reduce the accuracy of a conceptual model, and reduce the power of the statistical testing of hypotheses (Van de Vijver and Leung 1997).

Following Hofstede's dimensions (1984, 2010), the score of individualism for Korea and Taiwan are 18 and 17 respectively, which place Korea and Taiwan as highly collectivistic among their peer countries. However, Steenkamp and Baumgarther (1998) addressed that the measurement invariances have to be assessed for cross-national differences in relationships between scale scores and real differences in structural relations between constructs. Steenkamp and Baumgarther (1998) explains that at least the same pattern of factor loadings is required in order to establish whether a construct can be conceptualized in the same way across countries. However, Korea and Taiwan, by Hofstede dimension (1984) that has been invariably adopted in the recent dimensions (2010), have been already scored with relatively low individualism, that confirms their high level of collectivism. The reliability of Hofstede's dimension has been recently tested by Taras *et al.* (2010) in their study of a three-decade, multilevel, meta-analytic review of Hofstede's cultural value dimensions. Moreover, even Steenkamp *et al.* (2012), in their studies incorporating with Hofstede's dimensions, they report that there is strong evidence for the universal applicability of the transaction dimensions across Hofstede's conceptualization. Therefore, the measurement of invariance between Korea and Taiwan was not necessary for this book.

Instead, in this book, the methodological considerations were taken into account more importantly prior to beginning the data collection. This followed the guidelines of data collection given in the study of Cavana *et al.* (2001). Cavana *et al.* (2001) stated that there are three issues that are important when undertaking cross-cultural data collection: response equivalence, the timing of the data collection, and the status of the individual collecting the data.

Response equivalence can be ensured by following uniform data collection procedures for the different cultures or national samples. In this book, both the selection of interviewees and stratified random sampling followed the same procedure with categories and stratum. The same category of selection was applied for the interviewees in Taiwan and Korea. Even from an occupational perspective, there was one banker and two insurance cross-selling professionals chosen from both countries. For the questionnaire survey, the area of the survey was limited to the capital city and to the most urban areas of Korea – Seoul and Gyeonggi provinces of Korea, and in Taiwan – Taipei and Taipei County. In terms of the age band and gender proportion, the data collection standard followed the statistics of the local governmental researcher.

Cavana *et al.* (2001) proposed that data collection should be completed within an acceptable timeframe in the different countries – preferably within three to four months. The interviews with the Taiwanese participants were completed in November 2010, and the interviews with the Korean participants were completed in December 2010. The questionnaire survey in Taipei and Taipei County was conducted between October and November 2010, whereas the survey in Seoul and Gyeonggi provinces began in November 2010 and ended in January 2011. Both the data collection periods were in favour of the proposed timeframe.

Lastly, the status of the individual collecting the data was a concern raised from the study of Sekaran (1992). Sekaran mentioned that, when a foreigner comes to collect data, the responses may be biased for fear of portraying the country in an adverse manner. This concern was a small matter for this book, as the researcher who interviewed the Korean participants was a Korean, and the Taiwanese participants had been acquainted with the researcher for an average of three years prior to the interview. Both the questionnaire surveys were conducted by an outsourced local interlocutor who was of the same nationality as the participants of the survey.

Overall, in the data collection methods, the book respected the guidelines and concerns outlined by previous studies on cross-cultural research. Moreover, the book used researchers who were from the local countries, as these people were more familiar with the local markets of Korea and Taiwan.

This book applied triangulation as the main approach to data collection and analysis. Qualitative data from interviews and quantitative data from questionnaire surveys were obtained via local bank customers in Korea and Taiwan. Face-to-face interviews were selected as the method for qualitative data collection, as interviews offer rich data that provide an opportunity to establish rapport with interviewees. They also support an understanding of complex issues (Cavana *et al.* 2001). This method was crucial for the book, as the subject of cross-buying intentions of financial products was still a new phenomenon to the general participants. Understanding this concept required more in-depth experiences and insights from certain segmented participants. Personally administered questionnaires were used as a quantitative method with general participants who were collected by stratified random sampling (Tharenou *et al.* 2007). In order to proportion the population accurately, official statistics from the governments of Korea and Taiwan were pre-investigated and used as the basis for target sampling.

4.3 Data collection and characteristics

Qualitative data for interviews

Qualitative data rely on the responses from the questions asked during interviews or observations of the sample (Taylor and Bogdan 1998). Compared to quantitative data, which consist of results that can be measured in numbers, qualitative data can affect the quality of a study's results. In this book, qualitative data were collected through face-to-face interviews, which were conducted both in Taiwan and Korea. Interviewees were required to match certain criteria in order to ensure the study's validity. Each interviewee was required to be:

- A person who was working for a financial institution and engaged in a retail banking industry within the local market. It was imperative for the interview participants to have professional experience in customers' cross-buying activities in the banking industry in order to supplement the findings of the survey from the non-professionals;

- A person who had been engaged in the cross-selling activities of financial products in financial institutions for more than seven years. The seven year limit was chosen because cross-selling activities, such as bancassurance, were officially allowed in Korea from 2003, and Taiwan from 1998;
- A person who had experience in planning sales campaigns and conducting business performance monitoring, specifically in customers' cross-buying activities in the financial services industry.

There were six interviewees – three interviewees from each country, all of whom matched the above criteria. The interviews were arranged via the personal relationships and referrals of the researcher. All interviews were pre-arranged with the interviewees in accordance with their preferred date and time, and with an adequate venue. Prior to the interviews, the researcher shared the purpose of the meeting and the topic of the research with the interviewees in order for them to be prepared and comfortable with the process. The necessary information consent and disclosure wording was noted by all interviewees, and the researcher received their verbal consent, which was officially recorded on an MP3 player.

In the beginning of the interview, the interview participants understood the purpose of this research and identification of the researcher. Subsequently, the following paragraph has been read for their consent:

> The outcome of this interview will be solely used for the research. Your participation is on a voluntary basis and you may withdraw from the interview at any time without your withdrawal affecting your position, treatment or care.

Once the participant of interview agreed with the above statement, the definitions of a customer's cross-buying of financial products and the cultural value of collectivism were explained verbally based on the measurements identified through literature review. The participants were then questioned on each determinant of cross-buying intentions – perceived value, trust, image and satisfaction – and its relationship with collectivism. The interview ended with the final comments of the participants with their personal suggestion on the managerial implication of this study.

In Taiwan, the three interviewees were chosen via personal contacts and referrals. Two interviewees were from the joint-venture insurance companies of a bank, and one interviewee was directly from a bank. One of the interviewees had more than 15 years' experience in banking and insurance marketing in a global bancassurance company's Asian regional office in Hong Kong. This experience provided her with more insight that allowed a pragmatic comparison between the customers in other markets and the banking customers in Taiwan.

Another interviewee was the senior manager of a captive insurance company belonging to a global leading bank. He was in charge of developing business relationships with the bank's partners, from which he could share various aspects of the key drivers of customers' intentions to cross-buy financial products in the banking channels. The last interviewee was engaged in the cross-selling activities of financial products in Taiwan from the inception of bancassurance in Taiwan. He held a senior management position in a bank, which ranked in the top five of 40 banks in terms of asset size in Taiwan.

Each interviewee attended one hour of a one-on-one interview, which was based on a semi-structured questionnaire that was prepared according to a conceptual model with open-ended questions. The interviews were conducted in English, as all participants were fluent in English. All interviewees proactively participated in the interview because the topic of customers' cross-buying intentions was a subject that was frequently discussed and explored in their corporate strategic meetings. However, due to compliance issues and the companies' external communication guidelines, the names of the interviewees and their companies cannot be disclosed. The interviewees are instead referred to as T#1, T#2 and T#3. The details of interviewees T#1, T#2 and T#3 are shown in Table 4.1.

In Korea, three interviewees with the same qualifications as those from Taiwan were selected. The first interviewee was the head of a sales department in an insurance company. This interviewee was solely engaged in the cross-selling of insurance products to banking customers through bank branches. This interviewee had more than ten years' experience in the insurance field, and was established in a sales and training department of bancassurance from the inception of the bancassurance regulation in 2003. The other two interviewees were from the banking sector. One was from a captive insurance company set up by the seventh largest bank in Korea, and the other was from the insurance marketing department of an international bank, which was the sixth largest bank in Korea. The interviewee from the bank had more than 10 years' experience working in the insurance sector, and was then working in the banking sector.

Table 4.1 Profiles of interviewees in Taiwan

Taiwanese interviewees	Organization	Position	Experience
T#1	Joint venture insurance company between one of the largest banks in Taiwan and French insurer	Chief Executive Office	15 years
T#2	Captive life insurance company of global leading bank	Senior Vice President, Business Development	10 years
T#3	One of the largest banks which has strategic alliance with UK insurer	Head of Marketing and Strategy	12 years

Therefore, he could provide pragmatic views on customers' cross-buying intentions of financial products from the perspective of two different sectors of the financial services. He had previously undertaken a customer survey within the bank, which had a similar topic to this book, and he shared the results of this survey. In this survey, customers were asked about how the bank's image influenced their decision-making related to the cross-buying of different financial products in bank branches.

As in Taiwan, each interviewee from Korea attended a one-hour face-to-face interview. The same semi-structured questions and methodology were applied as in Taiwan. All interviews were conducted in Korean and were recorded with the interviewees' verbal consent. As with Taiwan, the Korean interviewees were also concerned about internal compliance and confidentiality. Therefore, the names of interviewees and their companies were not disclosed in the research, but were instead marked as K#1, K#2 and K#3. The details of interviewees K#1, K#2 and K#3 are shown in Table 4.2.

All the interviewees, regardless of their country and industry, showed a keen interest in this topic. This was because, of the six interviewees, four were employed by foreign financial institutions, where they experienced the differences in the marketing strategies between the headquarters of foreign financial institutions and the local entities. Furthermore, some of the interviewees had conducted similar customer surveys in-house. However, they could not reach an empirical reasoning regarding this phenomenon, nor could they determine clear theoretical explanations for their customers' behaviour. These interviewees requested to view the results and analysis. Therefore, the results will be distributed to them after the completion of the required process.

Quantitative data for the questionnaire survey

The data collection for the survey followed a generalized scientific guideline of the sample size, which was proposed by Krejcie and Morgan (1970), and confirmed by Cohen (1973) and Roscoe (1975).[1] Following this guideline, the sample size of 350 was drawn from each country. These samples were collected

Table 4.2 Profiles of interviewees in Korea

Korean interviewees	Organization	Position	Experience
K#1	One of the largest foreign banks in Korea	Head of Bancassurance team	12 years
K#2	Captive insurance company owned by one of the largest banks in Korea	Head of Product Development/ Implementation	10 years
K#3	The Korea branch of UK leading insurance company	Head of Sales and Training	12 years

in person and in public places of the metropolitan areas of Korea and Taiwan – where most banking branches are located – via active banking transactions (Beck *et al.* 2007; Honohan 2008). In Korea, Seoul and Gyeonggi provinces were selected, and in Taiwan, Taipei and Taipei County were selected.

Data was gathered using the probability sampling approach, which allowed for a generalized survey of the population, and ensured that the special random characteristics were distributed evenly across the sample (Cavana *et al.* 2001). However, in order to achieve greater precision, as was discussed in the previous chapter, the stratified random sampling method was applied to members of the same stratum to be as similar as possible within the respective population (Tharenou *et al.* 2007).

For example, as with Korea, the stratification of the sample attempted to follow the same proportion of gender and age published by the Commission of Korea Statistics[2] for Seoul and Gyeonggi provinces. The reason for the statistics being chosen only for Seoul and Gyeonggi provinces was that these areas represent the largest metropolitan area for the targeted survey. The methodology of sampling was aligned with the sample collected from Taiwan, in the Taipei and Taipei County, which is the capital area of Taiwan where the survey was conducted. This increased the reliability of the cross-cultural data collection by extracting the data that had the most similar characteristics (Ember and Ember 2009; Hult *et al.* 2008). The characteristics of the sample data for Seoul and Gyeonggi provinces[3] are exhibited in Table 4.3, with a comparison to the actual population.

According to Korea's national statistics, male statistics were 2 per cent less than female statistics, with an age band of thirties to forties. Females represented 51 per cent of the total population in this selected area. In the sample data, a similar proportion was applied, with slightly less percentage in the age band of twenties and thirties. For females, there was a moderately higher percentage in the age band of the forties.

The data sample collection was supported by Korea Statistics and Information Research, located at 3F and 4F, Jeil Building, Shinseol Dong, Dong Dae Moon Gu, Seoul, Korea. The data met the accurate approximate proportion, with

Table 4.3 Characteristics of samples from Korea (%)

Korea	Male		Female		Total by age band	
Age band	Population	Sample	Population	Sample	Population	Sample
20s	11	10	11	11	22	21
30s	13	14	14	13	27	27
40s	12	12	12	13	24	25
50s	7	7	7	7	14	14
60s and over	6	6	7	7	13	13
TOTAL	49	49	51	51	100	100

between three and five experienced data collection personnel located in the public area where most bank branches were located. The survey was conducted with the structured questionnaire prepared in accordance with the constructs based on the conceptual model of the research, and followed the required ethical consideration as approved by the Human Ethics Research Committee.

In Taiwan, the same methodology was applied, with the target survey arena being limited to Taipei and Taipei County,[4] which is similar to Korea, and the major metropolitan area of Taiwan. The comparison of the data collected and the total population is shown in Table 4.4.

In this region, the national population statistics showed that there were 3 per cent more females than males within the age band of the thirties to forties, who represented 42 per cent of the population. The age band of the forties was 1 per cent higher than the actual population; however, overall, the sample showed a similar proportion in meeting the requirements of the stratified random sampling. The data collection was supported by Doctor Jin-Lung Peng, an Associate Professor of the Shih Chien University, in the Department of Risk Management and Insurance in Taiwan. The experienced personnel of the academic survey were allocated to this project in consideration of the process used for the ethical considerations.

The total data sample size of 700, gathered from both countries, applied the stratified proportion of the total population in the target cities and provinces. By comparing the data from Korea and Taiwan, it was noted that Korea had a slightly younger age band than that of Taiwan. However, overall, it showed that they had a similar proportion of males and females. In the integrated characteristics of the sample, it was noted that there was a slightly lower proportion of the samples of the age band of the twenties, but a higher proportion in the age band of the forties and the over sixties. However, the differences between the stratified stratum were negligible and acceptable in meeting the requirements of stratified random sampling (Kotrlik and Higgins 2001).

The consolidated comparison between the samples and the actual population of Korea and Taiwan is displayed in Table 4.5.

Table 4.4 Characteristics of samples from Taiwan (%)

Taiwan	Male		Female		Total by age band	
Age band	Population	Sample	Population	Sample	Population	Sample
20s	10	9	9	9	19	18
30s	10	10	11	11	21	21
40s	10	11	11	11	21	22
50s	9	9	11	10	20	19
60s and over	9	9	10	11	19	20
TOTAL	48	48	52	52	100	100

Table 4.5 Characteristics of samples from Korea and Taiwan (%)

Korea & Taiwan	Male		Female		Total by age band	
Age band	Population	Sample	Population	Sample	Population	Sample
20s	11	10	10	10	21	20
30s	12	12	13	12	24	24
40s	11	12	12	12	23	24
50s	8	8	9	9	17	17
60s and over	8	8	9	9	16	17
TOTAL	49	49	52	52	100	100

The survey for Taiwan and Korea began on 1 November 2011, with the survey for Taiwan ending on 30 November 2011, and Korea ending on 10 December 2011. The Korean survey was slightly extended due to difficulties in collecting sufficient data for the age band of the over sixties.

4.4 Data analysis and findings

Data analysis of interviews

The interview data analysis assisted in bringing meaning to the study, rather than seeking the truth, which was pursued by the quantitative research (Ott and Long-necker 2008). Corbin and Strauss (2008) stated that it is important to acknow-ledge the interplay between the researchers and the interview data due to the extent of subjective selection and interpretation of the general data, regardless of the type of research. Furthermore, unlike quantitative analysis, qualitative ana-lysis, such as interview data analysis, commonly takes place during data collec-tion. For this, Silverman (2009) suggested considering a continuum of analysis, ranging from the mere accumulation of raw data to the interpretation of the data.

The analysis of the interview data in this book adopted two strategies: them-atic analysis and comparative analysis. Thematic analysis is an analysis con-ducted based on a certain theme. It differs from other methods in that it seeks to describe the patterns found in the qualitative data (Braun and Clarke 2006). Comparative analysis is used to compare and contrast data on specific topics between the different sets of participants. By using both analysis methods, the analysis of the interview data in this book could gain more reliability and valid-ity, which would also become the basis for qualitative analysis as the supple-mentary justification of the outcomes.

The interviews were first conducted in Taiwan, with a semi-structured approach based on the same variables that were used as the basis of the survey questionnaire. The focus of the interview was to seek the views of the interview-ees on the driving factors behind customers' intentions to cross-buy financial products in bank branches. The interview sought to extract the pragmatic insights that could supplement or enrich the findings from the data analysis of the survey questionnaire.

Interviewee T#1 stated that trust was the most important factor to induce customers to cross-buy financial products from a bank. T#1 defined trust in two ways: trust of the individual salesperson at the bank, and trust that the bank will keep its promises and deliver a quality service. T#1 placed more importance on the trust of the individual salesperson. However, T#1 emphasized that trust as relating to the capability of the individual salesperson to handle the related services for the customer. In other words, even though that salesperson is not professionally capable of handling the task, once there is a relationship built upon trust between the customer and the salesperson, the customer is willing to cross-buy financial products from that person. This comment was in line with Liu and Wu (2009, 2007), who stated that customers with a high level of collectivism tend to make purchase decisions based on the trust in the relationship with a salesperson, rather than the perceived value. As stated by T#1:

> The history between the customer and the bank is very important in Taiwan. The Taiwanese banking customers are usually driven by the history of the personal relationship with the salesperson, which sometimes bears a stronger influence in the customer's decision in the cross-buying of the financial products. For instance, a customer of long standing with a specific bank will build a relationship of trust towards this bank, and this is what motivates the customer in the cross-buying of financial products. However, in this long relationship with the bank, it is most likely an individual salesperson who has gained the trust of the customers – very seldom is it the bank, itself, that gained that trust.

Alongside trust, T#1 commented that the image of the bank may also affect customers' intentions to cross-buy financial products. This relates to the trust of the customer towards the bank, which helps build a good image of the bank for the customer. T#1 also mentioned that elderly people prefer to deal with a big bank that has a traditionally good reputation, which they will be able to link to their social status. In other words, the elderly person will use the image of the bank with pride and a face-saving component. This aligns with the study of Oetzel and Ting-Toomey (2000), who stated that people from a high collectivistic culture will have more emphasis on face-saving than their counterparts in a low collective culture. T#1 noted:

> It is true that size does matter in Taiwan.... If you are the customer of the largest bank in Taiwan, you are considered a person with a high social status.... This will further influence their relationship with the bank. In that sense, the image of the bank is also important in motivating customers to cross-buy.

Not much emphasis was placed on perceived value, as, in Taiwan, most financial products are similar. Furthermore, there is no significant difference between the financial products that customers can cross-buy through banks, and those products available on the market. As for satisfaction, T#1 commented that the concept is too broad and varied to define. However, satisfaction will still play an important role in the cross-buying of financial products, as it will accelerate the effect of trust and image when making decisions.

Interviewee T#2, who had more than 12 years' experience in various positions from product planning to sales management, commented that perceived value is the most important factor in customers' intentions to cross-buy financial products in bank branches. T#2 emphasized that the perceived value of the product itself was more important than the convenience or the capability of th ank salespeople. In other words, the first factor the customer will seek is the price of the product, and the benefit they will attain from the product. This is in line with the findings from the studies of Verhoef (2005, 2001) and Ngobo (2004), which were based on the Western context. T#2 stated:

> The Taiwanese are very smart with financial planning.... They will always compare the premium of the insurance or the pricing of the financial products that they find in their banks with ones that they find in other banks. They are not interested in the bank, only in the pricing.

T#2 emphasized that trust plays an important role in terms of motivating customers to cross-buy in a bank. However, the trust T#2 mentioned was the trust in a bank's financial stability and security, rather than the trust in a specific person or in the value of the bank. This is due to the financial crisis of 2003 and 2008 – Taiwanese customers are becoming more cautious when choosing a financial service provider in order to secure a long-term credit risk. To a certain degree, this trust could be related to the image of the bank, which T#2 placed as the third most important factor in influencing cross-buying intentions. T#2 stated:

> After the two financial crises in Asia, the customers are concerned about the banks ... especially those customers who bought investment-linked products and suffered financially due to these crises. Therefore, today, before the customer decides to cross-buy, they will first consider whether the bank can sustain them over time.... This is the reason why the banks and the insurance companies are endeavouring to build a strong image of financial stability, not only in attracting customers, but also in maintaining the existing relationships with their customers.... However, this may be an important and attractive point when it comes to long-term savings or investment-related products, but for other short-term or simple financial products, the customers might not be interested.... In other words, image of the bank must be related to trust of the bank. It is because the customers may take their decision based on the first impression [image] of the bank, but in order to grow the long-term relationship for cross-buying, trust must be built between the customers and the bank, in which case, the first image of the bank may not be so important to the customers.... If there is the right relationship under a firm, trust is there.

T#2 stated that the key factors that influence cross-buying intentions differ with regard to the types of financial products that customers cross-buy. The interests of a customer on a complicated long-term savings plan and those of a customer on a simple one-year protection plan are likely to be different. At the same time, age bands, which are a key factor in cross-buying intentions, would be different. This may not include an additional factor in this book – the factor of satisfaction. T#2 stated that the relationship of satisfaction was similar to that stated by T#1 – that it will not affect a customer's intention to cross-buy before the selling of the product, but will affect the duration of the customer's relationship with the bank, based on the quality of the overall services.

Interviewee T#3 was a banker with experience of 15 years, who held a senior position in selecting cross-selling products. T#3 stated that image was the most crucial factor instigating customers to cross-buy. This was because the cross-buying of different financial products at a bank branch is new to the Taiwanese market. Therefore, if a bank presents an image of new and innovative products, this will motivate customers to cross-buy from that bank. T#3 emphasized that, to transform an ordinary customer into a relationship-based customer who will cross-buy the products with a long-term commitment to a relationship with the bank, it is essential for the bank to invest in renewing the brand image. This positioning is in line with the findings mentioned in the studies of Reinartz (2004, 2003). Based on experience in his company, T#3 stated:

> Selling insurance or other financial products is still new to the Taiwanese customers. They are sceptical of a bank selling other financial products alongside their core banking business.... Therefore, it is important for the image of the bank to be that of an innovative financial services provider. Actually, image can be more important than a bank's actual capability. This will require an extensive advertising campaign.... Especially in Taiwan, where most bank branches are located closely with each other, for which the banks cannot be benefited for locational conveniences.

T#3 also stated that trust is another factor that influences customers to cross-buy financial products. A case in point is that bank customers in Taiwan seldom change their main bank due to their trust and relationship with their bank. Therefore, it is easier for a bank to cross-sell its products that affect customers' intentions. This, to a certain extent, was similar to the comments of T#1. T#3 added that perceived value, such as the pricing of the product, could be the other factor alongside trust and satisfaction. However, he was not sure whether perceived value and satisfaction had any influence on customers' behavioural intentions to cross-buy. In addition, T#3 commented on the general Taiwanese customers as follows:

> The Taiwanese indeed appreciate trust in their relationships. They will remain with the bank even though they are not always happy with their services or the financial terms that the bank offers, due to their relationship

with the bank. This may be different with the younger customers.... That is why it is important for the bank to build an image of trust and continually express that they are doing their best for their existing customers. This will add comfort and therefore a motivation for the customers to cross-buy.

All the interviewees from Taiwan had a positive response to the Taiwanese customers because of their high level of collectivism, as they put the benefit of their group before their individual interests, and preferred the collectivistic harmonious culture, rather than the individual characteristics. However, they stated that this could change in the near future due to the changing mindset of younger generations as a result of globalization.

The interviews in Korea were conducted after the interviews in Taiwan, in the same manner that they were conducted in Taiwan, but in the Korean native language. Interviewee K#1 had been employed in the insurance industry for 10 years and, at the time of the interview, was employed by the largest foreign bank in Korea. K#1 shared his views on customers' intentions to cross-buy a financial product over a bank counter. K#1 selected trust as the most important driver for this behavioural intention. His definition of trust was a combination of customers' trust towards a personal banker who assists them with their banking tasks, and the loyalty built throughout the customers' relationship with the bank. K#1 shared the results of an in-house marketing survey conducted by his bank, which stated that customers will continuously purchase additional products and services from the bank once trust has been established. The categorization of these additional products included the cross-buying of non-financial products. The second most important driver of the cross-buying intention was satisfaction. K#1 stated that satisfaction was closely linked to trust, and felt that these two factors should always incorporate one another:

> In our in-house survey, it was found that Korean customers cross-buy insurance products from the bank because they have trust in the bank.... This trust originated from the relationship between the salespeople and the satisfaction that the customers gained from their experience with the bank.... It is not only insurance products that the customers are willing to purchase.... Non-financial products and services are also purchased through the bank because they trust the bank.... Trust, based on satisfaction, makes this possible.

K#1 did not agree that the factors of image and perceived value would influence the cross-buying intentions of customers. K#1 stated that perceived value could trigger the interest of customers at a certain level, but would not be the ultimate factor influencing them to make a decision to cross-buy products. K#1 also stated that geographic convenience as a perceived value was no longer valid due to the introduction of ATMs, internet and mobile banking. The fact that Korean customers often have multiple bank accounts between the eight major banks in Korea made K#1 unsure whether customers take image as one of the factors that influence their decision to cross-buy financial products from a particular bank. These comments on perceived value and image contradict the findings of Roig *et al.* (2006) and Bravo *et al.* (2009). However, even these studies indicated that the benefits of perceived value and image can differ for geographic or corporate strategic reasons. K#1 made a very interesting comment:

> It is difficult to comment on the differentiation of a bank's image in Korea.... They have different styles of advertising, and many have a fancy catchphrase, but, in the end, the result is the same for the customers.... It is not linked to change the image of the bank or to influence the customer's cross-buying intention. For instance, it may influence some customers in switching from one bank to another, but once the relationship is formed and usually after the first transaction with the new bank, the image no longer influences the customer to cross-buy.... This phenomenon also applies to the perceived value. Initially, the interest rate, discount fees and additional benefits of the banking products are important; however, once the product has been purchased, the relationship moves on and becomes trust, and the customer is no longer concerned about the conditions of previous transactions.

Interviewee K#2 had different views from those of K#1. K#2 viewed perceived value as an important factor influencing customers' cross-buying intentions, as Korean customers are concerned about the value of the product they are buying. However, K#2 agreed that, at times, trust plays an important role, as Korean customers are inclined to make reckless decisions because of the relationship or value upon which their trust is based. This Korean behaviour is mentioned in the studies of Yoo *et al.* (2006) and Ha and Akamavi (2009).

K#2 stated that satisfaction might not be a factor that influences the cross-buying intention. This is because satisfaction is a broad term relating to the positive reaction of a customer. It is not easy to identify whether satisfaction supports a positive intention to cross-buy financial products. K#2 also placed less emphasis on the image of a bank as an influential factor in cross-buying intention, as most banks in Korea share a similar image. In his opinion, the image, such as the reputation of a bank, would not influence customers' intention to cross-buy once the initial relationship between the customers and the bank was established:

> The customers in the banking industry are getting younger.... The young generation is able to access the internet for competitive pricing or the conditions of financial products, and, should they find a more attractive offer, they will then subscribe to that product provider. In other words, they will not cross-buy financial products only because they have a bank account with that bank.... However, if the customer is willing to cross-buy from the bank, it should be because of the trust that the customer has with the bank, and this may stem from the satisfaction that the customers have gained in

many facets of the bank.... But image is not as important in Korea, as there are not many banks [and they] are all major banks with little differentiation in their image branding.

K#3 provided genuine feedback on customers' cross-buying intentions of financial products in the field. K#2 confidently stated that trust will drive customers to cross-buy financial products from a bank. For example, in the bancassurance business, even though the same product is sold by insurance agents, customers will buy the product from the bank because they trust the bank based on previous financial transactions. However, the antecedent factor to trust is satisfaction. Trust can only be built with satisfied customers. If customers are not satisfied with the services or products from a bank, trust cannot be established. Therefore, customers would have a negative inclination to cross-buy, even if the services or products offered by banks are superior to those of the insurance company. Based on his experience within this field, K#3 stated the following:

> Solely from a sales perspective, when cross-selling financial products in bank branches, we are not selling the products, but are selling the trust.... Each product is sold based on how much trust the customer has towards the bank salesperson. If the product is sold based only on competitive values, such as discounts, better terms with benefits, and even convenience of access, and we do not gain the trust of the customers, this trust will not last and the efforts put into the transaction will have been in vain.... There are a number of cases where a customer will buy the same insurance product, even with more expensive pricing, at a higher price from the bank, when they could have bought the product from an insurance sales agent. This is because the customer has more trust in the bank and the customer believes that he or she can benefit from this trust.

K#3 did not agree that image would influence customers' intentions to cross-buy. In the past, some banks have promoted an image of being able to provide all financial services through cross-selling activities, but this promotion was not reflected in their sales. K#3 stated that promoting or emphasizing a good image could be useful in informing the customer of a new financial service or product, but would not necessarily lead to an actual intention for a customer to cross-buy. This is because, once customers are informed of services or products new to the market, the customers will go to their own bankers and request the same services. This was in line with the statement made by K#1.

The perceived value of a bank could be important, but it may be limited or may differ in certain customer segments. For example, high net worth customers would not be as sensitive to the pricing of a product, but would be comfortable with the additional privileged services that they receive.[5] Meanwhile, ordinary customers would prefer competitive pricing of a product, even though they may sacrifice the convenience of buying or maintaining the product. However, these preferences to perceived value would not be as strong a factor in inducing customers to cross-buy compared to trust or satisfaction. This is because these values are important at the stage when the banks are initiating a relationship with the customers. Once a relationship has been formed, it is important to maintain trust and continuously ensure the satisfaction of customers. K#3 gave an example of the practices in the market:

> If you are extremely wealthy and are not concerned about 10 million Korean won [equivalent to US$12,000], then you are not concerned about the interest rate or discount fee from the bank.... Your concern would be the stability of the bank.... How secure the bank is and how the bank will maintain its stability in the long term. This is when the trust of the bank plays a major role with the customer's intention to cross-buy. However, if you are not wealthy and are an ordinary or mass-affluent customers, whose concerns about 1,000 Korean won [which is less than US$1], then the pricing or discount fees will be important to you. However, this may be important in a simple transaction, such as in using the ATM or cash remittance fees, but when it comes to the cross-buying of financial products, these values will not be as significantly important.

These interviewees from Korea, as with those from Taiwan, agreed that Korean customers make decisions with the general attitude of customers from a collectivistic culture. An interesting point that K#2 shared related to the collectivistic behaviour that is typically noted by Korean customers using internet banking. Korean customers are very sensitive to trends and brands, and tend to make purchase decisions based solely on this collectivistic thinking. K#2 noted that when customers are buying a product, they tend to follow the collectivistic trend, or recklessly follow other customers' purchase decisions. This once again confirmed that Koreans and Taiwanese are categorized as a people with high level of collectivism. K#2 stated that similar phenomena can take place in the financial market:

> When a new trend is introduced to Korea, the customers rush to follow.... For instance, if the trend is a new product, everybody will rush to buy that new product.... This is called 'purchase without any questions'. This kind of purchase behaviour is often noticed with financial products. The customers just buy the products from the bank because that product is in trend. An example is the Regular Payment of Investment Products, which was one of the traditional financial products that existed before with securities companies in Korea. However, in the early 2000s, the trend of cross-buying this financial product from the bank's branches was so popular that many people bought the Regular Payment of Investment Product without knowing what product they were investing in.

To summarize the key points from the interviewees from Taiwan and Korea, the following simplified outcomes are demonstrated in Table 4.6.

Table 4.6 Summary of results from interviews

Influence on cross-buying intentions	Perceived value	Trust	Image	Satisfaction	Influence of collectivism?
T#1	Negligible	Very strong	Positive	Strong	Yes
T#2	Strong	Strong	Negligible	Strong	Yes
T#3	Positive	Strong	Very strong	Negligible	Yes
K#1	Negligible	Very strong	Negligible	Positive	Yes
K#2	Very strong	Strong	Negligible	Negligible	Yes
K#3	No	Yes (strong)	No	Yes	Yes

The interviewees had varying views of perceived value. Three interviewees – T#2, T#3 and K#2 – out of six stated that perceived value would not play an important role in customers' cross-buying intentions, while others believed that it would be a positive driver when cross-buying financial products. Both the parties understood that, in Taiwan and in Korea, where the customers are from a strong collectivistic culture, perceived value would have less importance. However, they believed that this factor would still be taken into account by customers when making decisions. These answers align with the findings from the studies of Verhoef (2001) and Ngobo (2005). Nearly all interviewees stated that image was not a major driver in the banking industries of Korea and Taiwan. Only one interviewee, in Taiwan, believed that the image of new and innovative banks would provide more incentive for customers to cross-buy, as the activity of cross-buying is still a new phenomenon in Taiwan.

Factor analysis for quantitative data

A factor analysis is commonly conducted to identify the variability among the observed variables in terms of potentially lower factors, and to detect a structure in the relationships between these variables (Harman 1976). In a factor analysis, there are two main streams of approach: EFA and CFA. EFA is often conducted in the early stages of a scale development, and if there is no prior theory. In this situation, the research uses factor loadings to predict the factor structure of the data. On the other hand, CFA is used in data analysis to examine the expected causal connections between variables with a confirmed theory underlying their measurement model (Hurley *et al.* 1997). William (1995) stated that EFA would be preferred for a scale development, while CFA is more appropriate when measurement models have a well-developed underlying theory for the hypothesized patterns of loadings. Recent articles that have appeared in major organizational research journals have stated that the use of CFA is steadily increasing, while the use of EFA is gradually declining (Austin *et al.* 2002; Hurley *et al.*, 1997; Shook *et al.* 2004; Stone-Romero *et al.* 1995). For this book, both EFA and CFA were used to strengthen the appropriateness of the model.

First, the KMO measure of sampling adequacy and Bartlett's test of sphericity were conducted. The KMO measure of sampling adequacy is an index that examines the appropriateness of factor analysis. KMO should be 0.60 or higher in order to proceed with a factor analysis. It is commonly suggested that 0.50 should be used as the cut-off value, and a desirable value would be 0.8 or higher (Kaiser 1970). Bartlett's test of sphericity is used to test the null hypotheses that the variables are uncorrelated in the population, which means that the population correlation matrix is an identity matrix. An identity matrix is the matrix in which all diagonal elements are one, and all off diagonal elements are zero. If all off diagonal elements are zero, then the study needs to reject the null hypotheses (Dziuban and Shirkey 1974).

In the results, the KMO factor was 0.876, which is closer to one, and $x2 = 6062.543$, with $p < 0.001$. This satisfied the overall sampling adequacy

Based on this, EFA was performed by using principal axis factoring and varimax rotation. As factor loading for the measurements was above 0.7, this confirmed that the grouping of measurements was undertaken properly. As for the compound variance of each factor, factor one was 17.05 per cent, factor two was 33.98 per cent, factor three was 50.88 per cent, factor four was 66.64 per cent, and factor five was 79.1 per cent. This indicated that the extracted five factors explained 79.1 per cent of the total variance. However, through these procedures, Q3, Q7, Q15 and Q18 were deleted, with the result of factoring loading, as shown in Table 4.7.

In proceeding with the CFA, the study needed to confirm the fit of the model to the data, and evaluate the adequacy of the model. Once the factor model was fitted to the data, the factor loadings were chosen to minimize the discrepancy between the correlation matrix implied by the model and the actual observed matrix.

In CFA, as shown in Table 4.8, the estimated fitness of each index was measured based on the standard level. GFI, AGFI, RMR and RMSEA were measured for absolute fit. NFI, IFI, CFI and NNFI were measured for incremental fit. PNFI and PCFI were measured for parsimonious fit (Fornell and Larcker 1981; Marsh *et al.* 1988). As all of these indexes met the standard level, the efficacy of the measurement model was confirmed.

Table 4.7 Exploratory factor analysis (rotated component matrix)

Rotated component matrix[a]						Construct liability	
	Component						
	Factor 1	Factor 2	Factor 3	Factor 4	Factor 5		
Q4	0.129	−0.105	0.032	0.866	0.023	0.844	PV
Q5	0.177	−0.103	0.029	0.880	−0.042		
Q6	0.016	−0.034	0.018	0.864	0.058		
Q8	0.194	0.187	0.789	0.051	0.271	0.928	TR
Q9	0.249	0.127	0.836	0.019	0.297		
Q10	0.246	0.178	0.826	0.029	0.238		
Q12	0.014	0.098	0.284	0.041	0.781	0.821	IM
Q13	0.362	0.176	0.410	0.026	0.627		
Q14	0.310	0.185	0.249	−0.011	0.712		
Q16	0.826	0.179	0.179	0.063	0.163	0.904	SF
Q17	0.857	0.094	0.205	0.130	0.161		
Q18	0.797	0.152	0.250	0.200	0.108		
Q20	0.187	0.861	0.200	−0.086	0.075	0.884	CL
Q21	0.175	0.890	0.195	−0.090	0.060		
Q22	0.058	0.873	0.055	−0.098	0.246		

Notes
Extraction Method: Principal Component Analysis.
Rotation Method: Varimax with Kaiser Normalization.
a Rotation converged in 6 iterations.

Table 4.8 Confirmatory factor analysis

CFA	Index	Standard level	CFA results	Fitness
Absolute Fit Measure	GFI	Over 0.9	0.96	Confirm
	AGFI	Over 0.9	0.94	Confirm
	RMR	Less 0.5	0.027	Confirm
	RMSEA	Less 0.8	0.051	Confirm
Incremental Fit Measure	NFI	Over 0.9	0.965	Confirm
	IFI	Over 0.9	0.977	Confirm
	CFI	Over 0.9	0.977	Confirm
	NNFI	Over 0.9	0.97	Confirm
Parsimonious Fit Measure	PNFI	0.5 or 0.6	0.735	Confirm
	PCFI	0.5 or 0.6	0.744	Confirm

The result of CFA can be demonstrated with path analysis, as shown in Figure 4.1.

In addition to CFA, it is crucial to establish the convergent and discriminant validity, as well as the reliability. The one common practice proposed by Fornell and Larker (1981) is to measure this convergent validity and reliability with the average variance extracted (AVE) measure. This is a measure of the shared or common variance in a latent variable – the amount of variance that is captured by the latent variable in relation to the amount of the variance due to its measurement error (Raines-Eudy 2000).

In different terms, the AVE is a measure of the error-free variance of a set of items. A minimal demonstration of the validity of any latent variable should probably include the content or face validity of its indicators, the construct validity, and its convergent and discriminant validity. The validity of this latent variable would then be qualitatively assessed by considering its reliability and its performance over this minimal set of validity criteria.

The construct validity is concerned in part with the latent variable's correspondence or correlation with the other latent variables. The other latent variables in the study should be valid and reliable, and their correlations with the target latent variable should be theoretically sound. Convergent and discriminant validity involve the measurement of multiple constructs with multiple methods, and are frequently considered additional facets of construct validity. Convergent measures are highly correspondent across the different methods, while discriminant measures are internally convergent.

Latent variable reliability is a measure of the correspondence between the items and their latent variable and the correlation between the latent variable and its items. Correlations less than 0.7 ignore the measurement error. Fornell and Larker (1981) suggested that an adequately convergent latent variable should have measures that contain more than 0.50 explained the common variance in the factor analytic sense. It can be noted in Table 4.7 that the indexes of the construct reliability of all constructs were above 0.7 and the AVE were all

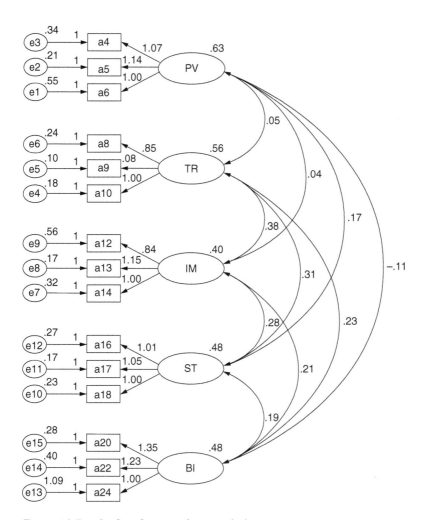

Figure 4.1 Result of confirmatory factor analysis.

above 0.5. Therefore, all the constructs – the questions used for the five latent variables – were used for the data analysis, with acceptable reliability.

The AVE can also be used to gauge the discriminant validity (Fornell and Larker 1981). If the squared correlation between the two latent variables is less than either of their individual AVE, this suggests that the latent variables each have more of an internal variance than the variance shared between the latent variables. In the results of the AVE, shown in Table 4.9, the average of each variable was well above the square of this phi – the correlation coefficient. This supports the validity and reliability of the model (Fornell and Larcker 1981).

Table 4.9 AVE table for discriminant validity

	Cross-buying intention	Satisfaction	Image	Trust	Perceived value
Cross-Buying Intention	0.7181				
Satisfaction	0.1459	0.7595			
Image	0.2134	0.3982	0.6103		
Trust	0.1866	0.3481	0.6496	0.8101	
Perceived Value	0.0320	0.0894	0.0074	0.0077	0.6455

Notes
AVE = $\sum$ (Standard Estimate^2)/$\sum$ (Standard Estimate^2) + $\sum$ measurement error.

Hierarchical regression analysis

In order to test the hypotheses from the conceptual framework built through the literature review, multiple regression analysis was applied (Cohen 2003; Pedhazur 1997). Multiple regression analysis is an extension of the simple linear regression to allow for more than one independent variable. Associated with this multiple regression is R^2, which was the per cent of variance in the dependent variable, explained collectively by all of the independent variables. R^2 is also called 'multiple correlations' or the 'coefficient of multiple determinations'. It is the per cent of variance in the dependent, explained uniquely or jointly by the independents. R^2 can also be interpreted as the proportionate reduction in error in estimating the dependent when knowing the independents. In other words, R^2 reflects the number of errors made when using the regression model to guess the value of the dependent, in ratio to the total errors made when using only the dependent's mean as the basis for estimating all cases.

Furthermore, by testing the difference of two R^2s, it is possible to determine if adding an independent variable to the model helps significantly. As a process of hierarchical regression, most variance in the dependent can be explained by one or a set of new independent variables, over and above that explained by the previous set. In this process, the estimates of *b* coefficients and constants should be used to construct a prediction equation and generate predicted scores on a variable for further analysis.

In this book, the interaction effects of collectivism were tested upon the independent variables of cross-buying intention – perceived value, trust, image and satisfaction. The interaction effect, collectivism – occasionally recognized as a moderator effect – which changes the relation between the independent variables and dependent variables, was the moderating variable. In other words, by adding collectivism as the moderator in the pre-identified relationship between the four independent variables and the dependent variable (cross-buying intention), the model could find changes in the relationship in order to validate the hypotheses from the conceptual model. These changes were identified through observing changes in R^2.

The changes in relationship were explained in terms of the significance of an interaction effect, which is the same as for any other variable, except in the case of a set of dummy variables representing a single ordinal variable. When an ordinal variable has been entered as a set of dummy variables, the interaction of another variable with the ordinal variable will involve multiple interaction terms. In this case, the F-test of the significance of the interaction of the two variables was the significance of the change of R^2 of the equation.

The F-test is used to test the significance of R, which is the same as testing the significance of R^2, which is the same as testing the significance of the regression model as a whole. If probability $F < 0.05$, then the model is considered significantly better than would be expected by chance, and the null hypotheses of no linear relationship of y to the independents can be rejected. F is a function of R^2, the number of independents, and the number of cases.

The hierarchical regression analysis (Baron and Kenny 1986; Bennett 2000) of this book was conducted in two steps by using SPSS version 12.0. Based on the relationship identified between the four independent variables (perceived value, trust, image and satisfaction) to the dependent variable (the cross-buying intentions of bank customers in Korea and Taiwan), the influence of collectivism was tested by entering the moderating effect of collectivism and the interactions with these variables, respectively. To test for the statistical significance of the moderating effect, the coefficients of determination, R^2, were monitored with consideration of F-statistics to validate the fitness of the model.

In this book, the hypotheses from the conceptual framework were verified via multiple regression analysis to test four independent variables (perceived value, trust, image and satisfaction), which reciprocally interacted with each other in order to affect the dependent variable (cross-buying intention). Subsequently, hierarchical regression analysis (Baron and Kenny 1986; Bennett 2000) was conducted in two steps by using SPSS version 17.0 to identify the moderating effect of collectivism on the interactions with these variables. This procedure is demonstrated in Table 4.10.

In Table 4.10, H1a, H2a, H3a and H4a were tested through multiple regression analysis (Cohen 2003) in Model 1, which resulted in validity, with $R^2 = 0.255$ and F-value $= 59.502$. This confirmed that hypotheses H1a, H2a, H3a and H4a were all supported. In other words, all the independent variables had positive correlations with cross-buying intention, except perceived value. The standardized coefficients of satisfaction (SF) were the highest among the independent variables, followed up by image. This means that most people appeared to have a higher intention to cross-buy financial products if their trust, image and satisfaction were strong towards the bank. This was in line with the literature review, in which these variables had a positive effect on cross-buying intentions, as was shown by Verhoef (2001), Ngobo (2004) and Soureli (2008). However, people who tended to have a high level of intention to cross-buy placed less importance on perceived value. Surprisingly, perceived value actually had a negative influence on cross-buying intentions.

Table 4.10 Hierarchical regression analysis for Korea and Taiwan

Overall (Korea and Taiwan)

Model	Variables	Unstandardized coefficients		Standardized coefficients	T	R-square	F-value
		B	Std. error	Beta			
1	(Control)	0.000	0.033		0.001	0.255	59.502***
	Perceived value	−0.261	0.037	−0.240	−7.093***		
	Trust	0.238	0.064	0.177	3.730***		
	Image	0.254	0.065	0.181	3.881***		
	Satisfaction	0.284	0.054	0.216	5.293***		
2	(Control)	0.000	0.027		0.001	0.505	349.748***
	Perceived value	−0.127	0.031	−0.117	−4.122***		
	Trust	0.172	0.052	0.128	3.295**		
	Image	0.177	0.053	0.126	3.313**		
	Satisfaction	0.167	0.044	0.127	3.774***		
	Collectivism	0.480	0.026	0.533	18.702***		
3	(Control)	−0.048	0.027	−0.018	−1.781	0.549	16.848***
	Perceived value	−0.019	0.036	−0.539			
	Trust	0.158	0.052	0.117	3.054***		
	Image	0.142	0.054	0.101	2.605***		
	Satisfaction	0.142	0.043	0.108	3.273***		
	Collectivism	0.480	0.028	0.533	17.347***		
	Interaction PV	0.011	0.028	0.013	0.394		
	Interaction TR	0.253	0.062	0.199	4.104***		
	Interaction IM	0.071	0.060	0.057	1.181		
	Interaction SF	−0.064	0.030	−0.061	−2.171*		

Notes
* $P < 0.05$.
** $P < 0.01$.
*** $P < 0.001$.

This outcome, which contradicts the findings of previous studies (Ngobo 2004; Verhoef *et al.* 2001), requires further specific study.

Hierarchal regression analysis was then conducted in three steps to verify hypotheses H1b, H2b, H3b and H4b. In Model 2, the moderator collectivism was entered to test the increment of R^2. Then, in Model 3, each variable was tested through interaction with collectivism in order to confirm the moderation effect of collectivism. In Model 1, R^2 was 0.255, which indicated that the model fitted 25.5 per cent. In Model 2, it increased to a better fitness of 50.5 per cent. By Model 3, it increased to a fitness of 54.9 per cent. It is noticeable that the incremental proportion from Model 2 to Model 3 was not as significant as from Model 1 to Model 2. Nevertheless, because there was a steady growth in the fitness of the model, it was confirmed that collectivism had a moderating effect on the relationship between all the independent variables and the cross-buying intentions of customers. Interestingly, in Model 3, the standardized coefficients of trust (TR) was the higher than image, which shows different outcome after hierarchal regression process.

In regard to perceived value and image in Model 3, the significance probability (*p*-value) of these variables was not statistically acceptable, as the results of measurement were more than 0.05. In other words, even though the overall model confirmed the moderation effect of collectivism on all independent variables, the significance of the model for the variables of perceived value and image were not acceptable. Meanwhile, the *p*-values for trust and satisfaction were less than 0.05, which confirmed the significance of the model on these two variables. Therefore, H1b, H2b and H4b were supported, while H3b was not supported.

This outcome was in line with the statement from interviewee T#1, who stated that perceived value was not the only factor motivating customers to cross-buy. T#1 stated that perceived value will only be considered and appreciated after the relationship between the customers and bank has been established. If the perceived value is emphasized without building an adequate relationship, this may negatively affect a customer's intention to cross-buy another financial product or service. Interviewee K#1 also made a quasi-comment that, in order to achieve the best performance of CRM, the bank has to respect a period in which it builds a relationship with the customer before approaching them to cross-sell financial products. These statements coincide with the studies from Kumar and Reinartz (2006) and Gounaris *et al.* (2007).

Several interviewees commented that image branding and recognition of the bank might be very important to promote the cross-sell strategy to customers. However, they stated that this is more applicable for Western customers, who are known to have more individualistic decision-making processes. Interviewees K#1 and K#2 stated that image might be more important at the stage of acquiring potential customers to build the relationship; however, once the relationship becomes concrete, the customers will be led to cross-buy based on this relationship, not by the bank's emphasis on image making. In Taiwan, T#2 mentioned that, even with the ongoing efforts of many Taiwanese banks to improve their images, it is difficult to change the mindset of customers towards a bank's image once a customer has a strong relationship with that bank. These statements were empirically proven from the literature of Nguyen and LeBlance (2001) and Bravo *et al.* (2009).

All interviewees confirmed that trust was the essential factor in building a relationship between the bank and customers, and was the main factor in influencing customers to cross-buy. Interviewees T#2 and T#3 also stated that satisfaction was an overall measure to identify the possibility of cross-selling financial products. However, interviewees K#1 and K#2 did not agree with this statement. K#1 stated that satisfaction of a Korean customer cannot be judged after the first sale of the product, as it would take a reasonable period for customers to develop satisfaction after a cross-buy or after receiving additional favour from the bank. K#2 also stated that satisfaction is rather post recognition from customers that should not affect customers' intentions to cross-buy in Korea or other East Asian countries. Nevertheless, in the outcome of data analysis of the survey, it was confirmed that collectivism influences the relationship of trust and satisfaction in customers' cross-buying intentions.

In order to test hypotheses H5, the same methodological approach and procedure were executed for each subjective country. For Korea, the outcome of hierarchal regression is summarized in Table 4.11.

In Table 4.11, from Model 2 to Model 3, the increment of R^2 was noted to confirm the moderation effect of collectivism. However, only trust showed statistical significance, and the other variables did not reach the standard p-value. This was implicated during the interviews with the Korean interviewees, as all of them commonly emphasized the importance of trust for Korean customers to cross-buy financial products. However, the Taiwanese interviewees emphasized satisfaction through trust. Table 4.12 shows the results from Taiwan.

Table 4.12 shows that the results from Taiwan were different to those from Korea. Most of the interpretation was the same on the data analysis, except for the fact that satisfaction was added as a variable that was considered statistically significant in the model.

By comparing Table 4.11 and Table 4.12, then with Table 4.11, it is noticed that, even between two countries with similar levels of collectivism, the moderating effect can be demonstrated differently with the same independent variable. In Korea, trust was the only variable with statistical significance, while, in Taiwan, satisfaction was also statistically significant. This was partially in line with the findings of Craig and Douglas (2006) and Watchraversingkan *et al.* (2008), who stated that, even in the same region, cultural values can influence customers' behaviour. Therefore, H5 is only partially supported. The level of collectivism that influences customers' cross-buying intentions in banking services is different in Taiwan and Korea. Table 4.13 exhibits the summary and consolidation of the outcomes of each hypothesis.

Table 4.11 Hierarchical regression analysis for Korea

KOREA

Model	Variables	Unstandardized coefficients		Standardised coefficients	T	R-square	F-value
		B	Std. error	Beta			
1	(Control)	0.018	0.052		0.340	0.263	30.780***
	Perceived value	-0.321	0.053	-0.295	-6.090***		
	Trust	0.234	0.099	0.168	2.361*		
	Image	0.257	0.105	0.178	2.448*		
	Satisfaction	0.255	0.078	0.184	3.256**		
2	(Control)	0.071	0.039		1.804	0.574	251.227***
	Perceived value	-0.165	0.041	-0.151	-3.983***		
	Trust	0.216	0.075	0.156	2.870**		
	Image	0.057	0.081	0.040	0.705		
	Satisfaction	0.165	0.060	0.119	2.755**		
	Collectivism	0.541	0.034	0.604	15.850***		
3	(Control)	0.008	0.041		0.198	0.630	12.913***
	Perceived value	-0.004	0.051	-0.003	-0.073		
	Trust	0.224	0.076	0.162	2.965*		
	Image	0.027	0.080	0.018	0.333		
	Satisfaction	0.135	0.057	0.098	2.392*		
	Collectivism	0.584	0.040	0.652	14.487***		
	Interaction PV	0.009	0.036	0.011	0.240		
	Interaction TR	0.426	0.099	0.347	4.296***		
	Interaction IM	-0.088	0.093	-0.072	-0.937		
	Interaction SF	-0.026	0.037	-0.025	-0.713		

Notes
* $P < 0.05$.
** $P < 0.01$.
*** $P < 0.001$.

Table 4.12 Hierarchical regression analysis for Taiwan

TAIWAN

Model	Variables	Unstandardized coefficients		Standardized coefficients	T	R-square	F-value
		B	Std. error	Beta			
1	(Control)	-0.039	0.045		-0.867	0.255	29.542***
	Perceived value	-0.178	0.052	-0.165	-3.444**		
	Trust	0.260	0.087	0.191	2.984**		
	Image	0.213	0.084	0.157	2.535*		
	Satisfaction	0.338	0.075	0.265	4.527***		
2	(Control)	-0.071	0.039		-1.820	0.441	114.312***
	Perceived value	-0.080	0.046	-0.075	-1.754		
	Trust	0.209	0.076	0.153	2.756**		
	Image	0.210	0.073	0.155	2.881**		
	Satisfaction	0.212	0.066	0.166	3.216**		
	Collectivism	0.414	0.039	0.452	10.692***		
3	(Control)	-0.082	0.039		-2.091	0.487	7.611***
	Perceived value	0.063	0.056	0.059	1.124		
	Trust	0.184	0.075	0.135	2.461*		
	Image	0.105	0.082	0.078	1.281		
	Satisfaction	0.215	0.068	0.169	3.165**		
	Collectivism	0.385	0.041	0.420	9.397***		
	Interaction PV	-0.088	0.050	-0.095	-1.766		
	Interaction TR	0.187	0.087	0.141	2.150*		
	Interaction IM	0.143	0.087	0.109	1.638		
	Interaction SF	-0.193	0.050	-0.177	-3.845***		

Notes
* $P < 0.05$.
** $P < 0.01$.
*** $P < 0.001$.

Table 4.13 Summary of results on hypotheses

H1a.	Customers' perceived value of their banks influences their cross-buying intentions in their banking service.	*Supported*
H1b.	Collectivism of the customers will not moderate the influence of their perceived value of their banks on their cross-buying intentions in their banking service.	*Supported*
H2a.	Customers' trust towards their banks influences their cross-buying intentions in their banking service.	*Supported*
H2b.	Collectivism of customers moderates the influence of their trust towards their banks on their cross-buying intentions in their banking service.	*Supported*
H3a.	Customers' image of their banks influences their cross-buying intentions in their banking service.	*Supported*
H3b.	Collectivism of customers moderates the influence of the image of their banks on their cross-buying intentions in their banking service.	*Not Supported*
H4a.	Customers' satisfaction towards their banks influences their cross-buying intentions in their banking service.	*Supported*
H4b.	Collectivism of customers moderates the influence of their satisfaction towards their banks on their cross-buying intentions in the banking services.	*Supported*
H5.	The moderating effect of collectivism on customers' cross-buying intentions in their banking services will be the same in Korea and Taiwan.	*Partially Supported*

4.5 Summary

As the research design of this book is based on the triangulation approach, the two sets of data collection methodologies were applied for the purpose of comprehensive data analysis. Face-to-face interviews were conducted for qualitative data collection, and questionnaire surveys were executed for quantitative data collection. These two methodologies supported each other because the interviews targeted field managers who were professionally engaged in the related local financial services area, while the questionnaire surveys were completed by the end customers who were the actual subjects to cross-buy financial products from the banks. By implementing these two data collection methodologies, the data not only provided richer details to the findings of empirical testing of the conceptual model (Denzin and Lincoln 2005), but also offered multiple dimensions to the conclusions (Creswell 2009).

As the study of this book took place in Korea and Taiwan, there were some practical concerns in terms of local execution, for which the study followed the guidelines given by Canana *et al.* (2001). First, response equivalence was ensured by applying stratified random sampling, which followed the stratum of the officially announced population statistics for the targeted areas – Seoul and Gyonggi provinces of Korea, and Taipei and Taipei County of Taiwan. Second, the timing of data collection, which was adhered to by the scheduling of the research, was well respected. The total data collection processes, including both the interviews and questionnaire surveys, were completed within a one to two month period. Lastly, the status of the individual collecting the data, which is often considered one of the most difficult tasks to overcome for foreign researchers, did not cause any issues. This was because the researcher was Korean and was acquainted with the Taiwanese financial services sector, and the questionnaire surveys were collected through trained local interlocutors for each country.

For the face-to-face interviews, there were six interviewees – three from Taiwan and three from Korea. The interviewees were selected based on predetermined criteria that consisted of practical working experience of more than seven years in the related fields. Each interview progressed for an average of one hour, and was conducted in Korean and English. Prior to beginning each interview, the required ethics confirmation process of the Human Research Ethics Committee of the University of South Australia was completed. The interviews were recorded in their entirety. For each country, there were two interviewees from bancassurance insurance companies or joint-venture insurance companies with the bank, and one interviewee from a bank that actively engaged in cross-selling financial products over the bank counter.

The sampling of the quantitative data collection followed the method of the probability sampling approach, particularly based on stratified random sampling. Seven hundred sets of data were collected from Taiwan and Korea. The Korea Statistics and Information Research supported the Korean survey, and the Department of Risk Management and Insurance in Shih Chien University conducted the local survey in Taiwan. The age bands of the sample data of the twenties and thirties were slightly less than the actual Taiwanese population. In Taiwan, the age bands of the forties and sixties were moderately higher than the population. However, the overall differences in proportions of these two sets of data were negligible, and were confirmed to fit into an adoptable data for the analysis.

The analysis of the interview data was conducted in a narrative manner. All interviewees commented that trust was the most important factor for driving customers in Korea and Taiwan to cross-buy financial products. This confirmed the findings from the studies of Liu and Wu (2009, 2007). Second to trust, the interviewees considered satisfaction to be the most influential factor. Four interviewees out of six agreed that, when customers are satisfied, they are more likely to cross-buy financial products from the banks. They similarly stated that satisfaction was a key factor to influence customers' intentions to cross-buy. However, they stated that satisfaction has a broad meaning, which means it is not easy to operationalize the concept, so customers will not recognize that their behavioural intentions of cross-buying are actually caused by satisfaction. This was in line with the points raised by Soureli (2008).

The quantitative data were gathered through the questionnaire survey. The CFA and EFA were both conducted on these data. In the EFA, KMO of sampling adequacy and Bartlett's test of sphericity showed a 'meritorious' level, as the KMO factor indicated 0.876. In the CFA, GFI, AGFI, RMR, RMSEA, NFI,

IFI, CFI, NNFI, PNFI and PCFI were all shown to be above the standard fitness level. In addition to the CFA analysis, to confirm the convergence and reliability of the model, the AVE was calculated. Respecting the standard given by Fornell and Larker (1981), all construct reliability were above 0.7, with all the AVE being above 0.50. The AVE was also used to measure the discriminant validity. In the analysis of the data in this book, all the squared correlations between the two variables were less than either individual AVE, which supported the model.

For testing the hypotheses of the book, hierarchical regression (Baron and Kenny 1986; Bennett 2000) was performed using SPSS 12.0. Four key factors to customers' cross-buying intentions (perceived value, trust, image and satisfaction) were all input as independent variables, with their relationship to cross-buying intention the dependent variable. With these relationships, collectivism was added as a moderating variable through the stepwise multiple regression process to observe the changes in the coefficient of the multiple determination, R^2.

As a result, all the independent variables had a positive influence on customers' cross-buying intentions in the banking service, except for perceived value. This result was contradictory to the qualitative data analysis results based on the interviews with interviewees T#2, T#3 and K#2. Collectivism was shown to influence the relationship between cross-buying intention and trust and satisfaction. However, as expected, the relationship between cross-buying intention and perceived value was not influenced by collectivism. The relationship between cross-buying intention and image was also not influenced by collectivism, which rejected the theoretical hypotheses, but confirmed the qualitative data analysis results from K#1, K#2, K#3, T#1 and T#2.

In the comparison of the data analysis results of Korea and Taiwan, it was noted that the level of collectivism that influenced customers' cross-buying intentions in the banking service was different in the Korea and Taiwan. This confirmed the findings from the studies of Craig and Douglas (2006), which stated that, even within countries with similar cultural values, there can be different outcomes in people's reactions. This also explains the fact that there were different answers to some of the interview questions from the interviewees in Taiwan and Korea. Therefore, from the consolidated data analysis of the quantitative and the qualitative approaches, H1a, H2a, H2b, H3a, H4b, and H4b were supported, but H1b, H3b, and H5 were not fully supported.

Notes

1 For populations of over 40,000, the sample size remains relatively constant, at slightly more than 380 cases.
2 www.kostat.go.kr.
3 www.kostat.go.kr.
4 www.moi.gov.tw/stat.
5 High net worth customers are a segment with a net worth of financial assets in excess of US$1 million. They are typically targeted by the private banking business.

5 Discussion and future studies

5.1 Introduction

This chapter focuses on the discussion of the outcomes from the quantitative analysis of 700 samples and qualitative analysis of interviews with practitioners in Korea and Taiwan. This discussion aims to outline this book's contribution to academics and practitioners. This book introduces new areas of research on customers' intentions to cross-buy financial products by taking an empirical approach from a cultural value perspective. This chapter aims to provide more insights into the practitioners, as the findings from this book may apply directly to actual practices in the finance services.

This chapter emphasizes that the application of the findings from this book should be viewed as more valuable to financial service companies that are operating or wish to operate internationally. This is because these companies have to understand the local customers' behaviour from various perspectives, including the cultural value perspective (Cunningham *et al.* 2006; Lovelock and Wirtz 2007; Ueltschy *et al.* 2009). This chapter also addresses the importance of the East Asian financial market by demonstrating how this service sector, particularly in the banking industry, has evolved since the Asian financial crisis of 1997. This chapter discusses the emergence of foreign companies, and the efforts of local banks to diversify the sources of their profits (Adams 2008; Mohanty *et al.* 2010), which has led East Asian countries to become the most influential players in the global financial market (Economist 2009; Peng *et al.* 2010).

Amid the rapid growth of financial services in East Asian countries, one of the most significant changes has been to allow customers to cross-buy financial products in bank branches, which has increased the importance of CRM in local banks (Foss and Stone 2002; Peppard 2000), and improved the diversification in banks' revenue generation (Adams 2008; Mohanty *et al.* 2010). This chapter provides business cases from globally reputable financial institutions, such as HSBC, Citibank, BNP Paribas and the AXA Group. It discusses how these groups have expanded their global presences in the last two decades, and examines their efforts to promote customers' cross-buying activities in the banking industry in East Asia.

Therefore, with these crucial considerations, this chapter reviews the relationships between the cross-buying intentions of customers and each determinant that was tested in Chapter 3. This chapter compares the outcomes of these relationships with the findings from the literature reviews presented in Chapter 2. As the main interest of this book, this chapter discusses the influence of collectivism on the relationships between the key determinants and cross-buying intentions. This chapter explores the contradictory outcomes, such as the relationship of perceived value and image to cross-buying intention, and the confirmative outcomes related to trust and satisfaction. The chapter also explains the different outcomes found in Korea and Taiwan by using references from the study of Craig and Douglas (2006).

Finally, this chapter provides three major managerial implications that offer a strategic direction with practical tactics that can be piloted in the cross-buying of financial services in Korea and Taiwan. These managerial implications mainly concentrate on the views of customers in order to avoid the critical issues raised in Chapter 1, which concerned the lack of objectivity in the studies related to customers' cross-buying intentions in the financial services. The most significant contribution of these managerial implications is that all future directions must be based on an understanding of Korean and Taiwanese customers' cultural values, such as their collectivistic cultural backgrounds.

As with other studies, this book leaves room for future studies to enhance this topic with further considerations. This chapter examines this study's three main limitations: its limitation in choosing countries, its restriction of using a single cultural value, and its concentration on only one service sector with a contractual setting – the banking industry. These limitations could be expanded in future studies to explore further aspects of the field of international marketing on customers' behaviour.

The value of this book lies in the fact that it may assist both academics and practitioners who wish to understand the cross-buying intentions of banking customers in Korea and Taiwan. This book answers its research questions by offering empirical evidence on how collectivism has driven customers' cross-buying intentions in Korea and Taiwan in the banking industry. To this end, this chapter concludes with the confidence that this book may sufficiently perform the role of being a cornerstone for related studies in the future.

5.2 Results

The influence of culture on customers' behaviour and perceptions towards various services has been a constantly challenging topic for both academics and practitioners. This topic has received increasing attention as more firms have begun to operate internationally, providing marketing services to local customers with different cultural backgrounds (Ueltschy *et al.* 2007; Wirtz and Lovelock 2007). Understanding customers' perceptions of services and their future needs has become an imperative element in the marketing area, particularly for firms to effectively compete in a globalized and multicultural industry (Cunningham *et al.* 2005; Javalgi and White 2002; Ueltschy *et al.* 2009). This is particularly the case in the context of East Asia. Ueltschy *et al.* (2009) stated that it is crucial to consider the culture of East Asia because each national culture may manifest in numerous facets of marketing and consumer behaviours.

The cross-selling of financial products in the East Asian banking industry has received increased attention throughout the past decade. Laeven (2005) stated that the banking system in East Asian countries became remarkably different following the East Asian financial crisis in 1997. This was because local banks became keen to improve their stability and performance through their engagement in various activities that may boost sales by economies of scope. Ghosh (2006) and Corbett (2007) stated that the liberalization and deregulation of financial services in Asia have offered local banks the opportunity to invest heavily in the activity of cross-selling financial products. Several market studies have shown that these changes in the financial services industry in East Asia have strongly affected their regional economies, placing East Asia as the main player in the global financial market (ADB 2009; Economist 2009; Prasad 2009; Peng *et al.* 2010). Subsequently, understanding bank customers' cross-buying intentions has become a focal point of interest. If there is insufficient motivation or intention from customers to cross-buy, then the banks' efforts to cross-sell may be futile (Ngobo 2004), or may even backfire (Güneş *et al.* 2010).

The major contribution of this book results from linking these two crucial topics in the contemporary financial marketing arena. This book offers a theoretical framework to recognize the interaction between customers' cross-buying intentions and their cross-cultural values, such as collectivism. Furthermore, this book examined this topic in the context of the East Asian countries of Korea and Taiwan. The trend of cross-buying activities of financial products in Korea and Taiwan began relatively late compared to European countries (Chen *et al.* 2009; Teunissen 2008). However, these two countries recorded tremendous growth in the past decade (Chen *et al.* 2009; Ghosh 2006; Swiss Re 2007), expressing great potential for their future roles in the global economy and financial market (Leung 2006; Peng *et al.* 2010). Therefore, the empirical findings from this book not only offer a thorough understanding of customers' cross-buying intentions in Korea and Taiwan, but also provide insights of how these activities function in the collectivistic culture.

Perceived value and cross-buying intentions of collectivistic bank customers

Perceived value was initially identified as one of the key factors that drive a bank's customers to cross-buy financial products (Ngobo 2004; Soureli 2008; Verhoef 2001). Verhoef (2001) stated that perceived value, such as payment equity of financial products, may induce customers to cross-buy financial products from the bank. Verhoef (2001) stated that perceived value plays a strong role in the length and depth of the relationship between the customer and the bank, which eventually leads the customer to cross-buy financial products.

Ngobo (2004) stated that perceived value, such as the convenience of cross-buying, has a positive effect on customers' cross-buying intentions. However, Soureli (2008) argued that customers will not have the intention to cross-buy solely because the bank offers the most competitive terms, unless there is a combined interrelationship with this and other factors. In other words, the effect of perceived value on a bank customer's cross-buying intention could be changed by the influence of other factors. This argument is similar to the findings from previous studies in the East Asian context. Liu and Wu (2007, 2010) found that perceived value, such as the location convenience, will not influence the cross-buying intentions of Taiwanese banking customers. However, location convenience will have a higher effect on cross-buying when it is mediated by satisfaction and trust. However, all of these previous studies were conducted in a single country, and the influence of cultural factors was not applied in their findings.

Therefore, the outcomes of this book, in relation to perceived value, offer significant insights to previous studies, as this study was undertaken in Korea and Taiwan, and it considers the effect of the cultural value of collectivism. Moreover, the findings in this book showed surprising results that were, in some ways, contradictory to previous studies undertaken in European countries. First, the perceived value of the bank did not have a positive influence on the cross-buying intentions of Taiwanese and Korean bank customers. This finding directly contradicts the outcomes of European studies, such as those of Verhoef (2001), Ngobo (2004) and Soureli (2008). However, this finding is somewhat in line with previous studies undertaken in East Asian countries. Liu and Wu (2007, 2010) stated that perceived value, alone, cannot influence customers' cross-buying in Taiwan. It can only do so via the mediating effects of other factors. However, in all these studies, whether in the European or East Asian context, perceived value had a positive influence over customers' cross-buying intentions in the banking industry.

In this book, perceived value influenced customers' cross-buying intentions. This supported the hypothesis H1a, but had a negative influence, rather than a positive influence, as was reported in other related studies. This leads to a discussion on the influences of the cultural value, collectivism, in the relationship between perceived value and the cross-buying intentions of customers. In building this hypothesis, it was assumed that customers from a collectivistic culture place less importance on the value of services in their purchase intentions for retail services (Jin and Sternquist 2003; Sternquist *et al.* 2004). This was based on the findings of Furrer and Liu (2000, 2001), who stated that collectivistic banking customers tend to tolerate poor service, as opposed to their counterpart customers from individualistic cultures.

However, surprisingly, through the testing of the moderate effects of collectivism, it was noticed that the level of collectivism does not have any influence on the relationship between perceived value and the customers' intentions to cross-buy financial products at their banks. In other words, regardless of the level of collectivism, Taiwanese and Korean customers were not motivated to cross-buy because of their perceived value of the bank. This suggests that caution should be taken when defining perceived value in East Asian countries.

In the survey questionnaire of perceived value in Table 3.1, Q3 caused disagreement during the survey and interviews. Q3 stated: 'My main bank branch is easy to find and access compared to other banks'. However, this survey question was believed to be less valid for perceived value because the survey was conducted in the metropolitan area of Korea and Taiwan, where most bank branches are heavily clustered. In other words, the customer may not consider geographic convenience as perceived value. The validity of this question was also queried in relation to the emergence of internet banking and ATMs – conveniences that further detract from the importance of a bank's location (Devlin 2001; Howcroft *et al.* 2003). This aligned with the statement from Liu and Wu (2009) that bank customers do not view locational convenience as their priority for cross-buying financial products in Taiwan.

This survey question also raised a debate from two interviewees in Korea and Taiwan. Interviewee K#1 stated that the location convenience of Korean banks was not directly related to a bank's perceived value. This was in line with previous studies that stated that most bank branches in Korea are unintentionally aggregated, as a result of bank consolidation and continuous mergers and acquisitions that began after the East Asian financial crisis in 1997 (Choe and Lee 2003; Kim *et al.* 2008). Even in Taiwan, where bank consolidation and mergers and acquisitions are not yet as active, interviewee T#3 mentioned that there are many bank branches geographically close to each other, so it is difficult for a bank to benefit from locational convenience in Taiwan. At the end of 2010, there were 40 retail banks registered in Taiwan (Financial Supervisory Commission ROC.[1] Therefore, it is noted that, in terms of adaptation for the independent variable and to use this in a study model, it is necessary to consider the local specific environments or constraints, particularly if the context is related to the East Asian market (Fang 2010; Meyer 2006; Peng *et al.* 2010).

However, as the previous chapter on data analysis indicated, if the standardized loading of a construct exceeds 0.5, and all constructs estimate over 0.8, it is considered valid for the measurement. Therefore, all the measurements of perceived value were used in the test of the conceptual model of this book.

Trust and cross-buying intentions of collectivistic bank customers

From the literature review, trust was shown to have a different outcome when influencing customers' cross-buying intentions in the banking services. Verhoef (2002) and Ngobo (2004) both stated that trust was not the major driver of customers' cross-buying intentions. From studying sample customers of financial services in the Netherlands, Verhoef (2002) found that there was no positive relationship between trust and the number of services purchased. Ngobo (2004) stated that trust was actually negatively associated with the cross-buying intentions of customers in the French banking services. However, the study of Liu (2007), which is one of the few studies that have been conducted in the East Asian context, indicated that trust plays an influential role in cross-buying. In fact, Liu (2007) concluded that the influence of trust is extremely strong, and that it can totally replace the direct effects of a bank's reputation and expertise in cross-buying in Taiwan. This demonstrates that, even the same construct – in this case, trust – can have different outcomes on cross-buying intentions in different countries.

It was no surprise that trust was confirmed to be highly influenced by collectivism when related to customers' cross-buying intentions. Even when trust was strongly related to a customers' loyalty (Lewis and Soureli 2006) and reduced the level of uncertainty possessed by banking customers (Lymberopoulos *et al.* 2004), in the studies of cross-buying intentions, there were mixed views on its influence. The findings of this book confirm that customers with a higher level of collectivism will be more influenced by trust in terms of their intentions to cross-buy banking services. Verhoef (2005, 2002) and Ngobo (2004) found that trust played a minor role in customers' cross-buying behaviour; however, Soureli (2008) and Liu and Wu (2007, 2009) found that trust played an important role in customers' cross-buying of financial products. The studies of Verhoef (2005, 2002) and Ngobo (2004) took place in the Netherlands and France, respectively, which are considered highly individualistic countries in terms of Hofstede's (1984b, 2010) cross-cultural dimensions. The studies of Soureli (2008) and Liu and Wu (2007, 2009) were based in Greece and Taiwan, respectively, which are countries with high collectivistic cultures (Hofstede *et al.* 2010; Hofstede 2007; Soares *et al.* 2007).

Therefore, by confirming the outcomes of this book, it can be stated that the customers of countries with higher collectivism will be inclined to have a higher intention to cross-buy banking services when the influential variable of trust is properly addressed. Trust is built upon a stable relationship with the service provider (Morgan and Hunt 1994), which is represented as the measurement of the relationship (Coulter and Coulter 2003; Gounaris 2005). In other words, trust is highly associated with the level of the relationship between banks and customers who are cross-buying financial products from the bank. Therefore, building a firm relationship with customers is a prerequisite to achieving the sufficient level of trust that will eventually lead to the success of customers' cross-buying from banking services. This relationship is particularly important in East Asian countries with high collectivistic cultures. This is because East Asian countries that have Confucian values, such as Korea and Taiwan, emphasize interpersonal harmony, relational hierarchy and traditional conservatism (Xu 1998). People from these countries generally place importance on maintaining harmonious relationships with others (Hofstede *et al.* 2010; Wei-Ming 1996; Yoo *et al.* 2006; Zhang *et al.* 2005).

This was confirmed through the interviews with field managers who had experienced actual reactions from customers. Interviewee K#3 explained that customers in Korea purchase financial products based on the relationship built with individual salespeople throughout their common history, rather than because of a direct comparison of the perceived value or image of the bank. T#1 agreed with this statement and stated that this phenomenon is even more significant in terms of customers' cross-buying intentions. This is because customers are making the choice to expand their relationship with the bank through cross-buying their products and this will only occur after a certain period of relationship building with the bank. These statements are in line with the findings and suggestions of several studies in Western countries (Kamakura *et al.* 2003; Kumar *et al.* 2008; Reinartz *et al.* 2008; Salazar *et al.* 2007).

In this book, trust was revealed, through the survey and interviews, as being important in the context of financial services. The customer's relationship with the service provider is aimed at being a long-term relationship, with barriers in place to try to prevent this relationship ending, such as high switching costs and complexity relating to the switching process (Reinartz and Kumar 2000). In other words, unlike other service industries or retail industries, customers are inclined to have long-term, comprehensive service care, and place emphasis on their trust in the financial service provider. In addition to this mindset of customers of the financial services industry, bank customers in Korea and Taiwan, who have suffered from two major Asian financial crises in 1997[2] and 2008,[3] place great importance on the trustworthiness of a financial service provider. This is in line with the statements of T#2, who addressed the concerns of financial products from Taiwanese customers' perspective. Liu and Wu (2007) confirmed, in their study of the cross-buying intentions of Taiwanese banking customers, that trust is the main driver of cross-buying, not only in a mediating role, but also as the indirect influence factor to the cross-buying intentions of customers. The outcome of this book proves that this also applies to Korean banking customers. In other words, despite the different local financial markets, the reaction of collectivistic customers towards the influence of trust to cross-buying was the same, which was not the case in Western countries that had low levels of collectivism.

Image and cross-buying intentions of collectivistic bank customers

Image can be expressed in various terms. It is complicated because the image of a bank is reflected in many terms, from the bank's reputation in the marketplace to the friendliness of the bank staff, which also includes the social responsibilities of the bank (Bravo 2009). Ngobo (2004) stated that if there is a low awareness of a bank's image, the performance of cross-buying will not be as active among French banking customers. This aligned with the findings from the study of Soureli (2008), which indicated that the cross-buying intentions of Greek bank customers are directly influenced by the image of the bank.

As the measurements for image, Soureli (2008) used the high opinion of the bank and the good impression of the bank, as perceived by its customers. Although these measurements were similar to those used in the study of Ngobo (2004), there was a gap between Ngobo (2004) and Soureli's (2008) studies, which were conducted in two different countries. The suspected reason for this is the different levels of collectivism in these two countries. For example, France – where Ngobo (2004) tested the effect of image on the cross-buying intentions of banking customers – scored 71 in terms of Hofstede's individualism level

(1984, 2005). Meanwhile, Greece – where Soureli's (2008) study was conducted – scored 36, as it is one of the least individualistic countries in Europe. The influence of collectivism becomes more evident when comparing these findings with the outcomes of the study from Liu (2009). Liu (2009) similarly tested cross-buying intentions in the Taiwanese banking industry. Liu (2009) demonstrated that customers in Taiwan – which is considered one of the most collectivistic countries, with Hofstede's individualism score of 17 – are directly influenced by a bank's reputation and size. Furthermore, the results from this book show that a bank's reputation has equal effects on cross-buying in similar and dissimilar product categories. It is speculated that this finding arises from the fact that collectivistic customers tend to depend on the overall corporate brand image, rather than personal interaction (Da Silva and Alwi 2008).

However, in the research, surprisingly, image was not identified as a variable that is influenced by collectivism. It was confirmed as one of the variables that affect customers' intentions to cross-buy financial products, but it was noted that collectivism does not have a moderating effect on image in a relationship with customers' cross-buying intentions. One of the reasons for this outcome is that the constructs of the survey questionnaire were too wide for the surveyed people to digest the rationale behind the questions. For example, Q13 stated: 'My bank is highly committed and contributes to the society'. This linked to the corporate social responsibility of the financial institution. However, this outcome did not align with the fact that, in East Asia, the concept of corporate social responsibility is unrelated to the pre-existing levels of economic development, but is related to the extent to which local companies engage in international trade (Matten and Moon 2008; Williams and Aguilera 2008).

During the interviews in Korea and Taiwan, some interviewees, particularly those from the local financial institutions, commented that this survey question might not be fully relevant to determine the image of a bank. T#2 mentioned that a bank's image or first impression is not a key factor that can influence customers to cross-buy. Interviewees also stated that the concept of corporate social responsibility is still new to customers in Korea and Taiwan. While customers may recognize these efforts from the corporation, they may not perceive this as being a good image of these corporations, but take it for granted as something that large corporation should do for the local society. This aligns with findings from the related literature that stated that, in East Asia, customers consider the social responsibilities of corporations as a legitimate and necessary activity (Matten and Moon 2008; Hu and Wang 2009). Therefore, similar to the outcome of perceived value, a proper definition of image, with a greater focus on East Asian customers, is required.

Satisfaction and cross-buying intentions of collectivistic bank customers

Satisfaction is commonly referred to as a composition of other key drivers of customers' cross-buying intentions, with strong correlations to perceived value, trust and image of the financial service provider (Ngobo 2004; Soureli 2008). It is stated that satisfaction is one of the antecedents to affective commitment, and is one of the most important factors used to strengthen a customer's relationship with their financial service provider. However, in the context of cross-buying activities, satisfaction did not have any direct influence on customers' cross-buying intentions. Ngobo (2004) stated that satisfaction is not directly related to customers' repurchase intentions or their cross-buying intentions. Soureli (2008) found that satisfaction played only an intermediate role to other key factors relating to customers' cross-buying intentions, and that it did not significantly affect cross-buying activities directly. Nevertheless, collectivistic customers tend to be more influenced by satisfaction than their individualistic counterparts. This is justified by the fact that, when collectivistic customers are satisfied, they tend to express more positive word-of-mouth (Ladhari 2009; Ozdemir and Hewett 2010). This eventually leads to satisfaction having a greater effect on collectivistic customers' purchase behaviour than their individualistic counterparts.

In the research, it was found that satisfaction plays a positive role for Korean and Taiwanese customers in cross-buying financial products. This differs from the findings of literature in the European context, in which it was implied that the influence of satisfaction in cross-buying intentions in financial services is negligible (Ngobo 2004). However, in this book, in which the survey and data analysis were conducted in Korea and Taiwan, satisfaction was shown to be more influential in cross-buying intentions. This could also be explained by the complexity of defining satisfaction in the financial services. Hansen and Sand (2008) and Steenkamp and de Jong (2010) stated that there are numerous specification aspects of satisfaction, including satisfaction with a product, satisfaction with consumption, satisfaction with sales representatives, satisfaction with specific product attributes, or satisfaction with pre-purchase evaluations. Therefore, satisfaction might be viewed as a general concept applicable to different levels of analysis, depending on the study question being examined.

Interestingly, satisfaction was one of the variables that showed a different outcome between Korea and Taiwan. Although satisfaction showed a positive influence in relation to customers' cross-buying intentions in both countries, only Taiwan showed collectivism to have a moderating effect on satisfaction. In Korea, only trust showed statistical significance in terms of being moderated by collectivism. This confirmed the hypothesis that, even in countries with similar cultural values, there exists a different level of influence on customers' behavioural intention. This is partially in line with the study of Craig and Douglas (2006), who referred to the de-territorialization of culture.

The contribution of the findings from this book is not only limited to cross-cultural studies of cross-buying intention in Asia. These findings can also be expanded to meet the imperative needs of practitioners who seek to examine a link between what has been practiced in Europe and how this can be applicable to the East Asian context. Furthermore, these findings provide insights into the reasons for the strong growth of the East Asian financial market – a topic that may enable practitioners to determine the factors that influence customers to cross-buy financial products.

This book clearly indicates that managerial practices should focus on trust and satisfaction as key factors, if practitioners aim to achieve success in customers' cross-buying intentions in banking services in the environment of a collectivistic culture. This contradicts the practices of most multinational financial institutions, which largely spend their energy and resources on perceived value and image, such as through pricing and through advertising their brands and reputations. These factors may be crucial for these multinational financial institutions to initiate their entry into the local market. However, in terms of expanding their relationship through stimulating customers to cross-buy, they must employ a different marketing strategy, either to strengthen customers' trust or to revamp existing customers' satisfaction towards these institutions. This is in line with the studies from Verhoef *et al.* (2007), Salazar *et al.* (2007), Gunes *et al.* (2008) and Aksin *et al.* (2010). This book has built upon this statement by discovering that, even among the proven cross-selling strategies of financial products, a customer's cross-buying intention may differ depending on their cultural background.

5.3 Managerial implications

The increasing interconnection in the global marketplace fuelled by rapid growth in worldwide investment and trade, the emergence of global media and the internet, and the expansion of world travel (Steenkamp and de Jong 2010) has become a fundamental challenge faced by companies around the globe (Westjohn *et al.* 2011). This challenge has encouraged financial service companies to expand the scope of their marketing in terms of geographical diversification. This has moved companies' traditional multi-domestic approach to a global approach, enabling them to market their services on a global basis (Steenkamp and de Jong 2010).

An example of this is HSBC, which is based in the UK and is one of the world's largest retail banks. In 1991, HSBC had 50 branches; as of 2011, it had 87 branches worldwide (HSBC Group 2010). In 1991, Citibank, one of the representative banks in the US, had a presence in 90 countries. As of 2011, it had a presence in 160 countries (Citigroup 2010). BNP Paribas, which ranked as the largest bank in the world by assets as of 2010[4] had about 70 international offices in 1993.[5] That had expanded to 85 international offices by 2011. As these international financial institutions expand, it has been noted that they are required to undertake strategic positioning to diversify the range of financial services that they provide to the local market.

For example, in 1996, HSBC, under the holding company of HSBC Holding, acquired insurance companies and branded them HSBC Insurance. HSBC Insurance began operating in 21 countries where HSBC had active retail banking business (HSBC Group 2010) based on cross-selling insurance products to HSBC bank customers. Citibank, in 1998, announced a merger between Citicorp and Travellers Group, which enabled Travellers Group to cross-sell mutual funds and insurance products to Citibank retail customers. This offered the banking divisions an expanded client base of investors and insurance buyers.

This merger and acquisition was based on the repeal of the Glass–Steagall Act and the establishment of the Gramm–Leach–Bliley Act. The Gramm–Leach–Bliley Act legislatively allowed banking institutions to provide a broader range of services, including underwriting and other dealing activities (Citigroup 2010). This deregulation was considered as being not only a significant achievement for Citibank, but for all other financial services companies offering a mix of commercial banking, investment banking, insurance underwriting and brokerage in the US (Francis *et al.* 2010).

Unlike the US, in Europe, cross-selling activities have been frequently conducted since the 1980s. These diversified financial services originated in France and expanded to other European countries (Swiss Re 2007). Based on its success in these activities, BNP Paribas, a French-based bank, expanded its insurance subsidiary units to other countries, propagating the model of cross-selling insurance to bank customers – the model known as bancassurance (Artikis *et al.* 2008). Cardif, an insurance arm of BNP Paribas, began its international expansion in 1991, with three countries in Europe. This had expanded to 36 countries by 2011 (BNP Paribas Cardif 2010).

Notably, among this trend of financial institutions' global expansion and engagement in cross-selling activities, East Asian countries have been recognized as the most promising venues because of their high velocity of growth.[6] In the PricewaterhouseCoopers report (2011), it was stated that the focus of global economic activity is shifting rapidly eastwards, as the prospects for growth in financial services markets are stronger in East Asia than in any other region. The Asian Banker 500 (2011) stated that the financial sector in the East Asia region will continue to grow, as economic and political risks plague the West and Middle East respectively. In the 2011 Asian Financial Service Congress in Singapore, there was a clear consensus among the panel speakers that, with the strong economic performance in the region, East Asian countries must position themselves as major players in the global financial landscape. It was also stated that global financial institutions should invest more effort into adapting or adjusting their business models to suit the East Asian markets.

The emerging potential of this growth has been strengthened by the reformation of the local regulatory and market structure of financial services following the Asian financial crisis in 1997. It has been noted that many emerging Asian economies have participated in the deregulation and liberalization of their financial sectors, including opening up their banking systems to foreign competition. Examples of this progress include reformist deregulation and liberalization of the banks to offer financial products that resemble those traditionally offered by other financial institutions. The one major and immediate motivation for undertaking this action was that East Asian countries needed the funds that foreign investors could bring to help recapitalize the banking systems following the Asia crisis of 1997–1998 (Bird and Rajan 2001). The banking authorities in East Asian countries received pressure to internationalize, which eventually made them enhance and harmonise their regulatory and supervisory procedures to include international practice (Rajan and Zingales 2003).

Beyond these funding benefits, it appears that foreign competition will bring additional benefits that may not have occurred with domestic competition alone. For example, the entry of foreign financial institutions should change the banking industry to reduce the extent of non-commercial or connected lending that local banks are politically susceptible to conduct. Instead, the industry should focus on profit-oriented business lines, such as fee-based business or diversified sales channels and customer segments (Gopalan and Rajan 2009). Local banks that have ownership or management from foreign financial institutions have a lower non-performing loan ratio than domestic banks in East Asian countries. This supports these banks to have better financial stability (Gopalan and Rajan 2009; Mohanty *et al.* 2010). Furthermore, the foreign financial institutions that entered the local market also stimulated banks to diversify their business lines and sales strategies, such as cross-selling to their existing customer base (Corbett 2007; Kumar *et al.* 2011).

Referring to the examples of foreign banks previously mentioned, HSBC Insurance, which was established with the strategy of cross-selling its insurance products to the local banks of HSBC, operates in seven Asian countries out of its total 21 international operations (HSBC 2011). As of 2010, Citibank obtained approximately 40 per cent of its non-interest income from fee-based business and cross-selling financial products. Out of this, 25 per cent was generated in East Asia (Citicorp 2010). In 2011, BNP Paribas Cardif in Asia, an insurance arm of BNP Paribas Bank, conducted 26.5 per cent of its international operation outside France. This premium income of BNP Paribas Cardif solely depended upon cross-selling insurance products through bank distribution channels (BNP Paribas Cardif 2011). AXA Group, the largest insurance company by asset,[7] has operated its bancassurance strategy in the East Asian region since 1995. AXA Group deployed its first bancassurance joint venture with Krung Thai Bank in 1998. The bancassurance joint venture has since been extended to include local banks in six countries out of the ten countries in which AXA is operating in Asia (AXA 2010).

From these examples, it can be understood that major international financial institutions have taken strategic positions of cross-selling various financial products in Asia (Corbett 2007; Lin *et al.* 2011; Mohanty *et al.* 2010). There have subsequently been increasing demands to understand the behaviour of banking customers. An understanding of customers from different cultural backgrounds has been the key to the success of these banks' strategies in Asia. To this end, understanding customers' perceptions of services and future needs has become a crucial element in the marketing arena, particularly for firms that aim to effectively compete in a globalized and multicultural environment (Cunningham *et al.* 2005; Javalgi and White 2002; Ueltschy *et al.* 2009).

Identifying the drivers of customers' cross-buying intentions has also become important to the academics and practitioners in the marketing arena (Kumar *et al.* 2008; Liu and Wu 2007; Ngobo 2004; Reinartz *et al.* 2005, 2008; Soureli *et al.* 2008; Verhoef *et al.* 2007). Promoting an understanding of these drivers is even more important than promoting cross-selling, as the benefits of cross-selling can only be achieved if customers are willing to cross-buy (Kumar *et al.* 2008; Ngobo 2004). Without identifying a customer's intention to cross-buy, cross-selling can actually be a threat to a customer relationship and can weaken a firm's relationship with the customer. This is because frequent attempts to cross-sell can render a customer non-responsive or can even motivate them to switch to a competitor (Kamakura *et al.* 2003).

The importance of this book and its contribution to practitioners must be noted. The implications of this book's findings about the relationships between the driving factors for cross-buying intention-perceived value, trust, image and satisfaction – will increase the efficiency of establishing optimal marketing strategies for banks that aim to promote customers' cross-buying activities. This establishment of proper marketing strategy becomes more crucial when academic findings related to these factors differ from the outcomes in Western countries. For instance, trust and satisfaction have a relatively stronger relationship with cross-buying intention of customers in collectivistic culture. In future studies, academics would utilize this finding as the basis of exploring the interrelationships between these factors – trust and satisfaction – and other possible factors. Simultaneously, this may provide the practitioners in collectivistic culture to focus more on these factors to optimize their resources in their future marketing. Therefore, without understanding the differences of these outcomes and the reasons for these differences, practitioners and academics cannot expect to achieve the desired outcomes with their marketing strategies and business models. For multinational financial service providers that are expanding into East Asian countries, it should be considered that this may directly lead to the success or failure of their business in the local banking market.

Considering these factors, the following three managerial implications are suggested, based on the outcomes of this book. These three managerial implications will support practitioners who wish to implement successful cross-buying strategies for customers in collectivistic cultures.

A Establish trust based on satisfaction before asking customers to cross-buy

The common reason for the failure of multinational financial service providers' marketing strategies in the East Asian market is that they are unwilling to adapt to the specific characteristics of Asian customers. Trust is one of the most important values in Asian nations, and is highly appreciated in Confucian values (Zhang *et al.* 2005; Zhang *et al.* 2008). Zhang *et al.* (2008) stated that Asian cultures are collectivist, traditional service cultures with a focus on the long-term. Therefore, any good customer-provider relationship requires a high level of trust and commitment. Smith (2009) confirmed that customers from collectivistic cultures are more likely to value assurance, which is largely based on having confidence and trust among members of the group. Therefore, finding the optimal strategy to gain the highest level of trust from customers is the key to a successful strategy of cross-selling products in a bank.

In the local markets of East Asia, it is often noted that multinational financial service providers disregard the factor of trust, or do not place sufficient importance on this issue. In other words, they tend to think that trust is something that will eventually build in the relationship, and does not have to be a goal of the marketing strategy. This phenomenon can be understood in the sense that these multinational financial providers, which are mainly driven by the profitability and return on their investment in the local market, are not keen to invest in long-term relationships with their customers. However, local financial service providers and banks are known to seldom engage in improper business transactions with bodies of corporations because political reasons mean they will lose the trust of their local customers (Gopalan and Rajan 2009). However, from the outcomes of this book, it is confirmed that both banks – foreign banks and local banks – should aim for a high level of trust from customers in order to successfully lead them to cross-buy more financial products.

At the same time, different to related studies in the Western context, this book demonstrated that satisfaction plays an important role in collectivistic customers' cross-buying intentions. It has been conventionally proven and understood that the satisfaction of customers is frequently changeable and cannot be reliable as a driving factor in cross-buying. This was found in studies conducted in the Netherlands (Verhoef 2001) and France (Ngobo 2004). However, from the outcome of this book, it was found that satisfaction plays a significant role in customers' cross-buying intentions in collectivistic countries. At the same time, it was noted that customers in a collectivistic culture tend to share the common status of emotions, which are usually driven by common satisfaction with the bank. In other words, if a person related to a customer expresses a feeling of satisfaction towards a specific bank, the customer tends to evaluate the bank with a higher level of satisfaction. This is in line with the findings from the study of Furrer and Liu (2001), in which it was demonstrated that customers from collectivistic cultures are more strongly influenced by word-of-mouth than their counterpart customers from individualistic cultures. This can be linked to the characteristics of collectivistic customers, who tend to follow other people's consumption patterns (De Mooji and Hofstede 2010). Therefore, customers in East Asia, who have a high collectivistic culture, would believe that the status of satisfaction should be shared among the group. Therefore, the responsibility of satisfaction in the cross-buying intention of a customer in a collectivistic country is greater than in Western individualistic countries.

By combining these two outcomes in consideration of their practical implications, it is suggested that banks operating from a collectivistic culture should focus more on enhancing the trust of customers through continuous monitoring of these customers' satisfaction in order to motivate customers to cross-buy. In order to enhance the trust of customers, the bank could consider increasing communication with existing customers through various channels. It has been proven that timely contact with customers will increase the loyalty of customers towards the bank, which will eventually deepen the relationship between the customer and the bank, and lead to strong trust (Kassim and Abdullah 2010; Ndubisi 2007).

However, in collectivistic countries in East Asia, it is also important to choose the right manner of communication. In individualistic cultures, customers prefer low-context communication with verbal communication. However, in collectivistic cultures, people are conscious that their identity is based on the social system in which they belong. Therefore, collectivistic cultures prefer high-context communication, with an indirect style of communication (Zhang *et al.* 2008). In practice, the parties in individualistic cultures want to get to the point fast, whereas, in collectivistic cultures, it is necessary to first build a relationship and trust between the parties. De Mooij and Hofstede (2011), therefore, suggested that communication in collectivistic cultures should focus more on creating trust than direct persuasion.

One of the most frequently and effectively used communication tools for banks and financial institutions is to promote the financial stability and soundness of its institutions. The commonly used standard tool is to prove financial stability and soundness with a credit rating given by a credit evaluation agency, or the solvency ratio published by the local governmental authority. Instead of directly communicating the perceived value or quality of service of the bank, it is advisable to demonstrate the ranking of the bank's credit rating or to compare the bank's solvency ratio with its peers. This could be recognized as more important to customers in the East Asian financial services industry, where numerous financial institutions have closed down or merged with other financial institutions as a result of the financial crises (Choe and Lee 2003; Kim *et al.* 2008).

Furthermore, as cross-buying intention is a representative act of a customer's willingness to extend their relationship with the bank, it is obvious that the importance of a bank's financial stability should be addressed. A customer can only be attracted by competitive pricing or convenience of services after first building a relationship with the bank. However, in order to retain and extend this relationship, the bank needs to ensure trust exists. The bank and financial service provider should continuously seek to maintain a good status in the financial stability and solvency ratio. In fact, maintaining a good status of financial stability and using this in communication with customers will be a better strategy to gain strong trust from customers in East Asia than focusing on competitive pricing or convenience of services.

The other way to increase trust from customers is to use other customers' testimonials. Using testimonials shares similar concepts, such as customer evidence marketing, customer reference marketing and customer advocacy marketing (Jalkala and Salminen 2010). Testimonials are usually used by practitioners to refer to the phenomenon of leveraging existing customers and the value delivered to them via marketing activities. Collectivistic customers in East Asia are known to be highly influenced by others (Furrer *et al.* 2000, 2001). They are inclined to follow the consumption patterns of other members of their group (Hofstede 2010). Moreover, they positively react to word-of-mouth, such as customer testimonials (Martin and Lueg 2011).

These testimonials must be expressed on the basis of customers' satisfaction. Unlike their Western counterparts, East Asian customers – particularly those with a collectivistic cultural background – are less likely to express their satis-faction with a service (Furrer *et al.* 2001). However, when they do express their satisfaction, they are keen to praise the service even more than their counter-parts. Therefore, if someone in the group or a customer from the same service provider offers a testimonial for the service, the effect on the intention to cross-buy will be amplified. This is more apparent in the financial services industry, particularly in banks, because customers who are willing to cross-buy are cus-tomers who already have a relationship with the bank. For these customers, the customers offering testimonials will be considered members of the same group, who share common goals and objectives in the collectivistic culture (Hofstede 2010). Therefore, the effect of word-of-mouth on satisfaction will be higher than for customers with no previous relationship with the service provider.

With the advent of social media, building the trust and credibility of financial institutions through internet or mobile platform increasingly becomes a popular marketing tool. Moreover, most of these marketing tools are based on consumer-generated content that it takes control over the advertising-intended messages from the brand manager of financial institutions (Farshid *et al.*, 2011). Therefore, utilizing these marketing tools, such as social media or internet blogs, would offer financial services providers a new source of tool to build the trust and share the word-of-mouth effect on cross-buying activities.

B Refrain from only emphasizing perceived value to cross-buy

The results of this book demonstrate that perceived value is not influenced by col-lectivism. This means that the level of collectivism does not affect the relationship between perceived value and customers' intentions to cross-buy financial products from the bank. However, it was still important to investigate how perceived value was recognized by collectivistic customers, and what could be the key factor to use this value to promote the cross-buying intentions of collectivistic customers. One common failure of multinational financial service providers in the local East Asian market is that they blindly adopt the same marketing practices that have been suc-cessful in Western or other regional markets (Meyer 2006; Tsui 2004; White 2002). In the Western market, cross-buying activities were far more advanced and frequently practiced by bank customers and bankers.

Supported by this experience and a long history of business cases, several studies have previously examined the topic of customers' cross-buying inten-tions in financial services. Among these studies, it is commonly stated that per-ceived value is the main driver to the cross-buying intentions of customers, as the customers will continuously measure the value of the financial products and services offered by the same bank. Terms used to define perceived value in a Western context included location convenience, price equity, competitiveness, level of knowledge and expertise of the bank staff (Roig 2006; Verhoef 2001). From this book, it was identified that there were two critical issues that might have been created simply by applying this same strategy to collectivistic coun-tries in East Asia.

First, the notion of perceived value was not similarly recognized for collectivistic Asian customers as it was for Western customers. Location convenience was not considered important, as most bank branches are located near each other in Korea and Taiwan (Choe and Lee 2003; Kim *et al.* 2008). The information and expertise of bank staff was not usually evaluated objectively by collectivistic customers, particularly for Asian customers with a historical background of Confucian values, because these customers tend to be more generous towards poor service and the mistakes of bank staff than their counterparts in the Western market (Furrer and Liu 2001, 2002). This was also affected by another common characteristic of collectivistic customers and customers from a Confucian values background, which is to appreciate harmony and avoid direct confrontation within the group and society (Hofstede 2010; Zhang *et al.* 2005). At the same time, the evaluation of the same value can be different for those inside and outside the group. Even perceived value may be evaluated differently depending on whether the bank has a relationship with the customer or not.

In this book, cross-buying activities take place after the first banking activity between the customer and bank has been executed. Therefore, the cross-buying intention should be determined by whether the customers already have a relationship with the bank or not. If a relationship is already formed between the customer and the bank, in collectivistic customers in East Asia, they will be less sceptical and more generous to the bank in terms of evaluating the perceived value. Collectivistic customers in Asia may think price equity or competitiveness is the most important factor in their cross-buying intention. However, when it comes to evaluating their main bank, with which they already have a relationship, customers may think that this will be compromised by the fact that they and the bank belong to the same bonding group. Therefore, relying on the simple comparison of the perceived value of banks can actually lead banks to have an incorrect strategic cross-selling strategy.

The other issue in regard to perceived value is that, if perceived value is solely emphasized, it may deteriorate the other positive factors of cross-buying intentions in financial products. In a society with strong collectivism, the affinity and ownership of the group to the members is highly emphasized (Hofstede 2010; Oyserman 2008). It is important to continually remind members that they belong to the group so that they are recognized as different to those who are outside the group. In that sense, if the bank focuses too much on the convenience of services or their expertise, it might be seen that these benefits are also available to people outside the group, which might reduce the perceived bond that customers have with that bank.

This was noted in the study of Berhad and Tyler (2002), which found that there was a problem with loyalty programmes for collectivistic customers. Berhad and Tyler (2002) found that customer loyalty programmes may appeal to self-interest-motivated Western customers, but these incentives may be less effective in non-Western markets. They also stated that there may be a cultural bias against flaunting wealth for Asian customers. This does not mean that loyalty programmes will not work for Asian customers. However, to Asian customers, especially to highly collectivistic customers, the loyalty programme should be considered more to reinforce the existing relationships and reward those who already have shown higher level of loyalty than other customers. To this end, the perceived value of cross-buying financial products should be considered within the benefits of customers that have a previous relationship with the bank, not solely expressed as a comparative capability of the bank. This proposition is also in line with the findings of Barrey *et al.* (2008). In other words, if a bank is to cross-sell insurance products through its branches, there should be better loyalty programmes or benefits for existing banking customers, compared to other walk-in customers. In this way, the affinity of existing customers will be increased, thus motivating them to cross-buy financial products. This also results in the most efficient marketing strategy for banks.

Therefore, it is advisable to refrain from only addressing the perceived value, but to use perceived value as one of the tools to strengthen a bank's relationship with its customers. This is more crucial with collectivistic customers, as they might not seem as influenced by perceived value, but are still affected by other factors. For example, instead of providing a discount in pricing or offering more financial information to existing bank customers, the bank could consider increasing the price of the cross-selling products or charge additional fees to non-bank or new customers. In this way, the perceived value will induce customers to increase their trust and satisfaction towards a bank – two key factors in driving collectivistic customers to cross-buy financial products. Furthermore, this process will ultimately extend the length of the relationship, which will create additional opportunities for the management of this customer base.

C Understand the image of the bank from a collectivistic perspective

The importance of the corporate image of banks and financial institutions is highlighted in a highly competitive market environment. Nevertheless, in practice, it has been shown that financial institutions seldom place high priority on the brand image of themselves in the market, but mostly focus on financial results and performance (De Chernatony and Cottam 2006). Despite this practice, it has been confirmed that the strong brand image of a bank can increase its success in financial results and performance in the short and long term (Bravo *et al.* 2009).

It is true that the level of collectivism does not have any moderate effect on the relationship between image and customers' cross-buying intentions. This means that there is no difference between individualistic and collectivist customers in terms of their intention to cross-buy due to the image of the bank. However, as was previously discussed, it is important to cautiously interpret the influence of image on Asian banking customers. Furthermore, the image of the bank in a collectivistic culture might have to be viewed from a different perspective, and requires careful appraisal when it comes to the cross-buying intentions of customers. For example, customers in high collectivistic cultures relate more to conformity and group behaviour than customers from high individualistic cultures, who tend to seek variety and hedonistic experiences (Erdem *et al.* 2006). Customers from high collectivistic cultures will find a brand image that reinforces group membership and affiliation more attractive, while customers from more individualistic cultures will favour a brand image that promotes strengthening independence and offering individual gratification. It is also known that brand image represents an important symbolic meaning for group identity in collectivistic societies (De Mooij and Hofstede 2011). Therefore, the terms and measurements that have been used to express image in previous studies of customers' cross-buying intentions in the financial services industry should be viewed and linked to the level of customers' trust and loyalty towards the bank.

However, statements on the importance of image and its role in a collectivistic culture might be differently applied at the stage at which customers' cross-buy financial products from the bank. From the outcomes of this book, it is clear that image has less effect on the cross-buying intentions of customers from a collectivistic cultural background. For example, brand image can be an important factor when a customer is choosing a bank for their first interaction. As described in previous studies, customers from a collectivistic culture are inclined to seek a bank that has a brand image of strong affiliation and conformity. However, once a relationship is established, the driver of customers to cross-buy financial products does not only rely on image. It is crucial to maintain the brand image of the bank to emphasize affinity and membership among bank customers. However, in addition to this, it is necessary to emphasize the credibility and trust of the bank. Collectivistic customers rely more on the brand choice of the group as a whole (Tifferet and Herstein 2010). This means that the positive effect of this credibility will become an element in enhancing customers' sense of belonging to the group.

A bank's proper strategy to position its image to promote a customer to cross-buy financial products should be to emphasize its credibility and trustworthiness, based on its capability to perform these cross-selling activities, particularly for existing bank customers. For example, instead of positioning the bank as a place where customers can buy different types of financial products, it is better to promote the trustworthiness of the bank, and, based on this trustworthiness, inform the customer that they can also buy different types of financial products.

One of the common branding strategies used in Korea when bancassurance began in the early 2000s was to promote a bank's image as a total financial services provider. Banks and some securities companies were promoting themselves in this way. However, according to the outcomes of this book, this rhetoric did not induce customers to cross-buy. It would have been better if these banks had promoted images of being trustworthy and capable of introducing other financial products to customers. In Taiwan, this was proven by sales of insurance by the Taiwan Cooperative Bank, which dramatically increased after the bank established their own captive insurance company, which solely positioned itself as part of the bank, and not as a separate insurance company.[8] This was successful because the bank's collectivistic customers preferred to bond with the bank with which they already had a relationship, rather than with a new service company.

From the customer's perspective, it is still the bank from which they are cross-buying the financial products. Therefore, creating a new image of a financial institution, which may confuse existing bank customers, would not help improve customers' cross-buying intentions. Particularly in collectivistic cultures, relying on reputation and a good image will not increase customers' cross-buying intentions. The process of building a good image must be supported by establishing trust between the customer and the bank. Focusing too much on the quality of the services or the perceived value of the bank will deteriorate the trust of the customers towards the bank, which will eventually have a negative effect on customers' cross-buying intentions.

Retaining customers through stimulating their intentions to cross-buy financial products is directly relevant to guarantee the continuity and further development of the relationship between the customer and the bank (Liu *et al.* 2010; Peelen 2005; Soureli 2008). Therefore, it is important to understand the characteristics and preferences of cross-cultural customers, particularly in the contemporary globalized market (De Mooiji and Hofstede 2010). Based on the empirical and practical findings of this book, practitioners and academics should continuously and actively seek to understand the managerial implications of working in a cross-cultural market. This may require them to change their organizational climate and culture as a foundation for long-term activities.

5.4 Limitations and future studies

Although this book offers an important theoretical proposition related to customers' cross-buying intentions in the banking services by using empirical findings from two collectivistic countries, there remain a number of areas to be explored.

One of the potential limitations of this book is that the survey and interviews were conducted in Korea and Taiwan with similar levels of collectivism. This may support the outcomes of this book, as it samples the behaviour of customers in collectivistic cultures generally, regardless of their nationalities (Hofstede *et al.* 2010; Hult *et al.* 2008; Zhang *et al.* 2008). However, this may also lead to discontent. For instance, if the book could have added one or two more countries with different levels of collectivism, the comparison of data would have led to more distinctive conclusions. Even though the study is reconducted based on the same conceptual model on two other countries with different level of collectivism, the relationship between the determinants of cross-buying and customers' cross-buying intentions could have been similar. However, for example, if, alongside Korea and Taiwan, two new countries with high levels of individualism were included, the outcome of this book would have been clearer.

There are a few countries that would have been suitable for this purpose. The US, which has Hofstede's individualism score of 91, would have been appropriate, as would Australia, which has a score of 90. Korea and Taiwan show comparatively higher scores of individualism than Korea, with 18, and Taiwan, with 17. Additionally, in the US, although cross-buying activities in the banking industry have been officially permitted since the establishment of Gramm–Leach–Bliley Act in 1999, the sales performance by banks has not been as significant as expected. This is in direct comparison to the rapid success of the same activities in the East Asia region (Chen *et al.* 2009; Swiss Re 2007). Therefore, it would be academically worthwhile to explore the effect of high individualism on the cross-buying intentions of US customers. Australia is also considered one of the most individualistic countries. However, here, the cross-buying of financial products in bank branches has been soundly established and functioning since its initiation in the late 1990s.

The regulatory framework and local business practices in these countries would have to be taken into account for future studies, but it would be interesting to compare the US and Australia by using the same conceptual model used in Korea and Taiwan. Japan could also be a good candidate for future study. Japan is one of the countries in Asia that has a relatively high score of Hofstede's (2010) individualism, with a rating of 46. Japan, to a certain extent, shares similar cultural values with Korea and Taiwan (Zhang *et al.* 2005); however, its population is known to express its national values in customers' purchase behaviour (Knight and Kim 2007). Japan may also provide practical interest for practitioners, as Korea and Taiwan usually reference Japan when developing economic growth plans and financial systems (Liu and Hsu 2006).

The second limitation of this book is that the data analysis did not consider the different classifications of the sample, such as age band, gender or the length of the customer's relationship with the bank. These classifications were intentionally disregarded in this study because, based on the literature review and common practices in other cross-cultural studies, the outcome of this book was anticipated to be the same, despite the differences in the sample's classification. This is because cultural values should be the same for the same group within a culture (Hofstede *et al.* 2010; Javidan *et al.* 2006; Soares *et al.* 2007). However, during the process of the interviews, it was noted that these classifications may be useful for a long-term, comprehensive analysis of a nation. In the short term, from a practical managerial perspective, considering these classifications could also be interesting in order to observe differences in the data. Even individuals with the same cultural values may respond differently to the factors identified for cross-buying intentions. For example, the cross-buying intentions of the 20-year-old customers might be different to the customers who were aged over 60. The cross-buying intentions of a woman in her forties working in the home might be driven by different factors to a male in his thirties working in an office.

Moreover, as has been commonly noticed in other studies on CRM, the length of a relationship could be affected by collectivism. This was also indirectly implied by some of the studies identified in the literature review. Liu *et al.* (2001) and Ozdemir and Hewett (2010) stated that customers from highly collectivistic cultures are unlikely to switch service providers – they tend to stay longer with a single service provider because they value the relationship with them. This means that the length of a relationship might correlate with the level of collectivism, or vice versa. Therefore, in future studies, it would be beneficial to analyse the subclass of the sample to understand the difference between these classifications.

In future studies, one of the critical operational issues to consider would be the accuracy of the data. It is more reliable to gain these data, such as a customer's age, gender and length of relationship with the bank, directly from the customer base of the bank. This is because these data would be used for classification purposes, so it is important to pursue accuracy as much as possible. If access to banks' customer databases could be obtained, then future studies could also consider investigating the correlation between customers' cross-buying intentions and actual cross-buying behaviour. Customers' behaviour is determined by their intention to perform, which is a function of their attitude towards the behaviour (Ajzen and Fishbein 1980). However, a customer's intention is not always the same as their behaviour. This book was limited by its lack of use of banks' customer databases.

Lastly, the conceptual model formed in the book might be differently applied in a different setting of the service industry. Customers' purchase behaviour, including their cross-buying intentions, would be different in a non-contractual setting than in a contractual setting (Kumar *et al.* 2008; Ngobo 2004; Reinartz and Kumar 2000). For example, in a contractual setting, such as the financial services industry, when a contract is terminated, the frequency of cross-buying products is reduced. However, in a non-contractual setting, such as in other retail businesses, the effect of service termination would be limited, as there are no contractual liabilities.

In a non-contractual setting, the switching cost is often not significant for the customers that the natural sequence of cross-buying should be less apparent. Service industries in non-contractual settings will be more driven by short-term transactions, rather than long-term transactions that require trust and continuous customer satisfaction. Therefore, the findings of this book, such as the fact that trust plays an important role in the banking industry in a contractual setting, might not be applied in a non-contractual setting, such as in traditional retailing. Conversely, the perceived value, which did not play a significant role in the cross-buying intentions of customers in a contractual setting, might be more influential in a non-contractual setting.

However, it will be the same group of people with the same cultural background who will be serviced in both the contractual setting and non-contractual setting in Korea and Taiwan. It could be challenged by the fact that the respondents' level of collectivism is unlikely to be high collectivists. However, the respondents to the survey were selected from two relatively high collectivistic samples – Korea and Taiwan – which scored low individualism and high collectivism from Hofstede's cross-cultural dimensions (1984, 2010). Therefore, it would be interesting to apply a similar data collection method and the conceptual model in this book to non-contractual setting service providers, such as mega retailers in Korea and Taiwan. However, for this purpose, two major considerations would require attention for future studies. First, the definition of cross-buying would be different in retailers than in the bank. For example, in mega retailers, there are no core service products; instead, there is a range of varied products, from groceries to hardware. This would create difficulty in identifying the sequences of purchasing procedures, or the starting point of the relationship. Therefore, the definition of cross-buying from a retailer should be based on the total number of different product categories that the customer has purchased from the same retailer since their first transaction. This is in line with the definition of cross-buying examined by Reinartz and Kumar (2003).

Another important consideration is that, in terms of creating the measurements for the questionnaire, there would need to be a strong practical and theoretical validation of the process. For example, the meaning of trust to the customers of a bank would be differently interpreted by the customers of retailers. The classification question DB1, which asks customers to identify their main bank and bank account, could be replaced by a question about customers' main retailer and membership from this retailer.

One of the alternative approaches to customers' cross-buying intentions in a non-contractual setting is the cross validation method used by Ngobo (2004). To empirically test the drivers of cross-buying intentions, he approached two industries – banking and retail – with the same questionnaires. However, with the retailer (the non-contractual setting), Ngobo (2004) limited the definition of cross-buying intention to a customer's cross-buying of financial products from the retailer. Therefore, the questionnaire remained the same, as it was a target to identify customers' intentions to cross-buy financial products. However, the samples of the survey were from two different service settings. As a result, there were few differences between the outcomes from the retailer samples and the bank samples, except in perceived value and image. For example, the customers of the retailer were more driven by the perceived value and image of the service provider than the customers of the bank.

It is interesting to note that, even with cross-buying intention related to the same products, such as financial products, the outcomes can be different based on the setting of the service. This may motivate future studies to apply the cultural value, collectivism, to observe changes in the relationship between the two variables (perceived value and image) and cross-buying intentions. For non-contractual settings, it is more interesting to note this because, through the conceptual model of this book, perceived value and image were the two variables that responded differently to that observed in previous studies on cross-buying intention in Western countries. Therefore, conducting the same empirical testing used in this book on retailers in Korea and Taiwan would broaden the knowledge of the cultural influences on cross-buying and its relationship with the different environmental settings of the service industries.

Despite the topics available for future studies, this book has diligently enhanced the knowledge of customers' behavioural intentions of cross-buying banking services in East Asian countries, particularly from a cross-cultural perspective. Based on this book, academics could test more candidate countries with different levels of collectivism. Using this book's conceptual model, future studies could empirically test the influence of the sample's other demographic factors, such as age, gender and length of the customer's relationship with the bank. Furthermore, the conceptual model established in this book could be tested in different business environments, such as in the retailing or entertainment industries. The conceptual model built and tested in this book will hopefully become a cornerstone for academics and practitioners who wish to study the rapidly globalizing financial services in East Asia.

5.5 Summary

The cultural value, collectivism, influenced customers' intentions to cross-buy financial products. This book is the first empirical study to prove this statement, and the first to provide evidence on how collectivism has influenced the drivers of customers' cross-buying intentions in the banking services of Korea and Taiwan. Therefore, the discussion in this book not only contributes to CRM in the marketing arena, but also contributes to the knowledge of cross-cultural studies for East Asian countries.

This book began with a review of the relationships between the four key drivers of customers' cross-buying intentions, and the outcomes of testing the conceptual model on the relationship between customers' cross-buying intentions and the moderating effect of collectivism.

First, it was found that collectivism had no moderating effect on the relationship between perceived value and cross-buying intentions of banking customers. Interestingly, this directly contradicts the findings from studies on cross-buying intention in European countries (Ngobo 2004; Soureli *et al.* 2008; Verhoef *et al.* 2001). However, these results were expected, to a certain extent, because of previous studies based in Taiwan and Korea (Fan *et al.* 2011; Kim and Kim 2010; Liu and Wu 2007). This is because East Asian countries, such as Korea and Taiwan, have expressed that perceived value does not play a significant role in customers' intentions to cross-buy financial products in the banking industry. Therefore, the hypothesis was established under the assumption that, due to the high level of collectivism, customers in Korea and Taiwan would be influenced by perceived value in cross-buying.

However, from the findings of this book, it has been proven that collectivism does not influence the relationship between perceived value and customers' cross-buying intentions. This may be because the measurements used for perceived value in this study might not have been considered as the real value to customers in Taiwan and Korea. The findings of this study imply that, if there is too much emphasis on perceived value, this could reduce the motivation of customers to cross-buy financial products from the bank.

Second, this book found that trust is influenced by collectivism – the more collectivistic customers are, the more they tend to cross-buy financial products. This result was perceptible from the beginning, as the collectivistic customers were more dependent on their relationship with the service providers with which they had built trust throughout their relationship. However, in this book, it was confirmed that collectivistic customers appreciate the importance of trust, not only in their common buying behaviour, but also in their cross-buying of financial products from the bank. Based on the results of the interviews from Korea and Taiwan, trust was considered the most important factor in cross-buying. This was in line with the literature review (Fan *et al.* 2011; Kim and Kim 2010; Liu and Wu 2007).

Several participants of the interviews confirmed that trust was important for new customers to the bank, but could be more important for existing customers who wish to expand their relationship with the bank. These assertions are in line with the findings from the studies of Coulter and Coulter (2003) and Gounaris (2005).

Third, in relation to image, surprisingly, customers were not influenced by the level of collectivism in their intention to cross-buy financial products from the bank. This unexpected finding suggests that the defined measurements for image in the survey questionnaire might have been misinterpreted by the survey participants. As a result, the measurements of image for collectivistic customers should receive further consideration. This outcome was particularly surprising in Taiwan, where two participants in the interviews stated that image would play an important role in Taiwanese customers' cross-buying intentions. This has also previously been verified, as was demonstrated in the literature review (Fan *et al.* 2011; Kim and Kim 2010; Liu and Wu 2007).

However, this book demonstrated that image was not led by the influence of collectivism. In contrast, the Korean participants in the interviews stated that image would not be an influential factor in cross-buying. This was because, in Korea, there are only a few major banks that do not have a distinguishable brand image. However, in the questionnaire survey given to the customers, it was noted that image did influence them to cross-buy, but was not moderated by collectivism. Therefore, from this finding, it is confirmed that there could be other factors that interface with the relationship between image and customers' intentions to cross-buy financial products in Korea and Taiwan, excluding the level of collectivism.

Finally, satisfaction, which is known as a composition of other key variables, was influenced by the level of collectivism. This study confirmed that the more collectivistic customers are, the more they are inclined to cross-buy financial products when they are satisfied. This is significantly different from the findings of studies based in European countries (Fan *et al.* 2011; Kim and Kim 2010). However, it is also surprising to note from the interviews in Taiwan that no interview participants stated that satisfaction influenced Taiwanese customers to cross-buy financial products from the bank. Nevertheless, the outcome of the quantitative data, which were collected from the end customers, exhibited that Taiwanese customers are influenced by satisfaction, which is moderated by collectivism. Therefore, this book found that there may be some discrepancy between the findings from the quantitative data analysis and those of the qualitative data analysis, depending on the data sample. This also implies that the bankers, who are cross-selling, and the customers, who are cross-buying, might differently view the role of satisfaction, and that collectivism is an important factor for the cross-buying intentions of customers in Taiwan.

From these findings and discussions, three major managerial implications are proposed, based on this study. First, banks need to do more than emphasize perceived value to customers in order to induce them to cross-buy financial products. In addition, the terms that have been frequently used to express and measure perceived value in the context of Western countries should not be used in East Asian customer studies. For example, the perceived value of locational convenience and the expertise of bank staff might not be seen as perceived value by the collectivistic customers of Korea and Taiwan.

Furthermore, if perceived value is too extensively emphasized, then the other positive factors of cross-buying in collectivistic societies may deteriorate. Rather than focusing on perceived value, the affinity of the group should be emphasized and addressed. This is in line with the implications of the quantitative data analysis. However, even the findings of the qualitative data analysis suggest that it is important to promote trust as the perceived value of the bank, rather than focusing on materialist values. Materialist values might be important to new customers, but they are not important to existing customers, who the banks hope will cross-buy financial products.

Second, trust and satisfaction must be established before asking customers to cross-buy financial products. This also aligns with the statements of Ngobo (2004) and Salazar (2007), who both indicated that efforts to cross-sell to a customer who is not willing to cross-buy are useless. The results of this study confirmed that collectivistic customers intend to cross-buy more when they are satisfied and trust the bank. Banks should focus more on providing trust and satisfaction with their existing services in order to cross-sell more financial products to collectivistic customers. One of the ways to achieve this could be to increase communication and contact with existing customers, which would offer more bonding with the bank, and help customers recognize their relationship with the bank. At the same time, banks, as with other financial institutions, should continue to monitor and maintain good financial stability in order to increase the trust of customers towards the bank.

Finally, the outcomes of this study indicate that the level of collectivism does not influence the relationship between image and customers' intention to cross-buy financial products. However, image is still a driving factor in customers' cross-buying intentions. Therefore, this study suggests that banks should build an image based on trust and customers' satisfaction in order to accelerate the cross-selling strategy. For example, instead of branding the bank as the total financial services provider – a goal that focuses more on perceived value – it is recommended that banks maintain their image. This will help strengthen trust towards the bank, which will enable the cross-selling of different types of financial products based on the trust established between the customer and the bank. At the same time, instead of directly advertising the perceived value of what the bank can offer the customers, it would be better to indirectly communicate customers' testimonials or compliments relating to cross-buying financial products. This will be more effective to collectivistic customers as they are more inclined to listen and follow the associated group in terms of purchase behaviour.

Despite these discussions and managerial implications based on the findings of this study, there remains room for enhancement by future studies. One of the limitations of this book is that the study was only based on the collectivistic countries of Korea and Taiwan. It would be interesting to include other countries with high levels of individualism, such as the US and Australia. Based on Hofstede's (2010) model of individualism-collectivism, the US and Australia scored 91 and 90, respectively, demonstrating that they are highly individualistic nations. Korea and Taiwan scored 17 and 18, respectively, demonstrating that they are highly collectivistic nations.

This book's other limitation was that it tested the model without considering the sample's different classifications, such as age, gender and the customer's length of relationship with the bank. Examining these classifications in future studies would enable the study of whether there would be differences among the different classifications in samples from the same cultural background. Additionally, to ensure the accuracy of the data sample and analysis, it is suggested that future studies should use actual transaction data from the subjective bank, rather than surveying customers on their behavioural intentions.

Lastly, the conceptual model established and used in this book could be used to study other service industries in different environment settings. For example, mega retailers or telecommunication companies that are planning to cross-sell financial products to their customers could be examined using the findings from this book.

Notes

1 www.fscey.gov.tw.
2 The crisis began in Thailand in 1997, when the Thai government decided to float the Thai baht, cutting its links to the US dollar. The crisis spread out to Southeast Asia, and to Japan and Korea. The currencies in these regions slumped, which devalued stock markets and other asset prices, and caused an increase in private debt.
3 The crisis officially began when the Lehman Brothers filed for bankruptcy protection on 15 September 2008. This remains the largest bankruptcy claim in US history, with the company having over US$600 billion in assets. The Dow Jones closed down just over 500 points (−4.4 per cent) on that day, which caused global financial markets to suffer from the bad debt and depreciation of over-valued commercial properties.
4 www.bankersalmanac.com; Bankersalmanac.com is the leading source of intelligent reference data for compliance and risk assessment. It began in 1845 as The Bankers' Almanac − a hardcopy directory of banking information. It established partnerships with Wolfsberg Group, the British Bankers' Association, the Bankers' Association for Finance and Trade, SWIFT and the International Financial Services Association.
5 Based on the report of Banque Nationale de Paris (BNP). In 1999, BNP acquired Paribas, which subsequently became BNP Paribas.
6 The Asian Development Bank (www.adb.org) defines East Asian countries as China, including Hong Kong, Korea, Taiwan and Mongolia.
7 AM Best Insurance Ranking (www.ambest.com), January 2011.
8 Taiwan Cooperative Bank (合作金庫銀行) is one of the most prominent banks in Taiwan, having the most branches among all banks in Taiwan. This bank established a joint venture insurance company with the BNP Paribas group in 2009.

6 Conclusion

6.1 Research questions and contributions of the book

The financial services industry has recently undergone many dynamic changes, including consolidation and globalization, due to the convergence of services sectors (Claessens 2009; Claessens *et al.* 2010; Moshirian 2008). As a result of this convergence, which has led to the deregulation and liberalization of the financial services, many banks are now able to offer different types of financial products in order to the meet the various needs of their customers (Chen and Wang 2009; Claessens 2009; Moshirian 2008). This new ability to offer different types of products is commonly referred to as the cross-selling of financial products. This form of banking was conceived as a new trend in European countries in the early 1980s, and was eventually implemented by East Asian countries in the late 1990s (Chen and Wang 2009). However, the growth of these changes in East Asian countries has rapidly outpaced the past development of European countries (ADB 2009; Artikis *et al.* 2008; Prasad 2010). This remarkable success has been led by Korea and Taiwan (Artikis *et al.* 2008; Chen and Wang 2009; Swiss Re 2007).

Several international financial institutions – HSBC, BNP Paribas, Citibank and AXA Group – have invested heavily in expanding into East Asian countries, particularly focusing on the area of cross-selling financial products to their core business customers. This strategy was to maximize their profit and sustain their growth in the region. The PricewaterhouseCoopers report (2011) stated that global economic activity is rapidly shifting eastwards because the potential growth in the financial service markets of East Asian countries is becoming stronger than any other region in the world.

With this in consideration, Korea and Taiwan have shown a significant lead in the area of cross-selling financial products. Both, Korea and Taiwan have recorded a remarkable growth rate and expanding market share compared to the average figures of European countries (Korea Life Insurance Association 2010; Taiwan Life Insurance Association Monthly Report 2010; CEA European Insurance and Reinsurance Federation 2010). Korea and Taiwan resemble each other in various aspects, from their industrialization process to their political evolutions (Chia *et al.* 2007; Peng *et al.* 2010), and their governmental support to the local economy (Jacobs 2007; Lim 2009). Moreover, the Asian Development Bank (2009) indicated that Korea and Taiwan represent 49 per cent of the money supply in the East Asian market, which confirms the important role of Korea and Taiwan in this region and in the world.

It has also been recognized that Korea and Taiwan share similar cultural values due to their historical roots in Confucian values from China (Xu 1998; Zhang *et al.* 2005). Due to the influence of these Confucian values, one of the most common cultural values noticed in Korea and Taiwan is their high level of collectivism. This has been reflected in various cross-cultural dimensions that have been established from previous studies, such as Hofstede's cultural dimensions (1984, 2010), Inglehart's study (2006) and House's study (2004). From these cross-cultural studies, Korea and Taiwan have been generally designated as nations with stronger collectivism than their peers in Western countries.

Several studies have confirmed that customers from a collectivistic culture express different purchase behaviour and perceptions of service quality. For example, Furrer *et al.* (2000, 2001) indicated that customers within collectivistic cultures tend to have higher likelihood of praising service providers when they experience positive service quality than customers within individualistic cultures. Bagozzi and Lee (2002) found that people from collectivistic cultures are more strongly influenced by identification processes, such as value expressive influence, while people from more individualistic cultures are more influenced by internalization processes.

This finding is in line with the book of Mourali (2005), which found that customers from collectivistic cultures are more susceptible to value expressive social influences than customers from individualistic cultures. Moon and Chadee (2008) found that customers from collectivistic cultures emphasize price sensitivities less than customers from individualistic cultures in regard to their purchase intentions. Ozdemir and Hewett (2010) confirmed that collectivism generally increases the importance of the relationship quality, rather than service quality, in regard to behavioural intentions. Therefore, this book began with the assumption that collectivism may affect customers' intentions to cross-buy financial products in Korea and Taiwan.

The cross-cultural value of collectivism has never previously been factored into studies examining the rapid growth of the Asian financial services industry, particularly in the sector of cross-selling financial products. This is understandable to a certain extent, given that cross-selling activities started relatively later in Asia than in European countries (Artikis *et al.* 2008; Das and Ghosh 2006). Bancassurance – the representative case of cross-selling financial products in the banking industry – has only been allowed in Korea and Taiwan since the late 1990s and early 2000s, whereas most European countries have used bancassurance since the early 1970s and 1980s (Artikis *et al.* 2008; Chen *et al.* 2009; Swiss Re 2007). The rapid growth of this sector in Korea and Taiwan – countries that share similar levels of collectivism – led to an interest in exploring this topic in the hope of identifying the factors that have driven this success.

Therefore, the key research questions of the book related to investigating the drivers behind the economic growth of these countries in the East Asian region, and identifying how these drivers interact among themselves to accelerate growth. This book attempted to take a different view to studies in the past. First, it examined this growth from the customer's perspective, not the financial service provider's perspective. In other words, this book focused on the customers' buying behaviour, rather than the efforts and strategies of the financial service providers' selling activities. Second, this book considered how the cultural value of collectivism has influenced customers to behave differently to their counterparts in Europe. This book focused on the cross-buying intentions of customers, rather than the cross-selling activities of banks.

The first standpoint of this book – to view the topic from the customers' perspective – was supported by the studies of Verhoef *et al.* (2001), Ngobo (2004), Liu and Wu (2007), Soureli *et al.* (2008) and Fan *et al.* (2011). Through these studies, it was confirmed that if customers do not have the intention to cross-buy, the bank cannot cross-sell. Moreover, without understanding the factors that drive customers to cross-buy, the ongoing efforts of the bank to cross-sell will weaken the relationship between the customer and the bank, and may eventually cause customers to switch to another financial service provider (Gunes *et al.* 2010; Kamakura *et al.* 2003). The second standpoint of this book was to view customers' cross-buying intentions based on the cultural value perspective of collectivism. This offers a unique contribution to the existing studies on this topic, and offers guidance to practitioners who seek to achieve success in the financial markets of Korea and Taiwan.

While there have been several previous studies on customers' cross-buying intentions in the banking services – such as the studies of Verhoef *et al.* (2001), Ngobo (2004), Liu and Wu (2007), Soureli *et al.* (2008), Kim and Kim (2008) and Fan *et al.* (2011) – none of these examined how cultural values might affect their findings. Furthermore, there was a clear discrepancy between the findings from a European context and those from an Asian context. This is believed to be caused by differences in cultural values, such as collectivism. Prior to this study, there was a lack of literature that attempted to examine this issue and fill this literature gap.

6.2 Review of the literature and the research gap

Through considering the aims of its research questions, this book conducted its literature review in a twofold manner. It conducted a review of previous cross-cultural studies on collectivism, and a review of customers' cross-buying intentions in the financial services industry.

In the first part of the literature review, this book scrutinized the different definitions and methods of the operationalization of culture. This book followed the operationalization process of culture directed by Sojka and Tansuhaj (1995), which was revisited by Soares *et al.* (2007), in which culture was operationalized via three approaches: language and communication, material possessions and artefacts, and values and beliefs. Among these approaches, the operationalization of culture through value and belief has been the most accepted approach in previous cross-cultural studies of international marketing (Fischer and Schwartz 2011; Soares *et al.* 2007; Zhang *et al.* 2008). In this approach, the cultural value of the nation is segregated from the practices of the nation, as the values of the nation remain consistent, while the practices of the nation may change over time. In other words, the practices of the nation, such as its symbols, rituals and heroes, might change throughout the history of the nation, but the cultural values that underpin these practices remain the same (Fischer and Schwartz 2011; Hofstede *et al.* 2010; Soares *et al.* 2007).

For example, in Europe, even with the formation of the economic union and progress toward the standardization of political and social infrastructure, the cultural values and beliefs of individual nations are still strongly rooted in history and appear unchanged over time (De Mooij 2000; De Mooij and Hofstede 2002). These findings align with the research by Arnett (2002), which stated that the new cultural values being widely embraced by various societies do not necessarily mean that people will reject their old values to adopt new ones. In Asia, cultural values, which are mainly underpinned by the Confucian value that respects harmony, hierarchy and conservatism (Chung and Pysarchik 2000; Zhang *et al.* 2005; Wang 2008), still influence nations to strive for the benefits of the collective group, rather than the individual (Zhang *et al.* 2005; Ueltschy *et al.* 2009; Wu 2009). This is reflected in the behaviour of customers.

The confirmation of this consistency in cultural values has encouraged several studies to establish cultural dimensions in various forms. Among these include the studies of Inglehart (2006, 2000), Schwartz and Bardi (2001) and House *et al.* (2004). The cultural dimensions of Hofstede (Hofstede 1984a; Hofstede *et al.* 2010) are recognized as the most adequate and frequently used theories in cross-cultural studies (Nielsen *et al.* 2009; Soares *et al.* 2007; Taras *et al.* 2010b). However, as one of the most frequently used dimensions, Hofstede has also been criticized by several academics, including Trompenaars and Hampden-Turner (1995), McSweeny (2002), Fang (2003) and House (2004). This book scrutinized Hofstede's answers to these criticisms, particularly by comparing Hofstede's dimensions with the GLOBE project (House *et al.* 2004).

This book confirmed that the major weakness of the GLOBE project (House *et al.* 2004) stems from the fact that, in terms of the methodological approach in its questionnaire, GLOBE did not clearly separate values and practices for most of its measurements of cultural values – particularly for collectivism. GLOBE was also heavily influenced by Hofstede's model, as it was an extension of the five dimensions that Hofstede established in his previous study. These statements were also in line with the criticisms from the studies of Smith (2006) and Hofstede (2010).

In the cultural dimensions of Hofstede (Hofstede *et al.* 2010; Hofstede 1984a), collectivism was commonly stated as the most frequently used cultural value in the international marketing arena (Brewer and Venaik 2011; De Mooij and Hofstede 2011; Ozdemir and Hewett 2010; Vandello and Cohen 1999;

Zhang *et al.* 2005), particularly when comparing Asian and Western customers (Hofstede 2007; Oyserman and Lee 2008; Schimmack *et al.* 2005; Ueltschy *et al.* 2009). At the same time, collectivism is known to highly correlate to the Confucian value, which is the traditional value that is geographically widespread in the countries near China. The Confucian value has also strongly influenced the lifestyle values of many East Asian countries (Chan 2008; Ma 2010; Xu 1998; Zhang *et al.* 2005). Therefore, this book adopted collectivism as the cultural value to analyse the different behavioural intentions of East Asian customers' cross-buying of financial products.

In the second part of the literature review, this book examined the importance of CRM, which has become popular in the relationship marketing arena in recent decades (Chen and Popovich 2003; Peelen *et al.* 2006, 2009; Peppard 2000). Through the review of studies on the evolution of relationship marketing studies, it was noted that increasing the retention of customers and expanding the scope of products with which customers engage enhances the value of each customer, which leads to greater profitability of the service provider (Bolton *et al.* 2000; Peelen *et al.* 2006; Salazar *et al.* 2007). In order to achieve these two goals of increasing the retention of customers and expanding the scope of customers' purchased products, this study confirmed that a cross-selling strategy is optimally used in the practices of the contemporary marketing arena (Kamakura 2008; Kamakura *et al.* 2003; Li *et al.* 2011; Salazar *et al.* 2007). However, cross-selling can be pointless if the service provider does not understand what motivates their customers to cross-buy. In other words, the focal point of interest in relationship marketing should be shifted from the service provider's strategic perspective to the customer's perspective (Reinartz and Kumar 2003; Verhoef *et al.* 2010; Wind 2001). To this end, this book indicated that the cross-buying intentions of customers should be more intensively investigated before establishing tactics in cross-selling.

This book also addressed the fact that the cross-buying intentions of customers in the financial services industry should be viewed differently from those in other service industries. This is because the financial services industry is mainly based on a contractual setting, in which the natural sequence of a product purchase is more complex than in a non-contractual setting, such as the traditional retail business (Kumar *et al.* 2008; Ngobo 2004). Furthermore, in the financial services industry, customers' product buying intentions are based on risk, uncertainty, trust and personal relationships on a long-term basis (Maas and Graf 2008), whereas in a non-contractual setting, these factors appear to be less significant.

Therefore, this book explored the literature that investigated customers' cross-buying activities or their intentions to cross-buy financial products in the banking industry. This literature included the studies of Verhoef *et al.* (2001), Ngobo (2004), Liu and Wu (2007), Soureli *et al.* (2008), Kim and Kim (2008) and Fan *et al.* (2011). Through the review of this literature, four key drivers of cross-buying intentions were identified: perceived value, trust, image and satisfaction. However, among the handful of studies that were identified as having examined cross-buying intention in the banking industry, there were significant differences between countries in terms of the relationship between these four key drivers and customers' intentions to cross-buy financial products.

For example, in the studies of Verhoef *et al.* and Ngobo (2004), perceived value was identified as one of the important factors that influence customers' cross-buying intentions. However, in the studies of Liu and Wu (2007), Kim and Kim (2008) and Fan *et al.* (2011), trust seemed to be a more important factor than perceived value. At the same time, in the study of Ngobo (2004) and Soureli *et al.* (2008), image of the bank did not have a strong influence on customers' cross-buying intentions, unless it interacted with other factors. In the study of Liu and Wu (2007), image of the bank played an important role in customers' cross-buying intentions. Verhoef *et al.* (2001), Ngobo (2004) and Soureli *et al.* (2008) did not place much importance on the direct influence of satisfaction on customers' cross-buying intentions, while Liu and Wu (2007) and Fan *et al.* (2011) stated that satisfaction may directly affect customers' cross-buying intentions.

This book assumed that these different findings were caused by differences in the cultural values of the countries in which the studies were conducted. The studies of Liu and Wu (2007), Kim and Kim (2008) and Fan *et al.* (2011) took place in Korea and Taiwan, where the level of collectivism was much higher than European countries, where the studies of Verhoef *et al.* (2001), Ngobo (2004) and Soureli *et al.* (2008) were conducted. This evaluation is based on the score of individualism-collectivism derived from Hofstede's cross-cultural dimensions (Hofstede 1984a; Hofstede *et al.* 2010), in which Korea and Taiwan exhibited individualism scores of 18 and 17, respectively, whereas the Netherlands of Verhoef *et al.*'s (2001) study scored 80; France of Ngobo's (2004) study scored 71; and Greece of Soureli *et al.*'s (2008) scored 36.

The research gap identified in the literature review was filled by this book by empirically testing the moderating effect that collectivism has on the relationships between these factors and the intention to cross-buy financial products. The conceptual model for these relationships was established based on theoretical reasoning of these factors and the behavioural intentions of customers in a collectivistic culture (Gounaris *et al.* 2007; Liu *et al.* 2001; Ozdemir and Hewett 2010; Zeithaml *et al.* 1996). This conceptual model was tested in Taiwan and Korea, which share a similar level of collectivism (Brewer and Chen 2007; Hofstede 2010; House *et al.* 2004; Yoo *et al.* 2006) and a similar position in the process of industrial evolution (Chia *et al.* 2007; Peng *et al.* 2010). The aim of testing the model in Korea and Taiwan was to identify any resemblances or deviations between these two set of participants in order to validate the conceptual model.

6.3 Conceptual model and methodology

The conceptual model of this book was twofold. First, the model confirmed the relationships between the key variables of cross-buying intention, which were identified from previous literature reviews. Second, the model demonstrated the moderating effect of collectivism on these variables on customers' behavioural intentions in the financial services. This was undertaken based on the studies of Zeithaml *et al.* (1996), Liu *et al.* (2001) and Ozdemir and Hewett (2010).

The definition of collectivism was based on Hofstede's (1984) cultural dimension of individualism-collectivism. The validity of this definition was confirmed by several other studies (Hofstede 2007, 2010; Oyserman and Lee 2008; Soares *et al.* 2007). Cross-buying was defined as purchasing different types of products from the same provider (Reinartz *et al.* 2008; Verhoef *et al.* 2001). Four key drivers – satisfaction, trust, perceived value and image – were identified from the studies of Verhoef (2001), Ngobo (2004), Kumar (2008), Soureli (2008) and Liu and Wu (2009). The behavioural intentions of customers can be expressed as loyalty, willingness to pay more, switching intentions, external response and internal response (Gupta and Zeithaml 2006; Zeithaml *et al.* 1996). These constructs of behavioural intentions can be theoretically linked to the four key drivers of cross-buying intention, which expediently confirmed the relationship between collectivism and the four key drivers.

These four key drivers – the bank's perceived value to the customer, the customer's trust towards the bank, the bank's image to the customer, and the customer's satisfaction towards the bank – were categorized as independent variables, and the customer's cross-buying intention in Taiwan and Korea was the dependent variable. The conceptual model was used to test the moderating effect of collectivism on the relationships between these independent variables and the dependent variable. The conceptual model was tested separately in Korea and Taiwan in order to observe if there were any differences between Korea and Taiwan. This was done to test the findings of Craig and Douglas (2006), who stated that, even in the same geographical region with the same cultural values, a different response can arise due to cultural de-territorialization. Consequently, the conceptual model generated ten hypotheses that were tested in Korea and Taiwan.

The test of the conceptual model was conducted in the formation of a triangulation approach (Creswell and Miller 2000), which combined a quantitative approach of structured surveys administered randomly to bank customers in Taiwan and Korea, with a qualitative approach of carrying out selective personal interviews with local field managers. A structured survey of bank customers was executed with closed-ended questions, while the interviews with local field managers were executed with open-ended questions. This second approach was used to seek more practical knowledge to validate the outcomes of the research (Creswell and Miller 2000).

For the structured survey of customers, the questionnaire was structured in five-point Likert scales, measuring four items for each construct that was employed in the conceptual model. All of the items used in the questionnaire were sourced from various literature reviews of customers' behaviour in banking services and cross-cultural studies. The measurements were extracted from previous studies, such as those of Roig *et al.* (2006), Liu and Wu (2007), Bravo *et al.* (2009), Ngobo (2004), Verhoef *et al.* (2001), Soureli *et al.* (2008) and

Hofstede (2010). The questions were translated into Korean and traditional Chinese, and then back-translated by professionals for validation. In each questionnaire, ethical considerations were paramount, and were supported by the clear statement of the name and contact details of the surveyor.

The survey followed the generalized scientific guidelines for sample size that were proposed by Krejcie and Morgan (1970). A sample size of 350 was drawn from each country, making a total of 700 samples. These samples were collected from the metropolitan areas of Korea and Taiwan, where the majority of bank branches are located (Beck *et al.* 2007; Honohan 2008). The data was gathered by using the probability sampling approach, which allowed the survey to be generalized to the full population, as it ensured that random characteristics would be distributed evenly across the sample (Cavana *et al.* 2001). Ember (2009) confirmed in her study that this approach is the most suitable for cross-cultural studies. This is because, apart from ensuring the functional equivalence of the concepts investigated for the population concerned, it provides matched samples that are ideal for data analysis. Therefore, in this book, stratified random sampling was adopted, with consideration of area sampling. The limitation of this cross-sectional research design was that it provides a snapshot of a sampling population at one point in time, which may not reflect changes in social characteristics over time. However, as stratified random sampling can be adopted to divide a population into meaningful and non-overlapping subsets (Cavana *et al.* 2001), this method was recognized as the most appropriate approach for this study (Mann 2003).

For the interviews, six field managers – three from Korea and three from Taiwan – who had been engaged in cross-buying activities in the banking industry for more than seven years, were selected based on the personal networks of the interviewer. The interviewer had experience of more than 12 years in this field in Korea and other East Asian countries, including Taiwan. Each interviewee was given approximately one hour to discuss the pre-structured questions regarding how the four key drivers of customers' cross-buying intentions (perceived value, trust, image and satisfaction) affected customers' cross-buying intentions, and to what extent collectivism influenced customers' cross-buying behaviour. At the beginning of each interview, the ethical comments and confidentiality agreements were spoken and recorded on an MP3 player.

6.4 Data analysis and discussion

To validate the appropriateness of using factor analysis on data, KMO of sampling adequacy and Bartlett's test of sphericity were conducted, with the result of 0.876 as KMO factor, which was closer to one, and $x^2 = 6062.543$, with $p < 0.001$. This satisfied the overall sampling adequacy. Based on this, EFA was performed by using principal axis factoring and varimax rotation. Through these procedures, some measurements in the questionnaire were deleted.

As the factor loadings of the measurements were all above 0.7, this confirmed that the grouping of measurements had been undertaken properly. The measurement of discriminate validity, the correlation coefficient, and the AVE for each variable was well above the square of phi, the correlation coefficient, which supported the discriminant validity of the model (Fornell and Larcker 1981).

In CFA, the estimated fitness of each index was measured based on the standard level. GFI, AGFI, RMR and RMSEA were measured for absolute fit; NFI, IFI, CFI and NNFI were measured for incremental fit; and PNFI and PCFI were measured for parsimonious fit (Fornell and Larcker 1981; Marsh *et al.* 1988). As all of these indexes met the standard level, the efficacy of the measurement model was confirmed.

In order to test the hypotheses from the conceptual framework, multiple regression analysis (Cohen 2003) was applied to test the four independent variables (perceived value, trust, image and satisfaction), which reciprocally interacted with each other to affect the dependent variable (cross-buying intention). Subsequently, hierarchical regression analysis (Baron and Kenny 1986; Bennett 2000) was conducted in two steps by using SPSS version 17.0 to identify the moderating effect of collectivism on the interactions with these variables.

As a result, it was identified that the four key drivers (perceived value, trust, image and satisfaction) that were identified in the literature review correlate with customers' cross-buying intentions in the Korean and Taiwanese banking industry. However, among the relationships between the four key drivers and cross-buying intention, collectivism showed a moderate effect only on trust and satisfaction. In other words, if customers are more collectivistic, they are more likely to be influenced by trust and satisfaction when they cross-buy financial products from the bank. These customers' cross-buying is also influenced by the image of the bank; however, in relation to collectivism, image has less influence than trust and satisfaction. Surprisingly, perceived value did not positively correlate to the cross-buying intentions of Korean banking customers, nor was it influenced by the level of collectivism.

The outcome of this book was also exhibited in two sets of data analysis. The same conceptual model was tested in Korea and Taiwan in order to observe if there were any differences in customer behaviour even among customers with similar cultural values (Craig and Douglas 2006). Collectivism showed a strong influence only on the relationship between trust and cross-buying intention in Korea, whereas it showed a strong influence on the relationship between both trust and satisfaction and cross-buying intention in Taiwan. Therefore, this partially supports the hypothesis that, even within the same region with similar levels of collectivism, there could be a difference in the outcomes.

6.5 Managerial implications and future studies

This book proposed a managerial direction with a focus on trust and satisfaction as key factors to motivate customers' cross-buying intentions in the banking services of collectivistic cultures. This challenges the predisposition of most multinational financial institutions that invest their energy and resources to compete in pricing, to advertise their brands, and to improve or maintain their reputation.

These factors are crucial to initiate a bank's entry into the local market, but in terms of expanding their relationship through stimulating customers to cross-buy, banks must employ different marketing strategies either to strengthen their customers' trust or to revamp their customers' satisfaction towards the bank.

This book also offered a number of implications for practitioners. For example, even though perceived value and image were less influenced by collectivism, when working with collectivistic customers, it is useful to use these factors to increase the trust and satisfaction of customers towards the bank. It is advised not to emphasize perceived value alone as this might deteriorate the existing relationship and could negatively affect collectivistic customers' cross-buying intentions. This book also demonstrated that customers' intentions to cross-buy will be influenced by different factors than those that affect their willingness to buy a banking product in the first transaction. Perceived value and image might play an important role when customers are choosing their main bank, but once the relationship with their main bank has been established, trust and satisfaction are more important to collectivistic customers. This interpretation was supported by the answers from the field managers that were interviewed in Korea and Taiwan.

Although this book offers an important theoretical proposition related to customers' cross-buying intentions in banking services by using empirical findings from two collectivistic countries, there remain a number of areas to be explored.

One of the potential limitations of this book is that the survey and interviews were conducted in Korea and Taiwan, which have similar levels of collectivism. This may support the outcomes of this book, as it samples the behaviour of customers in collectivistic cultures generally, regardless of their nationalities (Hult *et al.* 2008; Zhang *et al.* 2008; Hofstede 2010). However, in future studies, it is suggested that this research model be employed between two or more countries with different cultural backgrounds, as the value attributes found in this book may vary in other markets and countries (Mäenpää and Voutilainen 2011). Furthermore, in future research, it is suggested that other cultural values be explored, such as power distance (Dash and Guin 2006). This is suggested in order to identify the moderate effect on the determinants that were used in this research model.

Second, the data analysis did not consider different criteria within the sample. For example, the sample's age band, gender and length of relationship with the bank were not considered. This was based on the fact that the outcomes of the study were anticipated to be the same despite the differences in the sample's classification, because the cultural values should be same for the same group within a culture (Javidan *et al.* 2006; Soares *et al.* 2007; Hofstede 2010). However, during the process of the interviews, it was noted that using these classifications might be beneficial for future researchers.

Lastly, the conceptual model formed in this book might be differently applied in different settings of service industries, such as traditional retail services. Therefore, testing the conceptual model of this book in other service areas would enhance the knowledge of cross-cultural differences in the contemporary marketing arena, and would also offer a better understanding of the specific behavioural intentions of banking customers.

Despite these potential topics for future studies, this book has broadened the knowledge of customers' behavioural intentions in regard to cross-buying banking services in East Asian countries, particularly from a cross-cultural perspective. The book confirms the moderate effect of cultural value on customers' cross-buying intentions of financial products in banking services. The conceptual model built and tested in this book could help practitioners' understanding on East Asia, particularly in rapidly globalizing financial service arenas of the region.

References

Abe, M., Satō, Y. and Nagano, M. (1999) *Economic Crisis and Korea/Taiwan*, Institute of Developing Economies, IDE survey.

Abrams, J., O'Connor, J. and Giles, H. (2002) 'Identity and intergroup communication', *Handbook of International and Intercultural Communication*, 2nd edition, 225–240.

Adams, C. (2008) 'Merging East Asian banking systems ten years after the 1997/98 crisis', *Asian Development Bank Regional Economic Integration Working Paper*.

ADB (2009) *Key Indicator for Asia and Pacific 2009*, 40th edition.

Ajzen, I. and Fishbein, M. (1980) *Understanding Attitudes and Predicting Social Behavior*, Prentice-Hall.

Aksin, Z., Armony, M. and Mehrotra, V. (2007) 'The modern call center: a multidisciplinary perspective on operations management research', *Production and Operations Management*, 16: 665–688.

Alden, D., Steenkamp, J. and Batra, R. (1999) 'Brand positioning through advertising in Asia, North America, and Europe: The role of global consumer culture', *The Journal of Marketing*, 63: 75–87.

Alden, D.L., Steenkamp, J.-B. E.M. and Batra, R. (2006) 'Consumer attitudes toward marketplace globalization: Structure, antecedents and consequences', *International Journal of Research in Marketing*, 23: 227–239.

Ansell, J., Harrison, T. and Archibald, T. (2007) 'Identifying cross-selling opportunities, using lifestyle segmentation and survival analysis', *Marketing Intelligence and Planning*, 25: 394–410.

Antón, C., Camarero, C. and Carrero, M. (2007) 'The mediating effect of satisfaction on consumers' switching intention', *Psychology and Marketing*, 24: 511–538.

Appiah-Kubi, B. and Doku, A. (2010) 'Towards a successful customer relationship management: A conceptual framework', *African Journal of Marketing Management*, 2: 37–43.

Arasli, H., Mehtap-Smadi, S. and Katircioglu, S. (2005) 'Customer service quality in the Greek Cypriot banking industry', *Managing Service Quality*, 15: 41–56.

Arnett, J. (2002) 'The psychology of globalization', *American Psychologist*, 57: 774–783.

Artikis, P., Mutenga, S. and Staikouras, S. (2008) 'A practical approach to blend insurance in the banking network', *The Journal of Risk Finance*, 9: 106–124.

Augusto De Matos, C.A., Henrique, J.L. and De Rosa, F. (2009) 'The different roles of switching costs on the satisfaction-loyalty relationship', *International Journal of Bank Marketing*, 27: 506–523.

Austin, J.T., Scherbaum, C.A. and Mahlman, R.A. (2002) 'History of research methods in industrial and organizational psychology: Measurement, design, analysis', *Handbook Of Research Methods in Industrial and Organizational Psychology*, 3–33.

Bagozzi, R. and Lee, K. (2002) 'Multiple routes for social influence: The role of compliance, internalization, and social identity', *Social Psychology Quarterly*, 65: 226–247.

Baron, R.M. and Kenny, D.A. (1986) 'The moderator-mediator variable distinction in social psychological research: Conceptual, strategic, and statistical considerations', *Journal of Personality and Social Psychology*, 51: 1173–1182.

Barry, J.M., Dion, P. and Johnson, W. (2008) 'A cross-cultural examination of relationship strength in B2B services', *Journal of Services Marketing*, 22: 114–135.

Bearden, W. and Teel, J. (1983) 'Selected determinants of consumer satisfaction and complaint reports', *Journal of Marketing Research*, 20: 21–28.

Beck, T., Demirguc-Kunt, A. and Martinez Peria, M.S. (2007) 'Reaching out: Access to and use of banking services across countries', *Journal of Financial Economics*, 85: 234–266.

Belk, R. and Coon, G. (1993) 'Gift giving as agapic love: An alternative to the exchange paradigm based on dating experiences', *Journal of Consumer Research*, 20: 393–417.

Belk, R. and Costa, J. (1998) 'The mountain man myth: A contemporary consuming fantasy', *Journal of Consumer Research*, 25: 218–240.

Bennett, J.A. (2000) 'Focus on research methods-mediator and moderator variables in nursing research: Conceptual and statistical differences', *Research in Nursing and Health*, 23: 415–420.

Berger, A. (2007) 'International comparisons of banking efficiency', *Financial Markets, Institutions and Instruments*, 16: 119–144.

Berry, L.L. (ed.) (1983) *Relationship Marketing, Emerging Perspectives on Service Marketing*, Chicago IL.

Bhuian, S. (1997) 'Exploring market orientation in banks: an empirical examination in Saudi Arabia', *Journal of Services Marketing*, 11: 317–328.

Bijmolt, T.H.A., Leeflang, P.S.H., Block, F., Eisenbeiss, M., Hardie, B.G.S., Lemmens, A. and Saffert, P. (2010) 'Analytics for customer engagement', *Journal of Service Research*, 13: 341–356.

Bird, G. and Rajan, R.S. (2001) 'Banks, financial liberalisation and financial crises in emerging markets', *The World Economy*, 24: 889–910.

Blattberg, R., Malthouse, E. and Neslin, S. (2009) 'Customer lifetime value: Empirical generalizations and some conceptual questions', *Journal of Interactive Marketing*, 23: 157–168.

Bolton, R., Kannan, P. and Bramlett, M. (2000) 'Implications of loyalty program membership and service experiences for customer retention and value', *Journal of the Academy of Marketing Science*, 28: 95–108.

Bolton, R. and Lemon, K. (1999) 'A dynamic model of customers' usage of services: Usage as an antecedent and consequence of satisfaction', *Journal of Marketing Research*, 36: 171–186.

Bolton, R., Lemon, K. and Verhoef, P. (2004) 'The theoretical underpinnings of customer asset management: A framework and propositions for future research', *Journal of the Academy of Marketing Science*, 32: 271–292.

Bolton, R.N. (1998) 'A dynamic model of the duration of the customer's relationship with a continuous service provider: The role of satisfaction', *Marketing Science*, 17: 45–65.

Bolton, R.N., Lemon, K.N. and Bramlett, M.D. (2006) 'The effect of service experiences over time on a supplier retention of business customers', *Management Science*, 52: 1811–1823.

Bond, M.H. (1987) 'Chinese values and the search for culture-free dimensions of culture', *Journal of Cross-Cultural Psychology*, 18: 143–164.

Brace, I. (2008) *Questionnaire Design: How to Plan, Structure and Write Survey Material for Effective Market Research*, Kogan Page Ltd.

Brady, M., Cronin, J. and Brand, R. (2002) 'Performance-only measurement of service quality: a replication and extension', *Journal of Business Research*, 55: 17–31.

Brady, M., Robertson, C. and Cronin, J. (2001) 'Managing behavioral intentions in diverse cultural environments: An investigation of service quality, service value, and satisfaction for American and Ecuadorian fast-food customers', *Journal of International Management*, 7: 129–149.

Braun, V. and Clarke, V. (2006) 'Using thematic analysis in psychology', *Qualitative Research in Psychology*, 3: 77–101.

Bravo, R., Montaner, T. and Pina, J.M. (2009) 'The role of bank image for customers versus non-customers', *International Journal of Bank Marketing*, 27: 315–334.

Brewer, M. and Chen, Y. (2007) 'Where (who) are collectives in collectivism? Toward conceptual clarification of individualism and collectivism', *Psychological Review*, 114: 133–151.

Brewer, P. and Venaik, S. (2011) 'Individualism–collectivism in Hofstede and GLOBE', *Journal of International Business Studies*, 42: 436–445.

Briley, D. (2009) 'Cultural influence on consumer motivations: A dynamic view', in C. Nakata (ed.), *Beyond Hofstede: Culture Frameworks for Global Marketing and Management*, Basingstoke: Palgrave Macmillan, pp. 181–197.

Briley, D. and Aaker, J. (2006) 'When does culture matter? Effects of personal knowledge on the correction of culture-based judgments', *Journal of Marketing Research*, 43: 395–408.

Briley, D., Morris, M. and Simonson, I. (2000) 'Reasons as carriers of culture: Dynamic versus dispositional models of cultural influence on decision making', *Journal of Consumer Research*, 27: 157–178.

Brislin, R. (1970) 'Back-translation for cross-cultural research', *Journal of Cross-Cultural Psychology*, 1: 185–216.

Bruhn, M. (2003) 'Internal service barometers: conceptualization and empirical results of a pilot study in Switzerland', *European Journal of Marketing*, 37: 1187–1204.

Bruton, G. and Lau, C. (2008) 'Asian management research: Status today and future outlook', *Journal of Management Studies*, 45: 636–659.

Burton, D. (2009) *Cross-Cultural Marketing: Theory, Practice and Relevance*, Routledge.

Calomiris, C.W. (1998) 'Universal banking "American-style"', *Journal of Institutional and Theoretical Economics (JITE)/Zeitschrift für die gesamte Staatswissenschaft*, 44–57.

Carrillat, F., Jaramillo, F. and Mulki, J. (2007) 'The validity of the SERVQUAL and SERVPERF scales', *International Journal of Service Industry Management*, 18: 472–490.

Cavana, R., Delahaye, B. and Sekaran, U. (2001) 'Applied business research', *Applied Business Reserach: Qualitative and Quantitative Methods*, Australia: John Wiley and Sons.

Chadwick, R. and Berg, K. (2001) 'Solidarity and equity: New ethical frameworks for genetic databases', *Nature Reviews Genetics*, 2: 318–321.

Chan, G.K.Y. (2008) 'The relevance and value of Confucianism in contemporary business ethics', *Journal of Business Ethics*, 77: 347–360.

Chen, I.J. and Popovich, K. (2003) 'Understanding customer relationship management (CRM): People, process and technology', *Business Process Management Journal*, 9: 672–688.

Chen, M.F. and Wang, L.H. (2009) 'The moderating role of switching barriers on customer loyalty in the life insurance industry', *The Service Industries Journal*, 29: 1105–1123.

Chen, Z., Li, D., Liao, L., Moshirian, F. and Szablocs, C. (2009) 'Expansion and consolidation of bancassurance in the 21st century', *Journal of International Financial Markets, Institutions and Money*, 19: 633–644.

Chia, H., Egri, C., Ralston, D., Fu, P., Kuo, M., Lee, C., Li, Y. and Moon, Y. (2007) 'Four tigers and the dragon: Values differences, similarities, and consensus', *Asia Pacific Journal of Management*, 24: 305–320.

Choe, H. and Lee, B.S. (2003) 'Korean bank governance reform after the Asian financial crisis', *Pacific-Basin Finance Journal*, 11: 483–508.

Chung, J. and Pysarchik, D. (2000) 'A model of behavioral intention to buy domestic versus imported products in a Confucian culture', *Marketing Intelligence and Planning*, 18: 281–291.

Claessens, S. (2009) 'Competition in the financial sector: Overview of competition policies', *The World Bank Research Observer*.

Claessens, S., Dell'Ariccia, G., Igan, D. and Laeven, L. (2010) 'Cross-country experiences and policy implications from the global financial crisis', *Economic Policy*, 25: 267–293.

Cohen, J. (1973) 'Statistical power analysis and research results', *American Educational Research Journal*, 10: 225–229.

Cohen, J. (2003) *Applied Multiple Regression/Correlation Analysis for the Behavioral Sciences*, London: Lawrence Erlbaum.

Colgate, M., Tong, V., Lee, C. and Farley, J. (2007) 'Back from the brink: Why customers stay', *Journal of Service Research*, 9: 211–228.

Cooil, B., Keiningham, T.L., Aksoy, L. and Hsu, M. (2007) 'A longitudinal analysis of customer satisfaction and share of wallet: Investigating the moderating effect of customer characteristics', *Journal of Marketing*, 71: 67–83.

Corbett, J. (2007) 'Financial institutions and structures for growth in East Asia', *Integration*, 14: 22–23.

Corbin, J. and Strauss, A. (2008) *Qualitative Research*, California: Sage Publications.

Coulter, K. and Coulter, R.(2003) 'The effects of industry knowledge on the development of trust in service relationships', *International Journal of Research in Marketing*, 20: 31–43.

Crabtree, B. and Miller, W. (1992) 'Doing qualitative research: Research methods for primary care', *Research Methods for Primary Care*, 3: 3–28.

Craig, C.S. and Douglas, S.P. (2006) 'Beyond national culture: implications of cultural dynamics for consumer research', *International Marketing Review*, 23: 322–342.

Creswell, J.W. (2009) *Research Design: Qualitative, Quantitative, and Mixed Methods Approaches*, Sage Publications, Inc.

Creswell, J.W. and Miller, D.L. (2000) 'Determining validity in qualitative inquiry', *Theory into Practice*, 39: 124–130.

Cronin Jr, J. and Taylor, S. (1994) 'SERVPERF versus SERVQUAL: Reconciling performance-based and perceptions-minus-expectations measurement of service quality', *The Journal of Marketing*, 58: 125–131.

Cronin Jr, J., Brady, M. and Hult, G. (2000) 'Assessing the effects of quality, value, and customer satisfaction on consumer behavioral intentions in service environments', *Journal of Retailing*, 76: 193–218.

Crosby, L., Evans, K. and Cowles, D. (1990) 'Relationship quality in services selling: an interpersonal influence perspective', *The Journal of Marketing*, 54: 68–81.

Cummins, J. and Venard, B. (2008) 'Insurance market dynamics: Between global developments and local contingencies', *Risk Management and Insurance Review*, 11: 295–326.

Cunningham, L., Young, C. and Lee, M. (2005) 'Customer perceptions of service dimensions: American and Asian perspectives', *The Service Industries Journal*, 25: 43–59.

Cunningham, L.F., Young, C.E., Lee, M. and Ulaga, W. (2006) 'Customer perceptions of service dimensions: Cross-cultural analysis and perspective', *International Marketing Review*, 23: 192–210.

Curasi, C., Price, L. and Arnould, E. (2004) 'How individuals' cherished possessions become families' inalienable wealth', *Journal of Consumer Research*, 31: 609–622.

Curry, A. and Sinclair, E. (2002) 'Assessing the quality of physiotherapy services using Servqual', *International Journal of Health Care Quality Assurance*, 15: 197–205.

Das, A. and Ghosh, S. (2006) 'Financial deregulation and efficiency: An empirical analysis of Indian banks during the post reform period', *Review of Financial Economics*, 15: 193–221.

Davin, D. (1999) *Internal Migration in Contemporary China*, New York: St. Martin's Press.

Day, G. (2000) 'Managing market relationships', *Journal of the Academy of Marketing Science*, 28: 24–30.

De Chernatony, L. and Cottam, S. (2006) 'Why are all financial services brands not great?' *Journal of Product and Brand Management*, 15: 88–97.

De Mooij, M. (2000) 'The future is predictable for international marketers', *International Marketing Review*, 17: 103–124.

De Mooij, M. and Hofstede, G. (2002) 'Convergence and divergence in consumer behavior: Implications for international retailing', *Journal of Retailing*, 78: 61–69.

De Mooij, M. and Hofstede, G. (2011) 'Cross-Cultural Consumer Behavior: A Review of Research Findings', *Journal of International Consumer Marketing*, 23: 181–192.

Denzin, N. and Lincoln, Y. (2005) 'The discipline and practice of qualitative research', *International Journal of Qualitative Studies in Education (QSE)*, 19: 769–782.

Denzin, N.K. (1989) *The Research Act: A Theoretical Introduction to Sociological Methods*, McGraw-Hill.

Devlin, J.F. (2001) 'Consumer evaluation and competitive advantage in retail financial services: A research agenda', *European Journal of Marketing*, 35: 639–660.

Dimaggio, P. (1997) 'Culture and cognition', *Annual review of sociology*, 23: 263–287.

Donald, M. (1991) *Origins of the Modern Mind: Three Stages in the Evolution of Culture And Cognition*, Harvard University Press.

Donthu, N. and Yoo, B. (1998) 'Cultural influences on service quality expectations', *Journal of Service Research*, 1: 178–86.

Dowling, G. (1993) 'Developing your corporate image into a corporate asset', *Long Range Planning*, 26: 101–109.

Dziuban, C.D. and Shirkey, E.C. (1974) 'When is a correlation matrix appropriate for factor analysis? Some decision rules', *Psychological Bulletin*, 81: 358–361.

Economist, The (2009) *Asia: An Astonishing Rebound*.

Elsas, R., Hackethal, A. and Holzhäuser, M. (2010) 'The anatomy of bank diversification', *Journal of Banking and Finance*, 34: 1274–1287.

Ember, C.R. and Ember, M. (2009) *Cross-Cultural Research Methods*, Altamira Press.

Ennew, C., Waite, N. and Sciencedirect (2007) *Financial Services Marketing: An International Guide to Principles and Practice*, London: Butterworth-Heinemann.

Epstein, M.J., Friedl, M. and Yuthas, K. (2008) 'Managing customer profitability', *Journal of Accountancy*, 206: 54–59.

Erramilli, M.K. and Rao, C.P. (1993) 'Service firms' international entry-mode choice: A modified transaction-cost analysis approach', *The Journal of Marketing*, 57: 19–38.

Fader, P.S. and Hardie, B.G.S. (2010) 'Customer-base valuation in a contractual setting: the perils of ignoring heterogeneity', *Marketing Science*, 29: 85–93.

Fan, C.K., Lee, L.T., Tang, Y.C. and Lee, Y.H. (2011) 'Factors of cross-buying intention-bancassurance evidence', *African Journal of Business Management*, 5: 7511–7515.

Fang, T. (2003) 'A critique of Hofstede's fifth national culture dimension', *International Journal of Cross Cultural Management*, 3: 347–368.

Fang, T. (2005) 'From "onion" to "ocean": Paradox and change in national cultures', *International Studies of Management and Organization*, 35: 71–90.

Fang, T. (2010) 'Asian management research needs more self-confidence: Reflection on Hofstede (2007) and beyond', *Asia Pacific Journal of Management*, 27: 155–170.

Farquhar, J.D. (2005) 'Retaining customers in UK financial services: The retailers' tale', *The Service Industries Journal*, 25: 1029–1044.

Farshid, M., Plangger, K. and Nel, D. (2011) 'The social media faces of major global financial service brands', *Journal of Financial Services Marketing*, 16: 220–229.

Faure, G. and Fang, T. (2008) 'Changing Chinese values: Keeping up with paradoxes', *International Business Review*, 17: 194–207.

Featherstone, M. (2007) *Consumer Culture and Postmodernism*, Sage Publications Ltd.

Featherstone, M., Lash, S. and Robertson, R. (1995) *Global Modernities*, Sage Publications Ltd.

Felvey, J. (1982) 'Cross-selling by computer', *Bank Marketing*, July 25–27.

Ferraro, G. (2006) *The Cultural Dimension of International Business*, Prentice Hall.

Fields, L., Fraser, D. and Kolari, J. (2007) 'Is bancassurance a viable model for financial firms?' *Journal of Risk and Insurance*, 74: 777–794.

Fischer, R. and Schwartz, S. (2011) 'Whence differences in value priorities?: Individual, cultural, or artifactual sources', *Journal of Cross-Cultural Psychology*, 42: 1127–1144.

Foddy, W. (1993) *Constructing Questions for Interviews*, Cambridge University Press.

Fombrun, C. and Van Riel, C. (1997) 'The reputational landscape', *Corporate Reputation Review*, 1: 5–13.

Fornell, C. and Larcker, D.F. (1981) 'Evaluating structural equation models with unobservable variables and measurement error', *Journal of Marketing Research*, 18: 39–50.

Fornell, C. and Wernerfelt, B. (1987) 'Defensive marketing strategy by customer complaint management: A theoretical analysis', *Journal of Marketing Research*, 24: 337–346.

Fornell, C. and Wernerfelt, B. (1988) 'A model for customer complaint management', *Marketing Science*, 7: 287–298.

Foss, B. and Stone, M. (2002) *CRM in Financial Services: A Practical Guide To Making Customer Relationship Management Work*, Kogan Page Ltd.

Francis, C., Trimble, A. and Chekwa, C. (2010) *Changes in Financial Institution Regulations Associated with the Repeal of the Glass–Steagall Act of 1933*, 2010 IABR and ITLC Conference Proceedings, Orlando, Florida.

Furrer, O., Liu, B.S.C. and Sudharshan, D. (2000) 'The relationships between culture and service quality perceptions: Basis for cross-cultural market segmentation and resource allocation', *Journal of Service Research*, 2: 355–371.

Gale, B. (1997) 'Satisfaction is not enough', *Marketing News*, 32: 18.

Garbarino, E. and Johnson, M.S. (1999) 'The different roles of satisfaction, trust, and commitment in customer relationships', *The Journal of Marketing*, 63: 70–87.

Gelfand, M., Erez, M. and Aycan, Z. (2007) 'Cross-cultural organizational behavior', *Annual Review of Psychology*, 58: 479–514.

Ghosh, S. (2006) *East Asian Finance*, Washington, DC, The World Bank.

Gilbert, G., Veloutsou, C., Goode, M. and Moutinho, L. (2004) 'Measuring customer satisfaction in the fast food industry: A cross-national approach', *Journal of Services Marketing*, 18: 371–383.

Goldenberg, J., Horowitz, R., Levav, A. and Mazursky, D. (2003) 'Finding your innovation sweet spot', *Harvard Business Review*, 81: 120–130.

Gopalan, S. and Rajan, R. (2009) 'Financial sector de-regulation in Emerging Asia: Focus on foreign bank entry', *The Journal of World Investment and Trade*, 11: 91–108.

Gounaris, S. (2005) 'Trust and commitment influences on customer retention: Insights from business-to-business services', *Journal of Business Research*, 58: 126–140.

Gounaris, S.P., Tzempelikos, N.A. and Chatzipanagiotou, K. (2007) 'The relationships of customer-perceived value, satisfaction, loyalty and behavioral intentions', *Journal of Relationship Marketing*, 6: 63–87.

Gregory, I. (2003) *Ethics in Research*, Continuum Intl Pub Group.

Guba, E.G. and Lincoln, Y.S. (1994) 'Competing paradigms in qualitative research', *Handbook of Qualitative Research*, 2: 163–194.

Gudykunst, W.B. (2005) *Theorizing About Intercultural Communication*, Sage Publications, Inc.

Güneş, E.D., Akşin, O.Z., Örmeci, E.L. and Özden, S.H. (2010) 'Modeling customer reactions to sales attempts: If cross-selling backfires', *Journal of Service Research*, 13: 168–183.

Gupta, S. and Zeithaml, V. (2006) 'Customer metrics and their impact on financial performance', *Marketing Science*, 25: 718–739.

Gustafsson, J. (2009) 'Swedes in Australia and their thoughts about business communication and culture', *Högskolan i Halmstad/Sektionen för Hälsa och Samhälle (HOS)*.

Ha, H. and Akamavi, R. (2009) 'Does trust really matter in electronic shopping? A comparison study of Korean, Taiwanese, and UK consumers', *Seoul Journal of Business*, 15: 91–119.

Hall, S. (1997) *Representation: Cultural Representations and Signifying Practices*, Sage Publications Ltd.

Hannerz, U. (1990) 'Cosmopolitans and locals in world culture', *Theory, Culture and Society*, 7: 237–251.

Hansen, H. and Sand, J.A. (2008) 'Antecedents to customer satisfaction with financial services: The moderating effects of the need to evaluate', *Journal of Financial Services Marketing*, 13: 234–244.

Hansen, J.D., Singh, T., Weilbaker, D.C. and Guesalaga, R. (2011) 'Cultural intelligence in cross-cultural selling: Propositions and directions for future research', *Journal of Personal Selling and Sales Management*, 31: 243–254.

Harman, H.H. (1976) *Modern Factor Analysis*, University of Chicago Press.

Hellmann, T.F., Murdock, K.C. and Stiglitz, J.E. (2000) 'Liberalization, moral hazard in banking, and prudential regulation: Are capital requirements enough?' *American Economic Review*, 90: 147–165.

Hickman, L. and Longman, C. (1994) *Business Interviewing*, Addison-Wesley.

Hoffman, J.L. and Lowitt, E.M. (2008) 'A better way to design loyalty programs', *Strategy and Leadership*, 36: 44–47.

Hofstede, G. (1984a) 'Cultural dimensions in management and planning', *Asia Pacific Journal of Management*, 1: 81–99.

Hofstede, G. (1984b) *Culture's Consequences: International Differences in Work-Related Values*, Sage Publications, Inc.

Hofstede, G. (1997) 'Riding the waves: A rejoinder', *International Journal of Intercultural Relations*, 21: 287–290.

Hofstede, G. (2001) *Culture's Consequences: Comparing Values, Behaviors, Institutions, and Organizations Across Nations*, Sage Publications.

Hofstede, G. (2004) 'Geert Hofstede cultural dimensions', online. Retrieved 19 November 2004.

Hofstede, G. (2005) *Cultures and Organizations: Software of the Mind*, London: McGraw-Hill.

Hofstede, G. (2006) 'What did GLOBE really measure? Researchers' minds versus respondents' minds', *Journal of International Business Studies*, 37: 882–896.

Hofstede, G. (2007) 'Asian management in the 21st century', *Asia Pacific Journal of Management*, 24: 411–420.

Hofstede, G. (2010) 'The GLOBE debate: Back to relevance', *Journal of International Business Studies*, 41: 1339–1346.

Hofstede, G. and Hofstede, G. (1991) *Cultures and Organizations*, New York: McGraw-Hill.

Hofstede, G., Jonker, C. and Verwaart, T. (2009) 'Modeling power distance in trade', *Multi-Agent-Based Simulation IX*, 1–16.

Hofstede, G.H., Hofstede, G.J. and Minkov, M. (2010) *Cultures and Organizations: Software of the Mind: Intercultural Cooperation and its Importance for Survival*, McGraw-Hill Professional.

Holden, N. (2002) *Cross-Cultural Management: A Knowledge Management Perspective*, Pearson Education.

Holt, D. (2002) 'Why do brands cause trouble? A dialectical theory of consumer culture and branding', *Journal of Consumer Research*, 29: 70–90.

Hong, Y. and Chiu, C. (2001) 'Toward a paradigm shift: From cross-cultural differences in social cognition to social-cognitive mediation of cultural differences', *Social Cognition*, 19: 181–196.

Hong, Y., Morris, M., Chiu, C. and Benet-Martinez, V. (2000) 'Multicultural minds: A dynamic constructivist approach to culture and cognition', *American Psychologist*, 55: 709–720.

Honohan, P. (2008) 'Cross-country variation in household access to financial services', *Journal of Banking and Finance*, 32: 2493–2500.

House, R., Leadership, G., Hanges, P., Javidan, M., Dorfman, P. and Gupta, V. (2004) *Culture, Leadership, and Organizations: The GLOBE Study of 62 Societies*, USA: Sage Publications.

Howcroft, B., Hewer, P. and Durkinc, M. (2003) 'Banker-customer interactions in financial services', *Journal of Marketing Management*, 19: 1001–1020.

Hsieh, M.F. (2011) 'Similar opportunities, different responses: Explaining the divergent patterns of development between Taiwan and South Korea', *International Sociology*, 26: 364–391.

Hu, Y.C. and Fatima Wang, C.C. (2009) 'Collectivism, corporate social responsibility, and resource advantages in retailing', *Journal of Business Ethics*, 86: 1–13.

Hult, G.T.M., Ketchen, D.J., Griffith, D.A., Finnegan, C.A., Gonzalez-Padron, T., Harmancioglu, N., Huang, Y., Talay, M.B. and Cavusgil, S.T. (2008) 'Data equivalence in cross-cultural international business research: Assessment and guidelines', *Journal of International Business Studies*, 39: 1027–1044.

Hurley, A.E., Scandura, T.A., Schriesheim, C.A., Brannick, M.T., Seers, A., Vandenberg, R.J. and Williams, L.J. (1997) 'Exploratory and confirmatory factor analysis: Guidelines, issues, and alternatives', *Journal of Organizational Behavior*, 18: 667–683.

Ibáñez, V.A., Hartmann, P. and Calvo, P.Z. (2006) 'Antecedents of customer loyalty in residential energy markets: Service quality, satisfaction, trust and switching costs', *The Service Industries Journal*, 26: 633–650.

Inglehart, R. (2000) 'Codebook for world values survey', *Ann Arbor: Institute for Social Research*.

Inglehart, R. (2006) 'Mapping global values', *Comparative Sociology*, 5: 115–136.

Inglehart, R., and Oyserman, D. (2004) 'Individualism, autonomy, and self-expression', in H. Vinken, J. Soeters, and P. Ester (eds), *Comparing Cultures: Dimensions of Culture in a Comparative Perspective*, 74–96, Leiden: Brill.

Inglehart, R. and Welzel, C. (2009) 'How development leads to democracy – What we know about modernization', *Foreign Aff.*, 88: 33–48.

Inglehart, R., Aguir, C., Ahmad, A., Aliev, A., Alishauskiene, R. and Andreyenkov, V. (2000) 'World values surveys and European values surveys, 1981–1984, 1990–1993, and 1995–1997', *Ann Arbor-Michigan, Institute for Social Research, ICPSR version*.

Israel, M. and Hay, I. (2006) *Research Ethics for Social Scientists*, Sage Publications.

Jacobs, J. (2007) 'Taiwan and South Korea: Comparing East Asia's two "Third-Wave" democracies', *Issues and Studies*, 43: 227–260.

Jain, D. and Singh, S.S. (2002) 'Customer life time value research in marketing: A review and future directions', *Journal of Interactive Marketing*, 16: 34–46.

Jain, S. (1989) 'Standardization of international marketing strategy: some research hypotheses', *The Journal of Marketing*, 53: 70–79.

Jain, S. and Gupta, G. (2004) 'Measuring service quality: SERVQUAL vs. SERVPERF scales', *Vikalpa*, 29: 25–37.

Jalkala, A. and Salminen, R.T. (2010) 'Practices and functions of customer reference marketing – Leveraging customer references as marketing assets', *Industrial Marketing Management*, 39: 975–985.

Javalgi, R. and White, D. (2002) 'Strategic challenges for the marketing of services internationally', *International Marketing Review*, 19: 563–581.

Javidan, M., House, R., Dorfman, P., Hanges, P. and De Luque, S. (2006) 'Conceptualizing and measuring cultures and their consequences: a comparative review of GLOBEs and Hofstedes approaches', *Journal of International Business Studies*, 37: 897–914.

Jeng, S.P. (2008) 'The effect of corporate reputations on customer perceptions and cross-buying intentions', *The Service Industries Journal*, 31: 851–862.

Jin, B. and Sternquist, B. (2003) 'The influence of retail environment on price perceptions', *International Marketing Review*, 20: 643–660.

Johns, N., Avci, T. and Karatepe, O. (2004) 'Measuring service quality of travel agents: Evidence from Northern Cyprus', *The Service Industries Journal*, 24: 82–100.

Johnson, S., Boone, P., Breach, A. and Friedman, E. (2000) 'Corporate governance in the Asian financial crisis', *Journal of Financial Economics*, 58: 141–86.

Jones, M.A., Reynolds, K.E., Mothersbaugh, D.L. and Beatty, S.E. (2007) 'The positive and negative effects of switching costs on relational outcomes', *Journal of Service Research*, 9: 335–355.

Joy, A. (2001) 'Gift giving in Hong Kong and the continuum of social ties', *Journal of Consumer Research*, 28: 239–256.

Kacen, J. and Lee, J. (2002) 'The influence of culture on consumer impulsive buying behavior', *Journal of Consumer Psychology*, 12: 163–176.

Kaiser, H.F. (1970) 'A second generation little jiffy', *Psychometrika*, 35: 401–415.

Kamakura, W.A. (2008) 'Cross-selling', *Journal of Relationship Marketing*, 6: 41–58.

Kamakura, W.A., Wedel, M., De Rosa, F. and Mazzon, J.A. (2003) 'Cross-selling through database marketing: A mixed data factor analyzer for data augmentation and prediction', *International Journal of Research in Marketing*, 20: 45–65.

Kassim, N. and Abdullah, N.A. (2010) 'The effect of perceived service quality dimensions on customer satisfaction, trust, and loyalty in e-commerce settings: a cross cultural analysis', *Asia Pacific Journal of Marketing and Logistics*, 22: 351–371.

Keh, H.T. and Xie, Y. (2009) 'Corporate reputation and customer behavioral intentions: The roles of trust, identification and commitment', *Industrial Marketing Management*, 38: 732–742.

Kim, J.H. and Kim, S.H. (2010) 'Factors affecting cross-buying intentions in the banking industry', *Korea Marketing Journal*, 11: 57–89.

Kim, S., Lee, J.W. and Bank, A.D. (2008) *Real and Financial Integration in East Asia*, Asian Development Bank.

Kjeldgaard, D. and Askegaard, S. (2006) 'The glocalization of youth culture: The global youth segment as structures of common difference', *Journal of Consumer Research*, 33: 231–247.

KLIA 2011. Monthly Statistics, *Monthly*, 2011 June 28th edition, Korea Life Insurance Association.

Kluckhohn, C. (1961) *Anthropology and the Classics*, Brown University Press.

Knight, D.K. and Kim, E.Y. (2007) 'Japanese consumers' need for uniqueness: Effects on brand perceptions and purchase intention', *Journal of Fashion Marketing and Management*, 11: 270–280.

Knight, G. (1999) 'International services marketing: Review of research', 1980–1998, *Journal of Services Marketing*, 13: 347–360.

Knott, A., Hayes, A. and Neslin, S. (2002) 'Next-product-to-buy models for cross-selling applications', *Journal of Interactive Marketing*, 16: 59–75.

Koderisch, M., Wuebker, G., Baumgarten, J. and Baillie, J. (2007) 'Bundling in banking – A powerful strategy to increase profits', *Journal of Financial Services Marketing*, 11: 268–276.

Kongsompong, K., Green, R.T. and Patterson, P.G. (2009) 'Collectivism and social influence in the buying decision: A four-country study of inter- and intra-national differences', *Australasian Marketing Journal (AMJ)*, 17: 142–149.

Kotrlik, J.W.K.J.W. and Higgins, C.C.H.C.C. 2001. 'Organizational research: Determining appropriate sample size in survey research appropriate sample size in survey research', *Information Technology, Learning, and Performance Journal*, 19: 43–50.

Krejcie, R. and Morgan, D. (1970) 'Determining sample size for research activities', *Educational and Psychological Measurement*.

Kroszner, R.S. and Rajan, R.G. (1994) 'Is the Glass–Steagall Act justified? A study of the US experience with universal banking before 1933', *The American Economic Review*, 84: 810–832.

Kumar, V. and Reinartz, W. (2006) *Customer Relationship Management: A Databased Approach*, Wiley.

Kumar, V., George, M. and Pancras, J. (2008) 'Cross-buying in retailing: Drivers and consequences', *Journal of Retailing*, 84: 15–27.

Kumar, V., Sunder, S. and Ramaseshan, B. (2011) 'Analyzing the diffusion of global customer relationship management: A cross-regional modeling framework', *Journal of International Marketing*, 19: 23–39.

Ladhari, R. (2009) 'A review of twenty years of SERVQUAL research', *International Journal*, 1: 172–198.

Laeven, L. (2005) 'Banking sector performance in East Asian countries: The effects of competition, diversification, and ownership', *World Bank*.

Laforet, S. (2008) 'Retail brand extension – perceived fit, risks and trust', *Journal of Consumer Behaviour*, 7: 189–209.

Landrum, H., Prybutok, V. and Zhang, X. (2007) 'A comparison of Magal's service quality instrument with SERVPERF', *Information and Management*, 44: 104–113.

Laroche, M., Ueltschy, L., Abe, S., Cleveland, M. and Yannopoulos, P. (2004) 'Service quality perceptions and customer satisfaction: Evaluating the role of culture', *Journal of International Marketing*, 12: 58–85.

Lee, C.K. (2008) 'Organizational culture in East Asia', *Encyclopedia of Public Administration and Public Policy*, 2nd edition, 1–5.

Lee, J. and Kacen, J. (2008) 'Cultural influences on consumer satisfaction with impulse and planned purchase decisions', *Journal of Business Research*, 61: 265–272.

Lee, Z. (1999) 'Korean culture and sense of shame', *Transcultural Psychiatry*, 36: 181–194.

Leech, N.L. and Onwuegbuzie, A.J. (2007) 'An array of qualitative data analysis tools: A call for data analysis triangulation', *School Psychology Quarterly*, 22: 557–584.

Leung, K. (2006) 'The rise of East Asia: Implications for research on cultural variations and globalization', *Journal of International Management*, 12: 235–241.

Leung, K., Bhagat, R.S., Buchan, N.R., Erez, M. and Gibson, C.B. (2005) 'Culture and international business: Recent advances and their implications for future research', *Journal of International Business Studies*, 36: 357–378.

Levitt, T. (1983) 'The globalization of markets', *Harvard Business Review*, 70: 92–102.

Lewis, B. and Soureli, M. (2006) 'The antecedents of consumer loyalty in retail banking', *Journal of Consumer Behaviour*, 5: 15–31.

Li, S., Sun, B. and Montgomery, A.L. (2011) 'Cross-selling the right product to the right customer at the right time', *Journal of Marketing Research*, 48: 683–700.

Li, S., Sun, B. and Wilcox, R.T. (2005) 'Cross-selling sequentially ordered products: An application to consumer banking services', *Journal of Marketing Research*, 42: 233–239.

Lichtenstein, D., Ridgway, N. and Netemeyer, R. (1993) 'Price perceptions and consumer shopping behavior: A field study', *Journal of Marketing Research*, 30: 234–245.

Lim, H. (2009) 'Democratization and the transformation process in East Asian developmental states: Financial reform in Korea and Taiwan', *Asian Perspective*, 33: 75–110.

Lin, J.R., Chung, H., Hsieh, M.H. and Wu, S. (2011) 'The determinants of interest margins and their effect on bank diversification: Evidence from Asian banks', *Journal of Financial Stability*, 8: 96–106.

Lin, N., Tseng, W., Hung, Y. and Yen, D. (2009) 'Making customer relationship management work: Evidence from the banking industry in Taiwan', *The Service Industries Journal*, 29: 1183–1197.

Little, E. and Marandi, E. (2003) *Relationship Marketing Management*, Cengage Learning Business Press.

Liu, B., Furrer, O. and Sudharshan, D. (2001) 'The relationships between culture and behavioral intentions toward services', *Journal of Service Research*, 4: 118–129.

Liu, T. and Wu, L. (2007) 'Customer retention and cross-buying in the banking industry: An integration of service attributes, satisfaction and trust', *Journal of Financial Services Marketing*, 12: 132–145.

Liu, T. and Wu, L. (2009) 'Cross-buying evaluations in the retail banking industry', *The Service Industries Journal*, 29: 1–20.

Liu, W.C. and Hsu, C.M. (2006) 'The role of financial development in economic growth: The experiences of Taiwan, Korea, and Japan', *Journal of Asian Economics*, 17: 667–690.

Lovelock, C. and Wirtz, J. (2007) 'Services marketing: people, technology, strategy', Upper Saddle River, NJ: Pearson Prentice Hall.

Lymberopoulos, K., Chaniotakis, I. and Soureli, M. (2004) 'Opportunities for banks to cross-sell insurance products in Greece', *Journal of Financial Services Marketing*, 9: 34–48.

Ma, N. (2010) Zhengxu Wang, 'Democratization in Confucian East Asia: Citizen Politics in China, Japan, Singapore, South Korea and Taiwan', *East Asia*, 27: 209–210.

Maas, P. and Graf, A. (2008) 'Customer value analysis in financial services', *Journal of Financial Services Marketing*, 13: 107–120.

Maleske, R.T. (1995) *Foundations for Gathering and Interpreting Behavioral Data: An Introduction To Statistics*, Brooks/Cole Pub. Co.

Malthouse, E. and Mulhern, F. (2008) 'Understanding and using customer loyalty and customer value', *Journal of Relationship Marketing*, 6: 59–86.

Mann, C. (2003) 'Observational research methods. Research design II: cohort, cross sectional, and case-control studies', *Emergency Medicine Journal*, 20: 54–60.

Matten, D. and Moon, J. (2008) 'Implicit and explicit CSR: A conceptual framework for a comparative understanding of corporate social responsibility', *The Academy of Management Review (AMR)*, 33: 404–424.

Mattila, A. (1999) 'The role of culture and purchase motivation in service encounter evaluations', *Journal of Services Marketing*, 13: 376–389.

McCracken, G. (1990) 'Culture and consumer behaviour: An anthropological perspective', *Journal of the Market Research Society*, 32: 3–11.

McCracken, G. (2005) *Culture and Consumption II: Markets, Meaning, and Brand Management*, Indiana University Press.

McCrae, R.R., Terracciano, A., Realo, A. and Allik, J. (2008) 'Interpreting GLOBE societal practices scales', *Journal of Cross-Cultural Psychology*, 39: 805–810.

McSweeney, B. (2002) 'Hofstede's model of national cultural differences and their consequences: A triumph of faith-a failure of analysis', *Human Relations*, 55: 89–118.

Mearns, K. and Yule, S. (2009) 'The role of national culture in determining safety performance: Challenges for the global oil and gas industry', *Safety Science*, 47: 777–785.

Meyer, K. (2006) 'Asian management research needs more self-confidence', *Asia Pacific Journal of Management*, 23: 119–137.

Michalski, S. and Helmig, B. (2008) 'What do we know about the identity salience model of relationship marketing success? A review of the literature', *Journal of Relationship Marketing*, 7: 45–63.

Miller, J. (2002) 'Bringing culture to basic psychological theory – Beyond individualism and collectivism: Comment on Oyserman *et al.* (2002)', *Psychological Bulletin*, 128: 97–109.

Minami, C. and Dawson, J. (2008) 'The CRM process in retail and service sector firms in Japan: Loyalty development and financial return', *Journal of Retailing and Consumer Services*, 15: 375–385.

Mittal, V. and Kamakura, W. (2001) 'Satisfaction, repurchase intent, and repurchase behavior: Investigating the moderating effect of customer characteristics', *Journal of Marketing Research*, 38: 131–142.

Mittelman, J.H. (2004) 'What is critical globalization studies?' *International Studies Perspectives*, 5: 219–230.

Mohanty, M.S., Turner, P. and Settlements. Bank for International, M. (2010) *Banks and Financial Intermediation in Emerging Asia: Reforms and New Risks*, Bank for International Settlements, Monetary and Economic Department.

Moon, J., Chadee, D. and Tikoo, S. (2008) 'Culture, product type, and price influences on consumer purchase intention to buy personalized products online', *Journal of Business Research*, 61: 31–39.

Morgan, N.A., Vorhies, D.W. and Mason, C.H. (2009) 'Market orientation, marketing capabilities, and firm performance', *Strategic Management Journal*, 30: 909–920.

Morgan, R. and Hunt, S. (1994) 'The commitment-trust theory of relationship marketing', *The Journal of Marketing*, 58: 20–38.

Moshirian, F. (2008) 'Financial services in an increasingly integrated global financial market', *Journal of Banking and Finance*, 32: 2288–2292.

Mourali, M., Laroche, M. and Pons, F. (2005) 'Individualistic orientation and consumer susceptibility to interpersonal influence', *Journal of Services Marketing*, 19: 164–173.

Moutinho, L. and Smith, A. (2000) 'Modelling bank customer satisfaction through mediation of attitudes towards human and automated banking', *Marketing*, 18: 124–134.

Musalem, A. and Joshi, Y.V. (2009) 'How much should you invest in each customer relationship? A competitive strategic approach', *Marketing Science*, 28: 555–565.

Ndubisi, N.O. (2007) 'Relationship marketing and customer loyalty', *Marketing Intelligence and Planning*, 25: 98–106.

Newburry, W. and Yakova, N. (2006) 'Standardization preferences: A function of national culture, work interdependence and local embeddedness', *Journal of International Business Studies*, 37: 44–60.

Newman, I. and Benz, C.R. (1998) *Qualitative-Quantitative Research Methodology: Exploring the Interactive Continuum*, Southern Illinois University Press.

Ngobo, P.V. (2004) 'Drivers of customers' cross-buying intentions', *European Journal of Marketing*, 38: 1129–1157.

Nguyen, N. and Leblanc, G. (2001) 'Corporate image and corporate reputation in customers' retention decisions in services', *Journal of Retailing and Consumer Services*, 8: 227–236.

Nielsen, C.S., Soares, A.M. and Páscoa Machado, C. (2009) 'The cultural metaphor revisited', *International Journal of Cross Cultural Management*, 9: 289–308.

Oetzel, J. and Ting-Toomey, S. (2003) 'Face concerns in interpersonal conflict: A cross-cultural empirical test of the face negotiation theory', *Communication Research*, 30: 599–624.

Oliver, R. (1980) 'A cognitive model of the antecedents and consequences of satisfaction decisions', *Journal of Marketing Research*, 17: 460–469.

Oliver-Hoyo, M. and Allen, D.D. (2006) 'The use of triangulation methods in qualitative educational research', *Journal of College Science Teaching*, 35: 42–47.

Ormeci, E. and Aksin, O. (2009) 'Revenue management through dynamic cross-selling in call centers', *Production and Operations Management*, 19: 742–756.

Ott, L. and Longnecker, M. (2008) *An Introduction to Statistical Methods and Data Analysis*, Duxbury Press.

Oyserman, D. and Lee, S.W.S. (2008) 'Does culture influence what and how we think? Effects of priming individualism and collectivism', *Psychological Bulletin*, 134: 311–342.

Oyserman, D., Coon, H. and Kemmelmeier, M. (2002) 'Rethinking individualism and collectivism: Evaluation of theoretical assumptions and meta-analyses', *Psychological Bulletin*, 128: 3–72.

Ozdemir, V.E. and Hewett, K. (2010) 'The effect of collectivism on the importance of relationship quality and service quality for behavioral intentions: A cross-national and cross-contextual analysis', *Journal of International Marketing*, 18: 41–62.

Palmer, A. (2002) 'The evolution of an idea: An environmental explanation of relationship marketing', *Journal of Relationship Marketing*, 1: 79–94.

Parasuraman, A., Berry, L. and Zeithaml, V. (1993) 'More on improving service quality measurement', *Journal of Retailing*, 69: 140–147.

Parasuraman, A., Zeithaml, V. and Berry, L. (1985) 'A conceptual model of service quality and its implications for future research', *The Journal of Marketing*, 49: 41–50.

Parasuraman, A., Zeithaml, V. and Berry, L. (1994) 'Reassessment of expectations as a comparison standard in measuring service quality: implications for further research', *The Journal of Marketing*, 58: 111–124.

Parsons, T. and Shils, E. (1951) 'Values, motives, and systems of action', *Toward a general theory of action*, 33: 247–275.

Payne, A. and Frow, P. (2005) 'A strategic framework for customer relationship management', *Journal of Marketing*, 69: 167–176.

Pedhazur, E. J. (1997) *Multiple Regression in Behavioral Research: Explanation and Prediction*, 2nd edition, New York: Holt, Rinehart, and Winston.

Peelen, E., Van Montfort, K., Beltman, R. and Klerkx, A. (2006) 'A study into the foundations of CRM Success', *Nyenrode Research Papers Series*, 06–09, 1–27.

Peelen, E., Van Montfort, K., Beltman, R. and Klerkx, A. (2009) 'An empirical study into the foundations of CRM success', *Journal of Strategic Marketing*, 17: 453–471.

Peng, M.W., Bhagat, R.S. and Chang, S.-J. (2010) 'Asia and global business', *Journal of International Business Studies*, 41: 373–376.

Peppard, J. (2000) 'Customer relationship management (CRM) in financial services', *European Management Journal*, 18: 312–327.

Pieterse, J. (2009) *Globalization and Culture: Global Mélange*, Lanham, Rowman and Littlefield Publishers.

Porter, M. (1990) 'The competitive advantage of nations', *Strategic Management Journal*, 12: 535–548.

Prasad, E.S. (2009) 'Rebalancing growth in Asia', National Bureau of Economic Research Cambridge, Mass.

Prasad, E.S. (2010) 'Financial sector regulation and reforms in emerging markets: An overview', National Bureau of Economic Research.

Puccinelli, N.M., Goodstein, R.C., Grewal, D., Price, R., Raghubir, P. and Stewart, D. (2009) 'Customer experience management in retailing: Understanding the buying process', *Journal of Retailing*, 85: 15–30.

Punch, K.F. and Punch, K. (2005) *Introduction to Social Research: Quantitative and Qualitative Approaches*, Sage Publications Ltd.

Raines-Eudy, R. (2000) 'Using structural equation modeling to test for differential reliability and validity: An empirical demonstration', *Structural Equation Modeling*, 7: 124–141.

Rajan, R.G. and Zingales, L. (2003) 'The great reversals: The politics of financial development in the twentieth century', *Journal of Financial Economics*, 69: 5–50.

Reichheld, F. (1996) 'Learning from customer defections', *Harvard Business Review*, 74: 56–70.

Reichheld, F. and Sasser Jr, E. (1990) 'Zero defections: Quality comes to services?' *Harvard Business Review*, 5: 105–111.

Reinartz, W.J. and Kumar, V. (2000) 'On the profitability of long-life customers in a non-contractual setting: An empirical investigation and implications for marketing', *Journal of Marketing*, 64: 17–35.

Reinartz, W. and Kumar, V. (2003) 'The impact of customer relationship characteristics on profitable lifetime duration', *Journal of Marketing*, 67: 77–99.

Reinartz, W., Krafft, M. and Hoyer, W. (2004) 'The customer relationship management process: Its measurement and impact on performance', *Journal of Marketing Research*, 41: 293–305.

Reinartz, W., Thomas, J. and Kumar, V. (2005) 'Balancing acquisition and retention resources to maximize customer profitability', *Journal of Marketing*, 69: 63–79.

Reinartz, W., Thomas, J.S. and Bascoul, G. (2008) 'Investigating cross-buying and customer loyalty', *Journal of Interactive Marketing*, 22: 5–10.

Riley, P. (2007) 'Language, culture and identity: an ethnolinguistic perspective', *Sociolinguistic Studies*, 2.2: 285–289.

Ritzer, G. (2003) 'Rethinking globalization: Glocalization/grobalization and something/nothing', *Sociological Theory*, 21: 193–209.

Robertson, R. (1992) *Globalization: Social Theory and Global Culture*, Sage Publications Ltd.

Roig, J.C.F., Garcia, J.S., Tena, M.a.M. and Monzonis, J.L. (2006) 'Customer perceived value in banking services', *International Journal of Bank Marketing*, 24: 266–283.

Roscoe, J. (1975) *Fundamental Research Statistics for the Behavioral Sciences*, Nueva York, EUA: Holt, Rinehart and Winston.

Ryals, L. and Payne, A. (2001) 'Customer relationship management in financial services: Towards information-enabled relationship marketing', *Journal of Strategic Marketing*, 9: 3–27.

Ryan, A., Mcfarland, L. and Shl, H. (2006) 'An international look at selection practices: Nation and culture as explanations for variability in practice', *Personnel Psychology*, 52: 359–392.

Sackmann, S. and Phillips, M. (2004) 'Contextual influences on culture research: Shifting assumptions for new workplace realities', *International Journal of Cross Cultural Management*, 4: 370–390.

Salant, P. and Dillman, D.A. (1994) *How to Conduct Your Own Survey*, Wiley, New York.

Salazar, M.T., Harrison, T. and Ansell, J. (2007) 'An approach for the identification of cross-sell and up-sell opportunities using a financial services customer database', *Journal of Financial Services Marketing*, 12: 115–131.

Schein, E. (2004) *Organizational Culture and Leadership*, Jossey-Bass Inc Pub.

Schiffman, L., Hansen, H. and Kanuk, L. (2008) *Consumer Behaviour: A European Outlook*, Financial Times/Prentice Hall.

Schimmack, U., Oishi, S. and Diener, E. (2005) 'Individualism: A valid and important dimension of cultural differences between nations', *Personality and Social Psychology Review*, 9: 17–31.

Schwartz, S. and Bardi, A. (2001) 'Value hierarchies across cultures: Taking a similarities perspective', *Journal of Cross-Cultural Psychology*, 32: 268–290.

Seidman, I. (2006) *Interviewing As Qualitative Research: A Guide for Researchers in Education and the Social Sciences*, Teachers College Press.

Sekaran, U. (1992) *Research Methods For Business: A Skill Building Approach*, New York: John Wiley and Sons.

Sheth, J. (2006) 'Clash of cultures or fusion of cultures? Implications for international business', *Journal of International Management*, 12: 218–221.

Shih-Ping, J. (2008) 'Effects of corporate reputations, relationships and competing suppliers' marketing programmes on customers' cross-buying intentions', *Service Industries Journal*, 28: 15–26.

Shim, T., Kim, M. and Martin, J. (2008) *Changing Korea: Understanding Culture and Communication*, Peter Lang Pub Inc.

Shook, C.L., Ketchen Jr, D.J., Hult, G.T.M. and Kacmar, K.M. (2004) 'An assessment of the use of structural equation modeling in strategic management research', *Strategic Management Journal*, 25: 397–404.

Sieber, J.E. (2005) 'Empirical research on research ethics', *Using Our Best Judgment in Conducting Human Research: A Special Issue of Ethics and Behavior*, 14: 397–412.

Silverman, D. (2009) *Doing Qualitative Research*, Sage Publications Ltd.

Sin, L.Y.M., Cheung, G.W.H. and Lee, R. (1999) 'Methodology in cross-cultural consumer research', *Journal of International Consumer Marketing*, 11: 75–96.

Singhal, S. and Vij, M. (2006) 'Convergence in financial services industry, trends and issues in regulation and supervision', *Journal of Management Research*, 6: 48–56.

Sivakumar, K. and Nakata, C. (2001) 'The stampede toward Hofstede's framework: Avoiding the sample design pit in cross-cultural research', *Journal of International Business Studies*, 32: 555–574.

Smith, P., Dugan, S. and Trompenaars, F. (1996) 'National culture and the values of organizational employees: A dimensional analysis across 43 nations', *Journal of Cross-Cultural Psychology*, 27: 231–264.

Smith, P., Peterson, M. and Schwartz, S. (2002) 'Cultural values, sources of guidance, and their relevance to managerial behavior: A 47-nation study', *Journal of Cross-Cultural Psychology*, 33: 188–208.

Smith, P.B. (2006) 'When elephants fight, the grass gets trampled: The GLOBE and Hofstede projects', *Journal of International Business Studies*, 37: 915–921.

Soares, A.M., Farhangmehr, M. and Shoham, A. (2007) 'Hofstede's dimensions of culture in international marketing studies', *Journal of Business Research*, 60: 277–284.

Sofat, R. and Hiro, M. (2009) 'Challenges and emerging trends in banking – A globalised perspective', *Emerging Financial Markets.*

Sojka, J. and Tansuhaj, P. (1995) 'Cross-cultural consumer research: A 20-year review', *Advances in Consumer Research*, 22: 461–74.

Sondergaard, M. (1994) 'Research note: Hofstede's consequences: A study of reviews, citations and replications', *Organization Studies*, 15: 447–456.

Soureli, M., Lewis, B.R. and Karantinou, K.M. (2008) 'Factors that affect consumers' cross-buying intention: A model for financial services', *Journal of Financial Services Marketing*, 13: 5–16.

Steenkamp, J.B.E.M. and De Jong, M.G. (2010) 'A global investigation into the constellation of consumer attitudes toward global and local products', *Journal of Marketing*, 74: 18–40.

Sternquist, B., Byun, S.E. and Jin, B. (2004) 'The dimensionality of price perceptions: A cross-cultural comparison of Asian consumers', *The International Review of Retail, Distribution and Consumer Research*, 14: 83–100.

Stone-Romero, E.F., Weaver, A.E. and Glenar, J.L. (1995) 'Trends in research design and data analytic strategies in organizational research', *Journal of Management*, 21: 141–157.

Sultan, F. and Simpson, M. (2000) 'International service variants: Airline passenger expectations and perceptions of service quality', *Journal of Services Marketing*, 14: 188–216.

Sunikka, A., Peura-Kapanen, L. and Raijas, A. (2010) 'Empirical investigation into the multi-faceted trust in the wealth management context', *International Journal of Bank Marketing*, 28: 65–81.

Swati, G. (2006) 'East Asian finance: The road to robust markets', *World Bank*.

Swift, R. (2000) *Accelerating Customer Relationships: Using CRM and Relationship Technologies*, Prentice Hall.

Swissre (2007) 'Banc assurance: Emerging trends, opportunities and challenges', *Sigma*, 5: 1–39.

Taras, V., Kirkman, B. and Steel, P. (2010a) 'Examining the impact of culture's consequences: A three-decade, multilevel, meta-analytic review of Hofstede's Cultural Value Dimensions', *Journal of Applied Psychology*, 95: 405–439.

Taras, V., Steel, P. and Kirkman, B.L. (2010b) 'Negative practice-value correlations in the GLOBE data: Unexpected findings, questionnaire limitations and research directions', *Journal of International Business Studies*, 41: 1330–1338.

Tavassoli, N. and Lee, Y. (2003) 'The differential interaction of auditory and visual advertising elements with Chinese and English', *Journal of Marketing Research*, 40: 468–480.

Taylor, S.J. and Bogdan, R. (1998) *Introduction to Qualitative Research Methods: A Guidebook and Resource*, John Wiley and Sons Inc.

Teunissen, M. (2008) 'Bancassurance: Tapping into the banking strength', *The Geneva Papers*, 33: 408–417.

Tharenou, P., Donohue, R. and Cooper, B. (2007) *Management Research Methods*, Melbourne: Cambridge University Press.

Thompson, B. (2004) *Exploratory and Confirmatory Factor Analysis: Understanding Concepts and Applications*, American Psychological Association.

Tifferet, S. and Herstein, R. (2010) 'The effect of individualism on private brand perception: A cross-cultural investigation', *Journal of Consumer Marketing*, 27: 313–323.

Triandis, H. and Gelfand, M. (1998) 'Converging measurement of horizontal and vertical individualism and collectivism', *Journal of Personality and Social Psychology*, 74: 118–128.

Triandis, H.C. (2006) 'Cultural aspects of globalization', *Journal of International Management*, 12: 208–217.

Trompenaars, F. and Hampden-Turner, C. (1995) *Riding the Waves of Culture*, London: Brealey.

Trompenaars, F. and Hampden-Turner, C. (1998) *Riding the Waves of Culture*, N. Brealey Publishing.

Tsoukatos, E. and Rand, G. (2007) 'Cultural influences on service quality and customer satisfaction: Evidence from Greek insurance', *Managing Service Quality*, 17: 467–485.

Tsui, A. (2004) 'Contributing to global management knowledge: A case for high quality indigenous research', *Asia Pacific Journal of Management*, 21: 491–513.

Tsui, A. and Nifadkar, S. (2007) 'Cross-national, cross-cultural organizational behavior research: Advances, gaps, and recommendations', *Journal of Management*, 33: 426–468.

Tucker, L.R. and MacCallum, R.C. (1997). *Exploratory Factor Analysis*, unpublished manuscript, Columbus: Ohio State University.

Tung, R.L. and Verbeke, A. (2010) 'Beyond Hofstede and GLOBE: Improving the quality of cross-cultural research', *Journal of International Business Studies*, 41: 1259–1274.

Turner, B. (2003) 'McDonaldization: Linearity and liquidity in consumer cultures', *American Behavioral Scientist*, 47: 137–153.

Tylor, S. (1958) *Primitive Culture*, Harper.

Ueltschy, L., Laroche, M., Eggert, A. and Bindl, U. (2007) 'Service quality and satisfaction: An international comparison of professional services perceptions', *Journal of Services Marketing*, 21: 410–423.

Ueltschy, L.C., Laroche, M., Zhang, M., Cho, H. and Yingwei, R. (2009) 'Is there really an Asian connection? Professional service quality perceptions and customer satisfaction', *Journal of Business Research*, 62: 972–979.

Van De Vijver, F.J.R. and Leung, K. (1997) *Methods and Data Analysis for Cross-Cultural Research*, Sage Publications, Inc.

Vandello, J.A. and Cohen, D. (1999) 'Patterns of individualism and collectivism across the United States', *Journal of Personality and Social Psychology*, 77: 279.

Vandermerwe, S. and Chadwick, M. (1989) 'The internationalisation of services', *The Service Industries Journal*, 9: 79–93.

Vatanasombut, B., Igbaria, M., Stylianou, A.C. and Rodgers, W. (2008) 'Information systems continuance intention of web-based applications customers: The case of online banking', *Information and Management*, 45: 419–428.

Verhoef, P.C., (2003) 'Understanding the effect of customer relationship management efforts on customer retention and customer share development', *Journal of Marketing*, 67: 30–45.

Verhoef, P.C., and Donkers, B. (2005) 'The effect of acquisition channels on customer loyalty and cross-buying', *Journal of Interactive Marketing*, 19: 31–43.

Verhoef, P.C., Franses, P.H. and Hoekstra, J.C. (2001) 'The impact of satisfaction and payment equity on cross-buying: A dynamic model for a multi-service provider', *Journal of Retailing*, 77: 359–378.

Verhoef, P.C., Franses, P. and Hoekstra, J. (2002) 'The effect of relational constructs on customer referrals and number of services purchased from a multiservice provider: Does age of relationship matter?', *Journal of the Academy of Marketing Science*, 30: 202–216.

Verhoef, P.C., Van Doorn, J. and Dorotic, M. (2007) 'Customer value management: An overview and research agenda', *Marketing-Journal of Research and Management*, 3: 105–120.

Verhoef, P.C., Lemon, K.N., Parasuraman, A., Roggeveen, A., Tsiros, M. and Schlesinger, L.A. (2009) 'Customer experience creation: Determinants, dynamics and management strategies', *Journal of Retailing*, 85: 31–41.

Verhoef, P.C., Reinartz, W.J. and Krafft, M. (2010) 'Customer engagement as a new perspective in customer management', *Journal of Service Research*, 13: 247–252.

Voss, C.A., Roth, A.V., Rosenzweig, E.D., Blackmon, K. and Chase, R.B. (2004) 'A tale of two countries' conservatism, service quality, and feedback on customer satisfaction', *Journal of Service Research*, 6: 212–230.

Vyas, R. and Math, N. (2006) 'A comparative study of cross-selling practices in public and private sector banks in India', *Journal of Financial Services Marketing*, 10: 123–134.

Wagner, W. (2010) 'Diversification at financial institutions and systemic crises', *Journal of Financial Intermediation*, 19: 373–386.

Wang, Z. (2008) *Democratization in Confucian East Asia: Citizen Politics in China, Japan, Singapore, South Korea, Taiwan, and Vietnam*, New York, Cambria Press.

Watchravesringkan, K., Yan, R. and Yurchisin, J. (2008) 'Cross-cultural invariance of consumers' price perception measures: Eastern Asian perspective', *International Journal of Retail and Distribution Management*, 36: 759–779.

Wedeen, L. (2003) 'Conceptualizing culture: Possibilities for political science', *American Political Science Review*, 96: 713–728.

Wei-Ming, T. (1996) 'Confucian traditions in East Asian modernity', *Bulletin of the American Academy of Arts and Sciences*, 50: 12–39.

Westjohn, S.A., Singh, N. and Magnusson, P. (2011) 'Responsiveness to global and local consumer culture positioning: A personality and collective identity perspective', *Journal of International Marketing*, 20: 58–73.

White, S. (2002) 'Rigor and relevance in Asian management research: Where are we and where can we go?', *Asia Pacific Journal of Management*, 19: 287–352.

Williams, C.A. and Aguilera, R.V. (2008) 'Corporate social responsibility in a comparative perspective', *Oxford Handbook of Corporate Social Responsibility*, 452–472, Oxford: Oxford University Press.

Williams, L.J. (1995) 'Covariance structure modeling in organizational research: Problems with the method versus applications of the method', *Journal of Organizational Behavior*, 16: 225–233.

Wind, Y.J. (2001) 'The challenge of "customerization" in financial services', *Communications of the ACM*, 44: 39–44.

Winsted, K. (1997) 'The service experience in two cultures: a behavioral perspective', *Journal of Retailing*, 73: 337–360.

Wirtz, J. and Lovelock, C. (2007) *Services Marketing: People, Technology, Strategy*, New Jersey: Pearson Prentice Hall.

Wood, M. (2007) 'Seven habits of highly efficient banks', *Journal of Performance Management*, 20: 3–6.

Woodruff, R. (1997) 'Customer value: The next source for competitive advantage', *Journal of the Academy of Marketing Science*, 25: 139–153.

Wu, C., Lin, C. and Lin, Y. (2008) 'What forms of the bancassurance alliance model is customers' preference?', *Journal of Modelling in Management*, 3: 207–219.

Wu, X. (2009) 'The dynamics of Chinese face mechanisms and classroom behaviour: A case study', *Evaluation and Research in Education*, 22: 87–105.

Xu, A., Xie, X., Liu, W., Xia, Y. and Liu, D. (2007) 'Chinese family strengths and resiliency', *Marriage and Family Review*, 41: 143–164.

Xu, X. (1998) 'Asian values revisited: In the context of intercultural news communication', *Media Asia*, 25: 37–41.

Yang, Z., Wang, X. and Su, C. (2006) 'A review of research methodologies in international business', *International Business Review*, 15: 601–617.

Yeager, T., Yeager, F. and Harshman, E. (2007) 'The financial services modernization act: Evolution or revolution?', *Journal of Economics and Business*, 59: 313–339.

Yoo, D., Rao, S. and Hong, P. (2006) 'A comparative study on cultural differences and quality practices? Korea, USA, Mexico, and Taiwan', *International Journal of Quality and Reliability Management*, 23: 607–624.

Zeithaml, V., Berry, L. and Parasuraman, A. (1993) 'The nature and determinants of customer expectations of service', *Journal of the Academy of Marketing Science*, 21: 1–12.

Zeithaml, V., Berry, L. and Parasuraman, A. (1996) 'The behavioral consequences of service quality', *The Journal of Marketing*, 60: 31–46.

Zhang, J., Beatty, S.E. and Walsh, G. (2008) 'Review and future directions of cross-cultural consumer services research', *Journal of Business Research*, 61: 211–224.

Zhang, S. and Schmitt, B. (2001) 'Creating local brands in multilingual international markets', *Journal of Marketing Research*, 38: 313–325.

Zhang, Y. and Harwood, J. (2004) 'Modernization and tradition in an age of globalization: Cultural values in Chinese television commercials', *Journal of Communication*, 54: 156–172.

Zhang, Y.B., Lin, M.C., Nonaka, A. and Beom, K. (2005) 'Harmony, hierarchy and conservatism: A cross-cultural comparison of Confucian values in China, Korea, Japan, and Taiwan', *Communication Research Reports*, 22: 107–115.

Zhou, L. (2004) 'A dimension-specific analysis of performance-only measurement of service quality and satisfaction in China's retail banking', *Journal of Services Marketing*, 18: 534–546.

Zourrig, H., Chebat, J. and Toffoli, R. (2009) 'Consumer revenge behavior: A cross-cultural perspective', *Journal of Business Research*, 62: 995–1001.

Index

Page numbers in *italics* denote tables, those in **bold** denote figures.